Organizations and
Communication
Technology

Organizations and Communication Technology

Edited by:
Janet Fulk
Charles Steinfield

SAGE Publications
International Educational and Professional Publisher
Newbury Park London New Delhi

For information address:

SAGE Publications, Inc.
2455 Teller Road
Newbury Park, California 91320

SAGE Publications Ltd.
6 Bonhill Street
London EC2A 4PU
United Kingdom

SAGE Publications India Pvt. Ltd.
M-32 Market
Greater Kailash I
New Delhi 110 048 India

Printed in the United States of America

Cover Illustration: Harold Birch

Library of Congress Cataloging-in-Publication Data

Main entry under title:
Organizations and communication technology / edited by Janet Fulk &
    Charles W. Steinfield.
        p. cm. —
    Includes bibliographical references.
    ISBN 0-8039-3530-7. — ISBN 0-8039-3531-5 (pbk.)
    1. Management--Communication systems.   2. Management — Data
processing.   3. Information technology.   4. Organization.   I. Fulk,
Janet.   II. Steinfield, Charles William.
HD30.335.074   1990
658.4'038 — dc20   89-28042
                                                                 CIP

95 96 97 98 99 10 9 8 7 6 5 4 3

Contents

Preface

Imagine you find yourself lost deep inside an uncharted jungle. You look around and see many signs of life and glints of sun bursting through the overhanging boughs. You are surrounded by interesting sights, but what you don't see is a clear way to get out. You don't know how big the jungle is, how far you stand from any boundary, where food and water are located, or really anything else about the forest except those things that you observe right in front of you. If you are anything like us, you probably think, "Where is my National Geographic atlas when I need it?"

Editing a book of theoretical essays is like assembling a National Geographic team to begin charting that jungle. You go out and find really capable and creative people who are familiar with nature, cartography, and whatever data exists about the jungle. Then you offer each one a different part of the forest to work with, tell them your overall goals, and see what they come up with. When their reports are in, maybe you will have learned enough to construct a research proposal to fund further exploration.

Our theoretical explorers have generated interesting, insightful, and provocative essays about the interface of organization and communication technology. Each has something to say about one or more important yet unanswered questions: What forces shape the articulation of organizational and technological systems? What organizational, political and social processes constrain technological possibilities? How do technology and organization interact to shape organizational structures and processes? How do organization and information technology co-determine each other? These issues are critical to understanding organizational processes in an age of rapidly changing technological realities.

The fruits of these endeavors will have value to a wide variety of audiences. One audience is those who teach and conduct research on organizations. Organizational researchers exist in a variety of disciplines: management, communication, sociology, psychology, anthropology, economics, industrial and systems engineering, political science, public administration, and education. Regardless of disciplinary bounds, one fact is eminently clear. The changes taking place today in the organization/technology interface are so fundamental and well-recognized that organizational scholars who ignore them do so at their own peril.

The second audience is scholars of communication. These researchers have long had a concern with communication processes in the organizational context, and also have demonstrated considerable interest in new media. Several of the theoretical essays take a decidedly communication-oriented perspective. Effective communication is, in fact, at the very core of the goals driving the implementation of information technologies in organizations. Communication researchers, among the first to call attention to organizational challenges from new media, can benefit from the new frameworks this book provides for viewing existing issues.

A third audience is students, from undergraduate to graduate levels. The essays have three particular benefits for students. First, they deal with fundamental and timeless issues of communication and organization. We can learn a great deal about basic processes of communicating and organizing by studying the technology/organization interface. And, the treatment of these topics draws on key issues of relevance today. Second, the theoretical presentations are for the most part quite readable. They are accessible to newcomers to the field as well as to more established figures. Third, they cut a broad swath across key issues from individual behavior to interorganizational communication. Thus, in combination, these works paint a wide panorama of organizational communication.

A fourth audience is sophisticated management practitioners—those who are stimulated by intellectual dialog and are not bogged down by plentiful citations. Huber (Chapter 11) perceptively notes that the relative newness and volatility of the new technologies inevitably means that managers will not have sufficient past experience to rely on when making key decisions about technology implementation. Without experience as a guide, where do managers turn? Among the favored options is theory—theory which is both relevant and accessible. Reliance on theory for experimenting with new solutions and investigating new opportunities is not the same as applying time-worn principles. The practitioner who is looking for a straightforward "how to" might well invest efforts elsewhere. Several of the papers in this volume have been developed over time in response to feedback and ideas from such intellectually-oriented practitioners and have benefited tremendously from the input. These benefits can now be passed on to readers of this volume.

A fifth audience is policymakers. These individuals are constantly challenged to see the broad picture and to sketch the implications of changing trends for industry, society, and the global community. To the extent that theory can help make sense of the so-called "empirical swamp", it can help contribute to broader visions. The detailed citations and disciplinary terminology will be less the focus for policymakers than will be the broad outlines of the theoretical approaches proposed.

The book is organized to touch on issues from several different perspectives and levels of analysis. We begin in Part I with a chapter which lays out the basic rationale for this endeavor. The work centers on the role of theory for advancing our knowledge of communication technology in organizations. Part II presents two views on the nature of technology, task, and organization. Parts III, IV, and V deal with micro, group, and macro level conceptualizations. These distinctions in our sectional map are in part artificial, since each paper beneficially incorporates multi-level issues. Furthermore, the conceptual maps our explorers have created are linked at some points by shared concepts.

This work would not have been possible without the patience, help, and encouragement of many. The initial impetus for this volume was a special issue of *Communication Research* (Volume 14, Number 5, October 1987). Peter Monge provided the opportunity for us to edit the issue and gave us our first forum for extolling the value of conceptual development for the study of information technology and organizations. Sage Publications, and particularly Ann West, helped and encouraged us to take our cause further and develop this book. Harold Burch designed the cover artwork. Linnea Berg provided expert assistance in preparation of internal artwork for the volume. Rachel Osborn and Teresa Zamboni tirelessly worked to check references and prepare the name index. Joseph Schmitz contributed considerable time and effort to prepare the subject index. The Annenberg School of Communications provided sabbatical leave and internal resources for preparing final copy of manuscripts. The Ameritech Foundation provided generous fellowship support to Charles Steinfield, and Michigan State University provided valuable release time. Susan Russick gave up many a weekend outing while we worked on the volume. Marie and Neal Fulk are a continuing source of inspiration by demonstrating in their words and deeds the true value of scholarship. Our hearty thanks go to all these valuable contributors.

—Janet Fulk
Malibu, California

—Charles W. Steinfield
East Lansing, Michigan

PART I

Theorizing About Information Technology in Organizations

CHARLES W. STEINFIELD
JANET FULK

1. The Theory Imperative

We are in the midst of a data glut. Nearly two decades ago, in the face of wide-ranging speculations about the effects of new technologies on organizations, we heard the cry for more empirical data (Klemmer, 1973). We have heeded that call, yet our knowledge claims are still very limited. Why? The problem is that the accumulated data lacks a theoretical infrastructure—a tree to which individual findings can be grafted to generate the synthesis and integration needed to support knowledge claims. Even with the best crystal ball, the early framers of organization theory could not have envisioned the new organizational systems and processes that have evolved with the marriage of computers and telecommunications. Consequently, contemporary organization theory is ill-equipped to cope with these changing contexts. And, new theories have not arisen to fill the gap. In short, the field of communication technology in organizations is data rich but theory poor. And, as Blalock (1969, p. 2) notes, any good social scientist knows that the facts do not speak for themselves. Theoretical structures are critical.

Why Theory?

Why is the development of theoretical structures so critical to the study of new information technologies in organizations? First, theory provides a framework for synthesis and integration of empirical findings. Theory can help make sense of the jumble of research findings that have accumulated in the last two decades. Theory can (1) provide road maps as to what patterns to look for in the data, (2) point us toward explanations for the patterns, (3) help to resolve inconsistencies across studies, and (4) help to account for anomalous findings.

Theory also offers guidance as to where to direct *future* empirical attention and provides a structure for incorporating future research findings. Thus, it drives a more efficient and meaningful research effort. Theory also motivates integrated programs of research rather than fragmented individual studies. The overall consequence of theory-driven research efforts is a more coherent and defensible set of conclusions on which to base knowledge claims.

Second, the capacity of theory to *generate a priori hypotheses* adds an element of rigor to the research effort. It helps avoid the temptation to let the data suggest hypotheses that are then considered supported by those same data—with the resulting risk of false positive findings. These findings then serve as the basis for future studies, with the risk of a misguided research effort. Theory-driven research, of course, is not immune to false positive findings. However, theory makes the fallibility of empirical research much more manageable (Pickering, 1984).

Third, theory helps to focus research on *conclusions designed to be generalizable* across a spectrum of organizations and technologies. Information technology research is particularly vulnerable to generating idiosynchratic findings. Early research on "new" technologies inevitably focuses on exceptional organizations: early adopters and organizations willing to experiment with new technologies. Generalizable conclusions are difficult to draw when the evidence is obtained from outliers. This challenge is compounded when studies take place during the early stages of adoption. Initial periods of instability immediately after technological implementation may bear little resemblance to periods of stability that are achieved after the first year or so of implementation (Johansen, 1976). A well-conceived theory forces us to attend to issues of generalizability of conclusions.

Fourth, theory helps us see the forest as well as the trees. Theory provides perspective on the larger issues and *directs us toward more broadly-based knowledge claims*. Staw (1985, p. 97) notes:

> When research is literature- rather than theory-driven, contributions to knowledge are more conservative and incremental than they need to be. Because authors focus more on how their research fits with the previous literature than on the organizational problem itself, their research inevitably becomes directed toward controversies and gaps in the literature rather than toward a fresh look at the issues being studied.

Fifth, the existence of theory regarding the organization/technology interface appropriately *directs our research attention to central issues of organizational functioning* rather than misguided technological imperatives. Most researchers are trained to avoid Type I error (rejecting the null hypothesis when it is true), and Type II error (accepting the null hypothesis when it is

14

2. about Type II - why does it occur ?

false). Our greatest vulnerability, however, is in making Type III error: testing the wrong hypothesis (Mitroff & Featheringham, 1974). Type III error occurs when researchers have not succeeded in the most critical task of all: adequately representing the scientific problem for investigation. This error is most likely when our research is driven by the technological opportunities themselves, rather than basic issues of organizational communication and behavior. Theory can help guide us to important organizational issues and, it is hoped, steer us away from being enamored with the technology to the point where we are looking in the wrong place to find both questions and answers. Of course, the formulation of theory cannot guarantee that the scientific questions are appropriately posed. However, the process of theory development is likely, in itself, to assist us in preparing well-conceived questions.

Sixth, on a more practical level, theory provides a mechanism for integrating new and emerging fields with other related fields. The importation of theoretical premises from other fields that commonly takes place during the process of theory development sets up conditions for a more integrated social science. It also provides legitimization for young fields of study in relation to more mature disciplines. Contractor and Eisenberg (Chapter 7) note that the editors of the *Handbook of Communication Science* did NOT include a chapter on technological impacts. This occurred despite the editors' contention that the technologies would have considerable impacts, because the emerging field lacked "a unique theoretical focus." Theory, it seems, provides a key legitimizing function.

The goal of this volume is to provide a foundation for theory development on information technology in organizations. We make no claims to be comprehensive of all organizational processes nor all new communication technologies. Rather, we consciously have been quite selective. The authors who have agreed to contribute to this volume are individuals with considerable accomplishments in the conceptual domain. Their primary similarity is a strong drive for working on and formulating interesting problems. They all share a concern for the challenges facing organizations today as they are literally bombarded by new communication options in the face of considerable competitive pressures. And, they all share our goal of developing the knowledge base on information technology in organizations through the ongoing process of theory development. In short, they are all willing to take the first step in what will inevitably be a long and exciting process of developing a broad base of theories in the longer term.

Where Should Theory Come From?

The approaches to theory development employed in this volume are as diverse as the theories themselves. Most papers apply a variety of logics; a sampling is described below.

In the classic inductive model of theory building, researchers formulate theory based upon patterns of relationships observed in descriptive studies of communication technology uses and impacts. Patterns of uses and impacts are then explained by referring to the unique attributes of the technologies in question. Quite often, this approach is used to study a single new technology medium, such as electronic mail, rather than a range of new media. Much of the new information technology literature has followed this approach (for a good example, see Hiltz [1984] for a review of studies of computer conferencing). This approach, *if carried out in isolation from other logics*, is most vulnerable to false positive findings. As Popper (1981, pp. 72-73) noted,

> the belief that we can start with pure observations alone, without anything in the nature of a theory, is absurd. . . .It is quite true that any particular hypothesis we choose will have been preceded by observations—the observations, for example, which it is designed to explain. But these observations, in their turn, presupposed the adoption of a frame of reference: a frame of expectations: a frame of theories. If they were significant, if they created a need for explanation and thus gave rise to the invention of a hypothesis, it was because they could not be explained within the old theoretical framework, the old horizon of expectations.

Popper further suggests that a more productive approach is to acknowledge and articulate the theoretical frame of reference and subject it to critical tests and rules of critical argument. The profitable use of induction *in conjunction with deductive rules of argument is* illustrated by Markus' theory (Chapter 9). She generates expectations for use of interactive media based on deductions from an application of the Theory of the Critical Mass. She then proceeds to show how the patterns observable across previous research studies converge with the expectations derived from the theory.

A second approach found in previous literature is to conceptually analyze the attributes of new communication technologies, and use the resulting framework as a heuristic guide to develop propositions regarding uses and impacts. Miller and Vallee's (1980) conceptual framework for understanding electronic message systems is a good example of this approach, although they only considered a single type of new communication medium. Nass and *why is theory so important and where does it come from?*

Mason (Chapter 3) engage in such a conceptual analysis but consider a broader base of technologies and explicitly concern themselves with the organization/technology interface. They identify a range of technological and social dimensions that can be used to characterize all information technologies. One particular advantage of their approach is its conceptual breadth. It avoids the trap of being enamored with a particular technology to the point where the technology itself becomes the focus and driving force of the research. It frees the researcher to attend to more fundamental and timeless issues. It also provides a coherent foundation for cross-system and cross-technology comparisons.

A variant of the above strategy is to analyze the capabilities of new technologies along important organizational dimensions identified by previous theory. Then, predictions can be made for the organizational effects of new technologies by drawing on the expectations from theory. Huber's theory (Chapter 11) accomplishes this strategy very robustly. He analyzes the capabilities of new decision technologies and suggests how these capabilities are relevant to concerns within the realm of existing organizational theories. He then employs these theories to develop predictions for the effects of new decision technologies on organizational intelligence and decision making. Interestingly, he finds that current theories generate equally defensible yet *contrasting* predictions of effects. His piece, in particular, raises important questions about the ability of existing theory to directly confront the complexities of new decision technologies.

A third approach is to apply existing theory to the new context, where "new context" is the organizational setting in which new information technologies are employed. This model of modifying basic theoretical foundations to account for changed contexts is illustrated by the modifications that took place in organizational behavior theory with the influx of substantial numbers of women into the workplace. The revised theories recognized the new contexts for social and organizational relations. Organizational studies as a field is rich with theory. However, virtually all of this theory was developed prior to the very recent developments in computers and communications that are now being incorporated into organizations. Many of the conclusions from currently accepted theory need to be revisited. This process, we believe, will demonstrate that a great deal of existing social and organizational theory, *if appropriately modified*, is still relevant to the study of new media. Constructive alteration of current theory to new technological contexts offers more benefits than pursuit of either traditional theory or new technology research in a vacuum. Allen and Hauptman's model (Chapter 12) exemplifies this approach. They demonstrate how organizational information processing

17

theory can be effectively modified to account for new communication options in R&D settings. They argue that the theoretical trade-offs between functional and project goals are not inevitable in the context of new information technologies. Their model explicates how different communication options can substitute to some degree for both functional and project designs. Thus, new communication options make possible simultaneous project and functional designs without resorting to the cumbersome matrix structure. In the same vein, Zmud (Chapter 5) integrates tenets from information systems theory to create a model of strategic managerial information behavior via new information technologies.

Yet a fourth approach relies on reasoning by analogy from other concepts and theories. Historians and philosophers of science have long observed that scientists will frequently seek to understand new phenomena through the use of analogies and that these constitute the source of much innovation in science (Hesse, 1970; Knorr-Cetina, 1981; Pickering, 1980, 1984). By conceptually equating a less-understood with a better-understood phenomenon, scientists mobilize an existing body of knowledge to help deduce expectations for the new situation. Pickering argues that the study of high-energy physics advanced because theorists made an analogic connection between hadrons and nuclei. In the analogy, hadrons (e.g., protons and neutrons) were seen as composites of particles known as quarks, in the same way that nuclei are composites of protons and neutrons, and atoms are composites of nuclei and electrons. In another important instance of analogic theory construction, information theory was introduced into the social sciences from the physical science of thermodynamics (Shannon & Weaver, 1949).

An analogy produces a conceptual interaction between the two objects of comparison. By relating one object to a second, not only is the latter object viewed as similar to the former, but the former becomes more like the latter. In a parallel fashion, when using an existing theory to study information technology, not only do we view information technologies from the perspective of the theory, but we begin to view the theory from the perspective of the attributes of information technologies. Thus a natural consequence of the application of existing theory to the study of information technology is that each informs the other. This synergy may lead to valuable modifications in the original theory as well. Contractor and Eisenberg's model (Chapter 7) exemplifies this recursive process. They demonstrate how an analogy to social interaction theories not only benefits the emerging field of information technology in organizations, but also has implications back to the original social theories.

18

A number of other chapters in this book also borrow theory originally applied to different situations. In doing so, they provide a rationale for fitting the theory to the study of information technology, that is, they stress the "positive analogy" (Hesse, 1970) and deduce propositions to guide future research efforts.

This approach to theory development is not without its critics (Crane, 1980; Willer, 1967). Buck (1956, p. 225), for example, criticizes the use of analogy in general systems theory on two grounds. First, it goes little further than simply stating structural equivalence—it does not answer the question "so what?" Second, the subject of negative analogy (explicating the areas where the analogy does not fit) "is almost completely neglected by general systems theory." The problems Buck notes, however, lie in the development of that particular theory rather than in the process of employing analogies. What remains for information technology theorists, if we attend to Buck's recommendations, is to explicate the areas of negative analogy, and to specify the neutral analogy (where we do not know if the analogy fits). Hesse (1970) argues that this is the area of the greatest payoff.

Fulk, Schmitz, and Steinfield (Chapter 6) attend to Hesse's counsel. They argue that the dominant theoretical model of media use, the literal application of organizational information processing theory to the context of media choice, has created vast areas of negative analogy—so vast that it is time to search for a theory with a better "fit" to what is known about social and organizational behavior. They propose an alternative analogy using social influence theories, and show how the balance of positive to negative analogy is improved by employing the alternative model. Similarly, Poole and DeSanctis (Chapter 8) draw lessons from an integration of conflict theory and findings from studies of communication technology effects. Their efforts lead to a new theory, the Theory of Adaptive Structuration, which provides insights into not only group process in computer-assisted decision support systems but also to conflict management processes in general.

Analogic processes can be particularly fruitful when they bring to bear the tenets of theory developed in very different contexts. These analogies help us turn the kaleidoscope and reconfigure our notions about organizations and information technology. As Huber (Chapter 11) notes, linkages across fields provide important opportunities for synergy, and also improve the efficiency of social science research. Several of the chapters in this volume fruitfully apply theoretical approaches from such diverse fields as economics (Beniger, Chapter 2), sociology and public policy (Markus, Chapter 9; Thorn & Connolly, Chapter 10), and social psychology (Trevino, Daft, & Lengel, Chapter 4; Fulk et al., Chapter 6).

A fifth and final approach to theory development is to explicate the communication implications of theories that do not provide explicit propositions about communication. These implications link the theory base with the communication capabilities of new information technologies. The connecting tissue demarcates a rich new area for the development of propositions. One useful starting place for this type of exercise is Euske and Roberts (1987). Following the earlier example of Farace, Monge, and Russell (1977), Euske and Roberts examined the implications for organizational communication contained in seven categories of organization theory: classical, human relations, behavioral decision theories, systems theory, resource dependency, population ecology, and institutional. For example, among the implications from resource dependence theory are communication strategies for managing interdependence across firms, for coordinating the formation and maintenance of interorganizational networks, and for acquiring and controlling information as a source of power. Consider an interorganizational network comprised of a large, dominant manufacturer and a host of suppliers. Resource dependence issues are increasingly implicated as their transactions become mediated by new information technology. General Motors, for instance, has a network of many small supplies of parts and other materials that depend upon GM. GM now requires all suppliers to use electronic data interchange (EDI) in lieu of paper-based business transactions for order entry. However, in the absence of a universal EDI standard, GM requires all of its suppliers to use the GM promoted MAP standard. This further increases suppliers' dependency on GM, as they must invest scarce resources on a specific type of information system that may not permit links with other manufacturers.

The EDI example described above illustrates one of several ways that information technology concepts can be integrated into an existing theory via development of the theory's communication implications. Viewed from a different angle, employment of the new technology appeared to "reinforce" an existing structure of power relationships. An alternative perspective predicts that use of new communication technologies reverses existing structural trends. Thus, with deployment of new information technologies, a highly centralized organization will become more decentralized, and vice versa. (For a review of these two perspectives see Dutton & Kraemer, 1980. Nass & Mason, Chapter 3, also touch on this issue.) As we become more sophisticated in the development of organizational theory that is sensitive to new communication technologies, we can generate more complex conceptualizations than simple reinforcement or reversal approaches.

How Do We Assess Theory?

Increased effort at theory building will require ongoing efforts to evaluate and improve the resulting theory. Certainly the same classic metrics that are used to evaluate any theory pertain to theories of organizations and information technology. Theoretical frameworks must still be judged by their ability to target empirically accessible questions, provide for parsimonious explanations, and maintain internal consistency and logical coherence (Weick, 1987). Additionally, given the critical importance of information technology to organizational functioning, theories must also be judged by their ability to address issues of relevance to practitioners. As Huber (Chapter 11) notes, the newness and volatility of the "new" technologies create a vacuum of applicable managerial experience to guide management of impacts. This means that relevant, valid theory is doubly important.

The role of relevance as a criterion for evaluating organizational theories is stressed by Weick (1987, p. 105), who elaborates upon five properties of relevance developed by Thomas and Tymon (1982). Theories that have *descriptive relevance* address issues and phenomena that practitioners actually encounter. To the extent that outcomes of interest are addressed by theories, they have *goal relevance*. If the causal variables in a theory can in some way be controlled by practitioners, then Weick suggests that theory has *operational validity*. When theories exceed the complexity of common sense knowledge already used by practitioners, they meet the criterion of *nonobviousness*. Finally, Weick notes that *timely* theories are developed soon enough to deal with current problems. As Weick (1987) notes, however, not all good theories are so applied at the outset; many often lack descriptive relevance and timeliness in particular. Yet a theory that does not meet these two criteria might still prove to be relevant once applied to a specific situation. In so doing, the theory may be altered to conform to local conditions, and become both descriptively relevant and timely.

What Do These Theories Imply
for the Research Process?

Many authors in this volume take Huber's advice and suggest implications for management practice. For this chapter, we conclude with a brief consideration of several implications of the combined chapters for the practice of research.

First, we must employ methods that capture processes as they unfold over time. Consider the Critical Mass Theory developed by Markus (Chapter 9) to explain the process of adopting interactive communication technologies among communities. She develops several propositions regarding the paths to success or failure to achieve universal access to the technology. To appropriately test her notions, researchers must assess the production function for the innovation, and must look for the "tipping point" on the curve. This will require methods that are sensitive to the rate of change across time. In Chapter 6, Fulk et al. propose a process of social influence on media attitudes and behavior. One way to assess the patterns of social influence is to introduce information about a new medium selectively into an organization, and then to trace the influence process throughout communication networks over time. In Chapter 11, Huber notes that initial responses to communication options are influenced by novelty and by an incomplete understanding of the technology. He proposes that the initial, nonrational behavior is ineffective for survival; in the long term it will be replaced by rational use of the technology. This line of thinking demands a longer time horizon than is typically found in organizational information technology research. Longitudinal designs are also relatively uncommon in communication research, although scholars recognize the processual nature of organizational communication phenomena. New methods and analytical techniques are being developed and should be applied to the study of these phenomena (Monge, Farace, Eisenberg, Miller, & White, 1984).

Second, many models would benefit from field research in naturally occurring settings. Social information processing, social influence, and structural symbolic interactionism perspectives particularly emphasize prolonged exposure to cues from the social environment; laboratory experiments may not generalize well to real-life social contexts.

Third, we must attend more to both group- and macro-level variables. Current research excessively focuses on individual behaviors and attitudes. Poole & DeSanctis (Chapter 8) call our attention to the importance of group process for technology-mediated interactive tasks. Connolly and Thorn (Chapter 10), as well as Markus (Chapter 9), direct our attention to community behavior. Of particular interest in all three of these models is the interface between individual and group (or community) behavior in decisions about technology use. The development of the theoretical tissue for this interstice will be aided by research which accommodate cross-level relationships. Rousseau's (1985) treatise on multilevel and cross-level perspectives in organizational research serves as a useful resource for this endeavor.

Fourth, qualitative and interpretive methodologies should be employed to test several of these theories. Trevino et al. (Chapter 4), Fulk et al. (Chapter 6), and Contractor and Eisenberg (Chapter 7) all posit processes that are difficult to capture using other methodologies. These authors conceptually explore the symbolic meanings attached to media. Trevino et al. suggest a critical events methodology as one qualitative technique for identifying the meanings that respondents attach to objects in their environment.

Finally, Nass and Mason (Chapter 3) argue that research on information technologies must focus less on specific technologies, such as computer conferencing, fax, or local area networks. Rather, we should assess dimensions that apply across a wide spectrum of information technologies. This strategy allows us to construct theories that are not technology specific, and permits comparisons among information technologies. The net result is theoretical frameworks that are more generalizable to new contexts and new technological configurations. Methodologically, this suggests that researchers direct attention to a variety of information technologies in their empirical efforts. Generalizability can be further enhanced by selecting sets of technologies that in combination maximize variability along Nass and Mason's dimensions. One implication of this argument is that we should spend less effort trying to define and distinguish technologies and more time trying to understand the communication process that they imply. The level of specificity required for the definitional effort focuses our attention on the proverbial trees, at the risk of losing sight of the forest. Indeed, the theoretical approaches developed in this volume represent a set of frameworks that are independent of any specific information and communication technologies.

Conclusion

The broad set of perspectives presented in this compendium are designed to move us toward a more theory-rich field. The uses of the label *theory* are as diverse as the contents of the works themselves. Our goal was less to present closed deductive systems than to organize thought and energize conceptual development on a very important and timely topic for organizational communication studies. It has taken several decades to build the data component of this field of inquiry. To the extent that these contributions move us more rapidly toward developing the theory component and stimulating theory-driven research, we will have been successful in our undertaking.

References

Blalock, H. (1969). *Theory construction: From verbal to mathematical formulations*. Englewood Cliffs, NJ: Prentice-Hall.

Buck, R. C. (1956). On the logic of general behavior systems theory. In H. Feigl & M. Scriven (Eds.), *The foundations of science and the concepts of psychology and psychoanalysis* (pp. 223-238). Minneapolis: University of Minnesota Press.

Crane, D. (1980). Reply to Pickering. *Social Studies of Science, 10*, 502-506.

Dutton, W., & Kraemer, K. (1980). Automating bias. *Society, 17*.

Euske, N., & Roberts, K. (1987). Evolving perspectives in organization theory: Communication implications. In F. Jablin, L. Putnam, K. Roberts, & L. Porter (Eds.), *Handbook of organizational communication* (pp. 41-69). Newbury Park, CA: Sage.

Farace, R. V., Monge, P. R., & Russell, H. M. (1977). *Communicating and organizing*. Reading, MA: Addison-Wesley.

Hesse, M. (1970). *Models and analogies in science*. Notre Dame, IN: University of Notre Dame Press.

Hiltz, S. (1984). *Online communities: A case study of the office of the future*. Norwood, NJ: Ablex.

Johansen, R. (1976, May). *Pitfalls in the social evaluation of teleconferencing media*. Paper presented at the meeting of the Second Annual International Communications Conference, University of Wisconsin, Madison.

Klemmer, E. (1973). Preface to the special issue on interpersonal communication systems. *Human Factors, 15*(5), 435.

Knorr-Cetina, K. (1981). *The manufacture of knowledge*. New York: Pergamon.

Miller, R., & Vallee, J. (1980). Towards a formal representation of ems. *Telecommunications Policy, 4*(2), 79-95.

Mitroff, I., & Featheringham, T. (1974). On systemic problem solving and the error of the third kind. *Behavioral Science, 19*, 383-393.

Monge, P., Farace, R., Eisenberg, E., Miller, K., & White, L. (1984). The process of studying process in organizational communication. *Journal of Communication, 34*, 22-43.

Pickering, A. (1980). Exemplars and analogies: A comment on Crane's study of Kuhnian paradigms in high energy physics. *Social Studies of Science, 10*, 497-502.

Pickering, A. (1984). *Constructing quarks: A sociological history of particle physics*. Chicago: University of Chicago Press.

Popper, K. (1981). The myth of inductive hypothesis generation. In R.D. Tweney, M.E. Mynatt, & R. Clifford (Eds.) *On scientific thinking* (pp. 72-76). New York: Columbia University.

Rousseau, D. M. (1985). Issues of level in organizational research: Multi-level and cross-level perspectives. In L.L. Cummings & B. M. Staw (Eds.), *Research in organizational behavior* (pp. 1-37). Greenwich, CT: JAI.

Shannon, C., & Weaver, W. (1949). *The mathematical theory of communication*. Urbana, IL: University of Illinois Press.

Staw, B. M. (1985) Repairs on the road to relevance and rigor: Some unexplored issues in publishing organizational research. In L.L. Cummings & P.J. Frost (Eds.), *Publishing in the organizational sciences* (pp. 96-107). Homewood, IL: Irwin.

Thomas, K., & Tymon, W. (1982). Necessary properties of relevant research: Lessons from recent criticisms of the organizational sciences. *Academy of Management Review, 7,* 345-352.

Weick, K. (1987). Theorizing about organizational communication. In F. Jablin, L. Putnam, K. Roberts, & L. Porter (Eds.), *Handbook of organizational communication* (pp. 97-122). Newbury Park, CA: Sage.

Willer, D. (1967). *Scientific sociology: Theory and method.* Englewood Cliffs, NJ: Prentice-Hall.

Two Views of Information Technology, Tasks, and Organizations

A useful beginning point for a series of theoretical essays on information technology processes and effects is a conceptual analysis of the key construct—information technology. What is information technology? How does it differ from other types of technologies? What information processing features characterize different technologies? The two chapters in this section address these fundamental issues, and provide a conceptual foundation for emerging theoretical structures on information technologies in the organizational context.

In Chapter 2, James Beniger traces the historical development of organizational forms, illustrating the discontinuity that occurred with the development of industrial technologies. These technologies created a crisis of control, and resulted in the establishment of new bureaucratic forms capable of dealing with the added complexity engendered by rapid machine-based processes. For Beniger, information technologies are the latest innovation necessitated by this crisis of control, and as such are another manifestation of a "control technology." By comparing organizational forms to information technology architectures, Beniger isolates the central elements of these two technologies of control. He argues persuasively that to the degree that all controllers are similar with respect to information processing, an understanding of either organization or information technology cannot help but inform understanding of the other.

Clifford Nass and Laurie Mason contend that recent work on information technologies is limited because it lacks an integrated set of variables that apply to the entire range of information technologies. Current research, regardless of whether it focuses on a particular technology or the actions of individual actors, treats information technologies in holistic terms. The problem with treating specific information technologies as a whole unit is that findings cannot be generalized to other technologies. As an alternative, they suggest a variable-based approach. This approach explicates the key characteristics of information technologies as variables. Individual technologies are conceptualized as sets of variables rather than as whole units. The resulting framework permits comparisons across different technologies.

JAMES R. BENIGER

2. Conceptualizing Information Technology as Organization, and Vice Versa

About a decade ago, when personal computing briefly became a fad approaching a craze in the United States, many American reporters and commentators cast about for examples of important human tasks that would be difficult if not impossible to perform without computers. Because the so-called energy crisis was then still a vivid memory for many people, several writers independently decided to illustrate the computer's crucial role with a compelling example: the monitoring of the global movement of crude oil in ocean-going tankers.

Keeping track of tanker movements internationally may seem like a formidable data-processing task, but in fact it not only does not require a computer, but can be handled most effectively using only a pencil and a modest supply of 3×5 cards. Why? The explanation, as even cursory knowledge of information-processing and control technology would suggest, can be found in theoretical dimensions of the elements that organization and computers would control: the number of tankers, their speed, the complexity of their interactions, the predictability of their routes, and the probability and complexity of various contingencies.

Ocean-going oil tankers are relatively few in number, move extremely slowly, travel a small number of familiar routes known well in advance, and do not interact physically. What few simple contingency plans they have, for changes in political or weather conditions, are widely known and rarely used. All of these factors mean that the global movement of crude oil via tankers can be monitored quite effectively by merely reading a weekly trade paper and noting changes from the previous issue. Those reporters who wrote about such monitoring, presumably because little theory underlay their incidental knowledge of information technology and organizational control, were simply wrong in citing this example as something that could not be done without computers.

What example might have served? Consider again the basic theoretical dimensions of control: the number of at least partially independent elements, their speed, predictability, and interactions, and the probability and complexity of contingencies. This simple list would have led reporters to problems of controlling large numbers of high-speed objects (or rapidly changing variables) in real time—despite complex interactions of serious consequence—in a highly uncertain environment.

Transporting people from earth to the moon and back safely, for example, is without question something that could not be done without computers. Although sufficiently large and well-organized numbers of clerical personnel could perform the requisite calculations and other data processing, no arrangement of personnel could possibly execute these tasks fast enough to be effective (a conclusion which, because it hinges on the speed of communication among individuals, is actually subject to formal proof).

Similarly, air traffic control could not be maintained in anything like its present form without computers, although the airline reservation system could be, given modern telecommunications, although at a highly prohibitive cost. Centralized control of highway traffic, essentially the air traffic problem reduced from four dimensions (including time) to two, and confined to simple networks and to much slower speeds (though with proportionately tighter spacing), is clearly an intermediate problem—near the borderline of organizational control that might be effected (allowing for unlimited costs) without computers.

Computers and Organization

The question of what tasks would be difficult or impossible without computers might profitably be adopted as a general method for the study of organizations. It is introduced here to illustrate three points:

1. Theory is important to the practical understanding of information technologies in organizations (because lack of theory can lead, as we have seen, to seemingly plausible answers that are in fact quite silly).
2. Large-scale formal organization and computers have much the same practical functions in many applications (organization is often the most competitive alternative to computers, as we have also seen, in which case an economic tradeoff exists between the two).
3. To the extent that formal organizations and computers are homologous, understanding of the former can be informed by theories about information usually associated with the other, including those involv-

ing information processing, communication, decision, and control in the most abstract sense.

To appreciate the relationship between formal organization and computers, it is useful to consider the third major generalized information processor and hence controller available in even the earliest human societies, namely, the human brain. The unaided brain remains to this day the most awesome of all information-processing capabilities, a fact often overlooked amid the more recent adulation of computer technology. Undeniably computers can do many things better than can the brain, and many other things that the brain cannot do at all, as can also many organizations. Who amongst us, however, would want to replace the information-processing capabilities of our own brains with those of even the most efficient organization, or even the fastest and most powerful supercomputer?

Knowledge of the human brain, its capabilities and limitations, is crucial to the study of formal organization for at least two reasons: First, throughout history formal organization has emerged only as practical tasks involving information processing, communication, and control exceeded those same capabilities of the unaided human brain. Second, formal organization—itself a means of information processing, decision, and control—ultimately derives these capabilities from those of the individual brains of its human constituents, and thus cannot transcend their collective limitations and the constraints of their interconnectedness.

As expected from this perspective, the earliest known formal organizations arose (about 3000 B.C.) with the earliest known social systems that exceeded—in both scope and complexity—the information-processing capabilities of the unaided human brain. Best known among such early systems were the ancient nation-states of Mesopotamia and ancient Egypt and the later empires of Rome, China, and Byzantium. Until the industrialization of the nineteenth century, formal organization appeared only when collective activities needed to be coordinated by two or more brains toward explicit and impersonal goals, that is, needed to be *controlled*.

In terms of the various dimensions of control discussed above, however, preindustrial organization arose only when the number of elements, the scope and complexity of interactions and contingencies, or the volume of processing exceeded the capability of any one brain to control (as they did, most notably, in the early nation states, especially in their military operations). Preindustrial organizations were apparently never intended to control the *speed* of movements or flows, however, also expected from our

perspective, given that organizations are much slower at processing information than is the brain. Only when speed is accompanied by sufficient volume
of movements or flows do organizational capabilities exceed those of the
brain.

In short, formal organization might be seen as the best known means to
make a computer before the development of electronics, or as a prototypical
computer that uses multiple human brains as components, or as the computer that results from the coupling of various brains by means of formal
rules and channels of communication. Certainly many homologous relationships can be seen among formal organization, the computer, and the brain,
or among the various constituent brains in an organization and the components of a computer, or among the varied applications of these three generalized information processors. Not until the nineteenth century, however, did
advances in energy technology bring formal organization in the modern
sense—and with it, ironically enough, the need for purely technological
control that would eventually undermine the need for organization itself.

Industrialization and Organization

That formal organization did not begin to achieve anything approximat-
ing its modern form until industrialization can be seen in the growth of the
U.S. government. As late as the 1830s, for example, the Bank of the United
States, then the nation's largest and most complex organization with 22
branch offices and profits 50 times those of the largest mercantile house, was
managed by just three people: Nicholas Biddle and two assistants (Redlich,
1951/1968, pp. 113-124). In 1831, President Andrew Jackson and 665 other
civilians ran all three branches of the federal government in Washington, an
increase of just 63 employees (10.4%) over the previous ten years. Fifty years
later, however, in the aftermath of rapid industrialization, Washington's
bureaucracy included some 13,000 civilian employees, more than *double* the
total—already swelled by the American Civil War—only ten years earlier
(U.S. Bureau of the Census, 1975, p. 1103).

Much the same organizational revolution occurred—at about the same
time—in American marketing. As late as the 1840s, the staff of one of the
country's largest importers consisted of the owner, his son, two or three
clerks, and a porter; together they handled perhaps a quarter-million dollars
in annual sales (Tooker, 1955, pp. 64-65; 225). Just a quarter-century later
A.T. Stewart, then America's foremost dry goods distributor, had 2,000

employees and annual sales of $50 million; by 1873 the firm had a branch purchasing office in every major textile and apparel center in Great Britain and Western Europe (Resseguie, 1965).

Further evidence that a qualitatively new type of formal organization developed in response to industrialization can be found in the growth of concern about bureaucratization as a pressing social problem in the middle and late nineteenth century. The word *bureaucracy* did not even appear in English until the early nineteenth century, yet within a generation the phenomenon had become a major topic of political and philosophical discussion. As early as 1837, for example, John Stuart Mill wrote of a "vast network of administrative tyranny...that system of *bureaucracy*" (Burchfield, 1972, p. 391). A decade later Mill warned more generally of the "inexpediency of concentrating in a dominant bureaucracy . . . all power of organized action . . . in the community" (Mill, 1848, p. 529), followed in two years by Thomas Carlyle, who complained of "the Continental nuisance called 'Bureaucracy'" (Carlyle, 1850/1898, p. 121). The word *bureaucratic* had also appeared by the 1830s, followed by *bureaucrat* in the 1840s and *bureaucratize* by the 1890s.

Historians of formal organization also find qualitatively different organizational structures emerging with widespread industrialization in the middle and late nineteenth century. Harvard Business School historian Alfred Chandler, for example, hails the Western Railroad reorganization of the early 1840s as "the first modern, carefully defined, internal organizational structure used by an American business enterprise" (Chandler, 1977, p. 97). The first hierarchical organizational system of information gathering, processing, and telegraphic communication to centralize control in a manager's office (Erie Railroad) followed in 1853, formal line-and-staff control of an organization (Pennsylvania Railroad) in 1857, organizational structures (large wholesale houses) with a half-dozen or more operating departments controlled by a hierarchy of salaried managers in the late 1860s, and a centralized, functionally departmentalized corporate organization (General Electric) by the mid-1890s (Beniger, 1986, pp. 278-287; 390-399).

As final evidence that a qualitatively new type of formal organization developed in response to industrialization in the middle and late nineteenth century, consider that the first major theorist of modern organization, the German sociologist and political economist Max Weber (1864-1920), emerged during the same period. Those who have speculated about why Weber concentrated his attention on bureaucracy have tended to overlook—because of the ancient origins of formal organization—the possibility that he was simply attracted to the most revolutionary new technology of his age. If Weber were writing today, it follows, he might well apply much the same social analysis not to bureaucracy but to computers.

Technology and Organizational Control

Prior to industrialization, as we have seen, formal organization arose (prototypically in large nation states and their military operations) to control large numbers of elements, excessive scope or complexity of interactions and contingencies, or an otherwise unmanageable volume of processing—but never *speed* of movements or flows per se. We have already considered one reason: Organizations are much slower at processing information, other factors like volume held constant, than is the individual, unaided human brain. Consider now a second reason: Before industrialization, in effect the application of inanimate sources of energy (especially steam) throughout the material economy, few if any material processes—then driven by wind and water power, draft animal, and human muscle—could move nearly fast enough to exceed the capability of a single brain to control.

Seen in this way, industrialization, which at least potentially increased the speeds of most material processes 20 to 80 times virtually overnight, must have posed an unprecedented challenge and threat to formal organization, with its considerable disadvantages—relative to the individual brain—in controlling speed. Why, then, did industrialization not reverse the development of formal organization in favor of individual human control? Why, to the contrary, did industrialization in fact stimulate the rapid development of formal organization and corporate and state bureaucracies in their various modern forms (as we have just seen)?

The answer is that industrialization created both the need and the possibility for purely *technological* control (as opposed to either organizational or individual human control) of physical movements and flows. Control technologies, unlike formal organizations, can process at least highly constrained and routinized information faster than can the unaided brain. Because of the abstract and highly generalizable properties of control, however, technologies for the control of material flows can be readily adapted to the control of information and humans, and hence to control within organizations (computers being only one recent example). Thus by vastly increasing the speeds of material processing, industrialization created not only the need for modern organization but also both the need and possibility of control by technology, a factor that—ironically enough—would begin to erode the purpose of organization itself.

First Modern Organizations

To illustrate, consider the case of the railroads, already cited as the first modern organizational structures in American business. The earliest U.S. railroads, built between 1826 and 1830, used horses to draw cars along cast-iron rails. Steam power began to replace the horses in the early 1830s, thereby increasing operating speeds from 1 or 2 to more than 30 miles per hour literally overnight. Because early railroads operated for most of their length on only a single track, their most obvious control problem was to avoid head-on collisions. Lacking even the most rudimentary control technologies, early railroads adopted one of two solutions: On longer, lightly traveled roads (mostly in the rural West), all trains ran one way one day and the other way the next. Shorter and busier roads (mostly in the Northeast), for which this solution proved uneconomical or inconvenient, had the first of two trains scheduled to meet running in opposite directions wait on a siding until the other had passed.

The Western Railroad was—not incidentally—America's first inter-sectional line. With 156 miles of road connecting Worcester and Albany, the single-track Western was the first rail company forced, in order to maintain sufficient volume of traffic, to schedule as many as two passenger trains and one freight a day each way. This required nine daily "meets," times when trains had to wait on a siding for one going in the opposite direction to pass. On October 5, 1841, on a section of the road opened only the previous day, disaster struck: Two Western passenger trains collided head-on, killing two people, seriously maiming eight, and less critically injuring nine others. The public outcry, including an investigation by the Massachusetts legislature, reflected a preindustrial age not yet accustomed to travel at the speed of steam power, certainly not at the Western's operating speeds of up to 30 miles per hour—especially where horses had pulled cars only one-twentieth as fast less than a decade earlier (Salsbury, 1967).

As a result of the outcry and subsequent investigation, Western management instituted no less than America's first modern organizational structure: Control of the entire Western line and all of its various operations became centralized in a new headquarters in Springfield, Massachusetts. Because the Western was the first enterprise to extend beyond the span of a single manager's close personal contacts, a distance Chandler (1962, p. 21) sets for early railroads at roughly 100 miles, its headquarters was linked to three regional offices, each by three distinctly separate, carefully defined chains of authority and command. One chain passed through three regional "roadmasters" to control tracks, roadbeds, bridges, and buildings; a second stretched through three divisional masters and the various station agents to control all passenger and freight traffic; the third ran through master and deputy mechanics at each terminal and roundhouse to control all engines and rolling stock.

To command this new organizational structure, Western management reorganized its entire operations into a data-processing, communication, and control system that was, in effect, a prototypical computer. Innovations included regularity in data collection, formalization of information processing and decision rules, and standardization of communication with feedback. Responsibility for updating the three roadmasters on track conditions fell to conductors, enginemen, and stationmasters, who were required to pass a continuous stream of data along the regional hierarchies. Each roadmaster, in turn, was required to keep a journal of his operations and to make a formal monthly report to the chief engineer at headquarters. The company specified that "no alteration in the time of running or mode of meeting and passing of trains shall take effect until after positive knowledge shall have been received at the office of the superintendent that orders for such change have been received and are understood by all concerned" (Salsbury, 1967, p. 186).

Control of each train passed from the engineman, brakeman, and various other employees and became centralized in a conductor who had standardized detailed programming for responding to delays, breakdowns, and other contingencies. The conductor also carried a good watch, carefully synchronized with all others on the line, and moved his train according to precise timetables. He controlled all operations between origin and destination, including those of the engineman and brakeman, from his platform outside the first car of the train. Not only did he control the brake of this car, but he alone—except in sudden emergencies—determined when and where to stop and when to start, signaling his decisions by pulling a cord connected to the engine bell. The engineman, who formerly had exercised considerable control over his train, was reduced to little more than a programmable operator, dutifully following rules like "in descending grades higher than 60 feet per mile passenger trains are not to exceed 18 miles per hour and merchandise trains not over 10 miles per hour" (Salsbury, 1967, pp. 187-188).

To describe the conductor and engineman as "programmed" might at first seem anachronistic, a needless intrusion of contemporary jargon into the nineteenth century. In their control of trains, however, Western personnel might have been replaced in most of their functions by on-board microcom-

36

puters or, given modern telecommunications, by a more centralized means of computer control. Seen in this way, the Western conductors take on new significance: They are among the first persons in history to be used as programmable, distributed decision makers in the control of fast-moving flows through a system whose scale and speeds precluded control by more centralized structures, including the highly innovative organization of Western headquarters. This use of humans, not for their strength or agility, nor for their knowledge or intelligence, but for the more prosaic capabilities of their brains to store, retrieve, and process information, would become over the next century a dominant feature of employment in so-called information societies (Beniger, 1986, chaps. 7-9).

As illustrated by the Western Railroad and its early innovations in formal organization, the vastly increased speeds initiated by steam power and industrialization created the need not only for modern organization but also for technological control—a form of control quite distinct from that of either organization or individual human brains. Although second-by-second control of a Western train was largely independent of formal organization, at least before on-board telegraph, it might still seem highly dependent on human brains. Keep in mind, however, the new information technologies found on each train: the printed loose-leaf pages of rules and contingencies, the pocket watches synchronized throughout the system, the signal bell linking conductor and engineman, plus the various ways that the on-board employees had been made over into components of prototypical computer technology.

This final category, because it characterizes modern organization as well as most other technologies (at least before electricity) for controlling the speed of material movements and flows, foreshadows the technologies that would eventually begin to erode the need for organization itself. Just as microcomputers and telecommunications might replace many of the control functions of the on-board conductor, for example, so too might they replace many of the organizational tasks of workers in the Western headquarters. This equivalence of technological and organizational control, and ultimately of machine and brain, is one that Weber first identified as *rationalization*.

Rationalization and Organization

As mentioned, Weber must be considered among the first to establish that formal organization is itself a control technology, most notably in his *Economy and Society* (1922/1968). Among his defining characteristics of formal organization, he included several key elements of any control system: impersonal orientation of structure to the information that it processes, usually identified as cases, clients, customers, or patients, with a predetermined formal set of rules governing all decisions and responses. Any tendency to humanize formal organization, Weber argued, would be minimized through clear-cut division of labor and definition of responsibilities, hierarchical authority, and specialized decision and communication functions. The stability and permanence of organizations, he noted, are assured through regular promotion of career employees based on objective criteria like seniority.

Because of the abstract nature of the concept *formal* in *formal organization*, much of what Weber wrote about the latter subject might well have been written about the computer (or indeed any formal information processor and controller). Certainly computers, by virtue of being machines, have relative stability and permanence and maintain an impersonal orientation to the information that they process. Their programming (firmware as well as software) constitutes the formal set of rules governing all their decisions and responses, a priori and without prejudice about individual cases. Like formal organizational structure, computer structure can ordinarily be characterized as at least partially hierarchical, with clear-cut lines of authority (or priority) and specialized communication and decision functions. Indeed, virtually the only ways Weber characterized organizations that do *not* apply to computers concern problems associated with engineering actual human beings into such impersonal structures (those involving criteria of promotion like seniority, for example).

A far more subtle control technology, closely associated with that of formal organization, Weber called *rationalization*. Although the term has a variety of meanings, both in Weber's writings and in the elaborations of his work by others (Collins, 1986, chap. 4), most definitions can be subsumed by one essential idea: Control can be increased not only by increasing the capability to process information but also by decreasing the amount of information to be processed. The former approach to control was what Weber defined as formal organization and is today increasingly realized through computerization; the latter approach was what he usually meant by rationalization, what computer scientists now call *preprocessing*. Just as rationalization complemented and increased formal organizational control, according to Weber, so too does preprocessing—the destruction or ignoring of information in order to facilitate its processing—serve computerized control today.

Formal organization and rationalization intersect in the regulation of interpersonal relationships in terms of a formal set of impersonal and objective criteria. The early technocrat Saint-Simon, who lived to see only the earliest stages of industrialization, described such rationalization as a move "from the government of men to the administration of things" (Taylor 1975,

Pt. 3). The reason why people can be governed more readily *qua* things is that the amount of information about them that needs to be processed is thereby greatly reduced and hence the degree of control—for any constant capacity to process information—is correspondingly increased.

With sufficient rationalization, it is possible to maintain even the largest and most complex organizations, social systems and societies—ones that would be overwhelmed by a rising tide of information they could not process were it necessary to govern by the particularistic considerations of family and kin that characterize preindustrial societies. One example in formal organization is the development of standardized business forms, a major preprocessing technology. Because proliferation of paperwork is usually associated with a growth in information to be processed and not with its reduction, the development of business forms might at first seem to undermine control. Imagine how much more processing would be required of an organization if each new case were recorded in a completely unstructured way, however, and not limited to formal, objective, and impersonal information required by the standardized form.

Organizational Control Through Preprocessing

what is preprocessing, + give examples

Industrialization and the development of information societies provide many examples of innovations in preprocessing—the destruction, filtering out, or ignoring of information in order to facilitate its processing—that have enhanced control by organizations. Major innovations in organizational control through preprocessing include:

Time zones. As long as transportation moved at only a few miles per hour, the fact that neighboring towns often had slightly different times (differences in so-called "sun time") posed no problem in information processing—travelers could adjust watches at their leisure. With industrialization, however, steam moved complex rail networks, extending over thousands of miles of track, at upward of 40 miles per hour, thereby threatening—through information overload—organizational control of transportation. In 1883, at the initiative of the American Railway Association, North America was divided into five standardized time zones, thereby defining away almost all information about differences in sun time among cities (organization of world time into 24 zones came the following year). With sufficiently cheap and powerful distributed computing, ironically enough, it may soon be at least feasible to return to a transportation system based on local solar time, thereby shifting control from preprocessing back to processing—where it resided for centuries before steam power pushed humans beyond the pace of the sun across the sky.

Standardized grading. With the increasing growth and complexity of the rail system, in the 1850s, and the greater speed and volume of rail shipments, it became increasingly difficult for transporters to keep track of farm produce "in separate units as numerous as there were owners" (Clark, 1966, p. 259). This control crisis eased only with innovations in preprocessing: the various standardized methods of sorting, grading, weighing, and inspecting farm products still familiar today. These innovations greatly reduced the information processing necessary to control shipments of agricultural products, in effect by defining away all but a limited set of differences among the harvests of individual farmers. In less-developed countries, by contrast, even humble commodities such as ice cream cones sold by street vendors are still individually weighed to determine price. Consider how much more expensive, say, grocery shopping would be if commodities such as eggs were sold by individual weight rather than in set numbers of standardized grades.

Fixed prices. In the bazaars of less-developed countries, sellers still bargain individually, asking prices based on each buyer's social position, apparent need, and manifest interest in an item. Imagine the information-processing problems such a system would pose for inventory and employee control, accounting and related investment decisions. It is hardly surpising that efforts to preprocess away these control problems through fixed prices followed closely the advance of industrialization in the West, led—as might be expected—by the first mass retailers, the department and chain stores. The pioneering Paris department store Bon Marché had a fixed-price, one-price policy as early as 1852; ten years later Stewart's department store introduced the policy in the United States. F.W. Woolworth, who adopted the idea in his first "Five and Ten Cent Store" in 1879 (it had become a chain of 59 stores by 1900), further rationalized the preprocessing technology in *price lining*, the mass production of items expressly chosen or designed to sell at a predetermined price.

Trademarks. Brand names, labels, and trademarks constitute one of the most important preprocessing technologies of the industrial era. Because they help goods (and increasingly even services) to "sell themselves," trademarks reduce the information and associated costs of advertising, marketing and promotion in control of demand—and make such activities more cost effective as well. The first U.S. trademark legislation, enacted in 1870, attracted no registrants for more than three months and only 121 during the year. As might be expected, interest in trademarks awaited development of sufficient mass production of consumer goods, with the resulting need to control demand.

In 1880, on the eve of continuous-processing manufacturing, when the old trademark law was declared unconstitutional, Congress quickly passed new legislation—and businesses raced to register (Smith, 1923). Economic value of the new technology was easy to chart: Within the decade, royalties to use the Baker Chocolate name and trademark reached $10,000 a year; by 1905 *Printers' Ink* estimated the value of Royal Baking Powder's trade name to be $5 million, "a million dollars a letter" (Pope, 1983, p. 69).

The concept of preprocessing as an information-processing and control option available to organizations helps to explain a recent anomaly—the growing importance of *brand equity*, which varies according to the associations and behaviors of a brand's customers that enable it to earn greater volume or margins of sales. Increasingly brand names have acquired values that actually may exceed all of a firm's other assets. Evidently trademarks, brand names and labels, even though they are nothing more than information (albeit information in the heads of possibly millions of consumers), now constitute a means of capital investment beginning to rival opportunities in more traditional capital forms.

General Classes of Organizational Control

As these and earlier examples suggest, there exist general classes of organizational opportunities, functions or requirements that are intrinsically information-processing, communication, and control problems—problems for which computers and other information technologies are likely to be useful. Because these are *general* classes of problems, they have not changed much since their earliest appearance under industrialization. Study of organiztional control problems as members of these general classes will argue the value of theory in understanding information technology as organization, and vice versa.

To illustrate, consider the following ten general classes of control problems that have confronted organizations, listed in the order of their first appearance in the United States (often the earliest in the world) with a recent manifestation included for comparison:

1. Control of independently moving objects to prevent them from colliding: Organization of railroads following the Western crash of 1841; air traffic control.

2. Control of a great many objects in a complex network to prevent them from getting lost: Organization of freight car traffic on the Erie Railroad, America's first great trunk line, in the early 1850s; similar problems of automobile and trailer rental companies.

3. Control of movements or flows of individually unique commodities among many buyers and sellers in complex markets in order properly to charge receivers and compensate senders: Rationalization of commodity markets—through standardization of methods of sorting, grading, weighing, and inspecting—in the 1850s; royalty compensation of multiple authors of works written on computer networks, or of authors whose works are distributed by means of rental libraries, photocopying, etc.

4. Control of movements or flows through complex networks so that control might pass—simultaneously with the flows themselves—to adjoining, autonomously controlled networks: Monitoring by railroads of the location and mileage of "foreign" cars on their lines, by means of car accountant offices and through bills of lading, in the 1860s; control of cellular telephone calls among various "cells."

5. Control to push movements or flows as fast as possible past fixed capital (both to maximize returns and to prevent capital shifts to other investments): Struggle of rail mills adopting the Bessemer process in the late 1860s to control increasing throughput speeds in the production of steel; organizational innovations to speed customers through fast-food restaurants and theme parks such as DisneyWorld.

6. Control to push as much inventory as possible past fixed retailing capital (again to maximize returns and to prevent capital shifts to other investments): Struggle by large wholesalers and retailers (such as department stores) in the late 1860s to maintain high rates of stock turn; similar problems in "just-in-time" inventory control in large mail-order operations.

7. Control of increasingly differentiated units of organization in order to integrate and coordinate them in a larger organizational structure: Struggle in the 1870s by the large wholesale houses, the most differentiated organizational structures in the nineteenth century, to integrate a growing number of highly specialized operating units; the control problems that constitute the central focus of organization and management theory, management information (MIS) and decision support systems.

8. Control of consumer demand to match production flows: Efforts after the 1880s by the first companies to adopt continuous-processing technologies—including producers of oatmeal, flour, soap, cigarettes, matches, canned foods, and photographic film—to stimulate and control consumption using national advertising of brand names directly to the mass household market; modern demand-driven manufacturing.

9. Control of multiple and diverse inputs to complex assembly or other value-added processing: Efforts after the 1880s by metalworking industries—from castings and screws to sewing machines, typewriters, and electric motors—to control throughputs at the volume and speed of the metal producers; PERT charting and related technologies in manufacturing and other large-scale organized projects.

10. Control of information processing itself as it expands in one of the above-mentioned applications: Efforts by large companies after the 1880s to contain the growing scope, complexity, and speed of information processing—including inventory, billing, and sales analysis—necessary for control of new organizational systems; airline reservations and billing systems following the explosive growth of international air travel.

As these ten classes of problems suggest, the opportunities, functions, and requirements of formal organization intrinsically involve information processing, communication, decision, and control. These factors, in turn, combine in a relatively small number of general control problems—problems which have changed little except in specifics since their earliest appearance under industrialization. This suggests, first, that formal organization will be most usefully understood in the broader context of the human brain, the computer, and other technologies (including rationalization and preprocessing) with which it might be substituted, in part or in whole; and second, that general theory about information, communication, and control will be indispensable for this broader understanding.

Summary

Like brains and computers, organizations are *controllers*, that is, they exist primarily to process information—and thereby at least partially to control external factors—toward some predetermined set of goals (which of course might be modified as this process unfolds). To the extent that all controllers are homologous with respect to information processing, decision, and control, understanding of either formal organization, the human brain, or computers and related information technologies might be informed by theory involving information usually associated with any of the others.

To the extent that all controllers are homologous, they can be expected to have much the same functions in many practical applications. Just as formal organization has often provided the most competitive alternative to the unaided human brain, especially following industrialization during the middle and late nineteenth century, computers and related technologies usually afford the most competitive alternative to organization in the so-called information societies of the late twentieth century. In general, technologies that fill homologous functions—by constituting alternative means to similar ends—must be considered as economic tradeoffs in relevant applications.

Thus we can see that the two major topics of this edited volume, namely organizations and information technology, are related at the highest levels of generality. As such, they merit joint study for theoretical as well as practical reasons. Guided by any good theory involving information processing, communication, decision, and control, we can expect that any insights gained from the study of either organizations or information technology will immediately inform our understanding of the other. Similarly, we can expect that such knowledge of both organization and information technology—as information processors, deciders, and controllers—will inform economic and other practical decisions in even the most mundane applications.

Here, then, are the rewards, practical no less than theoretical, that we might expect from the continued development of a general theory of information, communication, decision, and control, and from the corresponding conceptualization of information technology as organization—and vice versa.

References

Beniger, James R. (1986). *The control revolution: Technological and economic origins of the information society.* Cambridge, MA: Harvard University Press.

Burchfield, R. W. (Ed.). (1972). *A supplement to the Oxford English dictionary*, vol. 1. Oxford: Oxford University Press, Clarendon.

Carlyle, Thomas. (1850/1898). *Latter-day pamphlets.* New York: Charles Scribner's Sons. (Original work published 1850)

Chandler, Alfred D., Jr. (1962). *Strategy and structure: Chapters in the history of the industrial enterprise.* Cambridge, MA: MIT Press.

Chandler, Alfred D., Jr. (1977). *The visible hand: The managerial revolution in American business.* Cambridge, MA: Belknap Press.

Clark, John G. (1966). *The grain trade in the old northwest.* Urbana: University of Illinois Press.

Collins, Randall. (1986). *Max Weber: A skeleton key.* Beverly Hills, CA: Sage.

Mill, John Stuart. (1848). *Principles of political economy, with some of their applications to social philosophy*, 2 vols. Boston: Little, Brown.

Pope, Daniel. (1983). *The making of modern advertising.* New York: Basic Books.

Redlich, Fritz. (1951/1968). *The molding of American banking, men and ideas.* New York: Johnson Reprint Corporation. (Original work published 1951)

Resseguie, Harry E. (1965). Alexander Turney Stewart and the development of the department store, 1823-1876. *Business History Review*, *39*(3): 301-322.

Salsbury, Stephen. (1967). *The state, the investor, and the railroad: The Boston and Albany, 1825-1867*. Cambridge, MA: Harvard University Press.

Smith, Clayton Lindsay. (1923). *The history of trade marks*. New York: Thomas H. Stuart.

Taylor, Keith (Ed.). (1975). *Henri Saint-Simon (1760-1825): Selected writings on science, industry, and social organization*. New York: Holmes & Meier.

Tooker, Elva. (1955). *Nathan Trotter, Philadelphia merchant, 1787-1853*. Cambridge, MA: Harvard University Press.

U.S. Bureau of the Census. (1975). *Historical statistics of the United States, colonial times to 1970*, 2 vols. Washington, DC: Government Printing Office.

Weber, Max. (1922/1968). *Economy and society: An outline of interpretive sociology*, 3 vols. (Guenther Roth & Claus Wittich, Eds.). New York: Bedminster Press. (Original work published 1922).

CLIFFORD NASS
LAURIE MASON

3. On the Study of Technology and Task: A Variable-Based Approach

If one were to categorize the numerous studies of communication technology and organizations, two clear types would emerge: object-centered and actor-centered. One set of studies would be *object-centered*; that is, the researcher has initiated these studies because the technology, as a material thing, has some particularly interesting feature or features. Usually these studies are motivated by the uniqueness (and usually newness) of a technology. Rather than looking for similarities across technologies, the justification for performing a study is that this technology, as a material object, is different from all previous technologies.

These object-centered studies have a number of other features in common. First, they tend to focus on the technological object as a whole; that is, the question under study, at least implicitly, is "What is the difference between organizations that have this technology and those that do not?" or "How have organizations that have adopted the technology changed?" These studies include work on computers (Forester, 1980, chap. 8), electronic mail (Hiltz & Turoff, 1978), teleconferencing systems (Johansen, Vallee, & Spangler, 1979), telephones (Pool, 1977), and a host of other specific technologies. Second, these studies tend to assume that the technology is a *determinant* of organizational change; that is, each technology necessitates new organizational activities and structures and changes the features of already existing activities and structures. A given communication technology, under this view, changes level of alienation (Form & McMillen, 1983; Vallas & Yarrow, 1987), control of work (Patrickson, 1986), educational requirements (Bell, 1973), gender segregation (Morgall, 1983), goal formation (Tikhomirov & Gur'yeva, 1986), health (Kleeman, 1982), notions of self (Turkle, 1984), productivity (Rice & Bair, 1984), and skill levels (Dickson, 1980; Zuboff, 1988), to give a

Authors' Note: This chapter has benefitted from the comments of Michael Basil, Steven Chaffee, Janet Fulk, Barbara Levitt, John Rawlings, and Charles Steinfield.

few examples. Third, the causes of the appearance and/or use of a particular technology are outside the scope of research; that is, the social determinants of the invention, diffusion, and utilization of a technology are not addressed. A given technology appears *sui generis* in an organization and having appeared, prompts the organization and its participants to adapt; technological growth is fundamentally autonomous (e.g., Ellul, 1964; Rostow, 1971; for a critique of this view, see Winner, 1977). Finally, the nature of a given technology dictates its use; users are relatively passive actors. Even if a variety of uses is socially approved, as in the case of the telephone, eventually the logic of the technology overcomes societal demands and expectations (Pool, 1983).

This object-centered research, using paradigms drawn from history (despite an obsession with newness) and engineering, has much to recommend it. The respect for specificity (Fischer, 1985) has provided important and interesting case studies concerning the individual- and organizational-level effects of particular technologies. The sensitivity to newness has led to a decreasing lag between the introduction of a new organizational communication technology and attempts to characterize its effects (Beniger, 1986), thus providing good opportunities for true pre/post-studies of organizational structure and behavior (in contrast to the dearth of early work on the effects of the introduction of radio and television).

In sharp contrast to the object-centered view are those studies that focus on a social actor or social actors. These *social-actor-centered* studies focus on characteristics of individual-, occupation-, team-, and organization-level variables concerning behaviors and attitudes. That is, the researcher has initiated these studies because one of the elements of the organizational environment that is related to the behavior and attitudes of social actors in organizations (or organizations themselves) is technology. Rather than focusing on the distinctions between a given technology and other technologies, however, social-actor-centered researchers focus on models of attitudes and behaviors toward a technology or technologies, models that are presumed valid across social actors.[1]

The social-actor-centered approach differs from the object-centered approach in other ways as well. First, although both approaches view each technology as a whole, the social-actor-centered approach understands individuals and social aggregates in terms of variables. That is, the question under study is, "How does technology serve as a backdrop against which characteristics associated with individuals and social aggregates are related?" One cannot study a particular organization and conclude simply that workers in the organization acted in relation to some set of variables

47

differently from workers in most organizations; one must identify precisely which characteristics of the organization or organizational participants are relevant. To argue that the organization had never been studied before would be futile; one is required to specify a characteristic (or characteristics) that varies across organizations and for which the organization had a particular value or values that warranted special attention.

The literature on organization is rich with sets of potential variables. For individuals, these include asymmetry in value (Thorn & Connolly, this volume), job tenure (Parcel, Wallace, Kaufman & Grant, 1988), motivation (Gallo, 1986), organizational climate (Margulies & Colflesh, 1982), occupation (Reese, 1988), sense-making (Barley, 1988), symbolic cues (Trevino, Daft, & Lengel, this volume), technological acceptance (Weikle, 1986), and technological optimism (Parcel, Wallace, Kaufman, & Grant, 1988). For organizations, variables include decision processes (Levitt & Nass, 1989), diffusion milieu (Feller & Menzel, 1977), division of labor (Greenbaum, 1976), final product (Machlup, 1962), goals (March & Simon, 1958), and level of formalization (Weber, 1977).

A second characteristic of social-actor-centered studies is that they tend to assume that technologies are the _result_ of individual (and aggregate) behaviors and attitudes, and of changes in behaviors and attitudes; that is, individual and aggregate characteristics determine when and how a technology will be adopted and used and how that technology will alter other aspects of organizational behavior (Fischer, 1985). Third, and conversely, variables associated with social actors are never determined by technology and are relatively stable. Individual differences, almost by definition, are stable traits across time and situations, and do not fit into _process_ theories. Fourth, a given technology, under this view, has relatively few intrinsic features; the dynamic in the technology/social actor relationship is found in the attitudes and behaviors of the social actors.

The social-actor-centered approach, drawing on traditions of psychology and sociology, also provides insights into the relationship between communication technology and organizations. As it is easier to find a large number of individuals and organizations than a large number of different yet related technologies, studies in this tradition have fewer problems with external validity and provide the opportunity to make broad theoretical statements, but the breadth is across social actors rather than across technologies. Because this approach looks for enduring characteristics of individuals and organizations, these studies have successfully identified continuities in organizational behaviors.

Despite these clear differences, the object-centered approach and the social-actor-centered approach have a critical similarity: both perspectives take a *holistic* view of technology. In the object-centered approach, researchers have an explicit fascination with the technology as a whole; that is, with the technology *qua* material entity. In the social-actor-centered approach, a given technology is treated as a whole out of a fundamental lack of interest; it is variation across individuals and social aggregates, not across technologies, that motivates the research.

The holistic view of technology represented by both categories of research *explain* has a critical limitation: *theories that are specified or operationalized in terms of one technology can never be applied to any other technology, whether extant or potentially available.* Thus, they cannot be true theories of technology. The reason for this limitation is that when a technology is said to have a given effect or is said to be affected by some social variable, we do not know what feature or characteristic of the technology has been caused or has led to the effect under study. That is, any single technology represents a particular value on a *number* of variables, and it is almost always impossible to determine contextually which characteristic or characteristics is relevant for a given study. For example, consider a study that demonstrates that personal computers have led to de-skilling in the workplace. If having a value of "very rapid" on the characteristic "processing speed" is the key to the de-skilling of workers, then, *ceteris paribus*, technologies that process information rapidly, such as adding machines, and technologies that preprocess information, such as sorting machines, should also lead to de-skilling (Beniger, 1986; Nass, 1987). However, if the key feature is having the value "keyboard" for the variable "input device" (Morgall, 1983), then typewriters, type-setting machinery, and push-button phones should lead to de-skilling of workers. If the pivotal criterion is "fits on a desktop" for the variable "size" (Dertouzos & Moses, 1979), then telephones, staplers, and reading lamps should lead to de-skilling. If "potentially serious risks" for the variable "health hazards," then microwave ovens or x-ray machines would also be likely de-skillers. If "very humanlike" (Turkle, 1984) for the variable "mode of operation," then robots will be engines of de-skilling; and if "recently" for the variable "when introduced," then almost every technology leads to de-skilling in its time (Mumford, 1935). This same confusion also appears when technology is treated as a result of organizational change.

The critical problem with the nonspecification of key characteristics engendered by this holistic approach is that neither the causes nor the effects of radical new inventions, significant innovations, or even virtual imitations

(Rosenberg, 1976, chap. 2) of a technology can be predicted from the study of the previous technology, because we do not know whether relevant features have been changed.

To address this problem, one must focus on variables that describe technologies. Unfortunately, in contrast to the literature on organizations, there exists today no fundamental list of key variables for the study of technologies; that is, there is no specified set of attributes or dimensions that vary across technologies and that are causes or consequences of organizational phenomena. This absence of technology variables has not always been the case. In 1808, Babbage initiated the formal study of the relationship between technology, including communication technology, and organizations in his book, *On the Economy of Machinery and Manufactures* (Babbage, 1833). The book is filled with analyses of the relationships between characteristics of particular machines and between characteristics of particular processes (manufactures). The Babbage tradition was carried on in the United States by the Scientific Management school (see Scott, 1981, chap. 3). Taylor (1911, 1947), often considered the father of Scientific Management, had a clear concern with the variables associated with information processing and communication technologies.

Despite the utility of the variable-based approach (Hage, 1972), by the 1940s it had fallen out of fashion and had been replaced by the present holistic approach, probably due to two primary causes: (1) the emergence of a holistic approach to individuals in organizations, exemplified by the rise of the human relations school (Mayo, 1945) and the falling out of favor of the Scientific Management approach (Bendix, 1963); and (2) the rise of the Chicago school (Ogburn, 1957), with its emphasis on detailed studies of single sites. In sum, a list of variables is the one thing that students of organizations have that students of technology do not have (Baum, 1966).[2]

Variable-Centered Perspective on Technology

In preparing a list of technological variables, direct reference to Babbage and his immediate successors has three limitations. First, most of the research in the Babbage tradition was developed before information-processing and communication technology became a pivotal part of organizational life and before the post-World War II boom in scholarship on the history of technology. Second, most of the research focusing on large-scale industrial production was limited to technological variables relevant to such processes. Finally, scholars in the Babbage tradition did not develop explicit lists of variables (although one might derive lists from their discussions).

Therefore, the present chapter provides a new list of technology-related variables. Each variable on the list has four key features. First, the variables *vary* across communication technologies. That is, each value of each variable is manifested in at least one communication technology. For example, for the variable "speed of copying," some communication technologies duplicate information very rapidly (a web press); some duplicate information fairly rapidly (fast photocopiers); some relatively slowly (hand-driven printing press); and some extremely slowly (pen plotters). Second, the variables on the list have been designed to apply to communication technologies of the past, present, and future; that is, the variables suggest continuities and differences across historical time, a departure from the usual focus on *new* technologies. Third, the variables highlight both similarities and differences between technologies. For example, both linotype machines and most personal computers have keyboard input, suggesting that manual dexterity is a key criterion for use of both technologies; however, linotype machines cannot produce new information, while personal computers can. Finally, the variable can be independent, intervening, or dependent, depending on the research question.

The variables we identify are divided into two types: those that describe technologies as a "box" and those that describe the tasks that technologies perform; that is, the static and dynamic aspects of a technology, respectively. For example, an answering machine is sometimes a transmitter of information (e.g., "the person is not at his or her desk") and sometimes a recorder of information (e.g., the message left by the caller). Each of these tasks will have different values on the task variables. However, the answering machine will have the same value for the "box" variables, regardless of the task the machine is performing. Because of the complex relationships between form and function in information-processing and communication technologies, the distinction between "box" variables and "task" variables can be blurred.

Both categories of variables seem relevant to the study of organizations. When an organization or individual in the organization uses a technology, the social actor uses that particular technology instead of, or in addition to, any other technology. Because the characteristics of the box can cause and be caused by a variety of organizational characteristics, static variables can be very revealing.

On the other hand, organizations generally use a technology because it performs one or more tasks that are relevant to the goals of the organization (other reasons for using technologies, such as legitimacy, as in Meyer & Scott, 1983, are relevant to social variables rather than technological variables). Understanding the characteristics of each task that the technology performs

Table 3.1
Variables for Technology as "Box" Variables

Analog or Digital
Complexity
Controller Type
Cost
Diffusion, Level of (see Rogers, 1983)
Form
Integration
Medium versus Sender versus Receiver (see Williams, 1974)
One-to-One versus One-to Many versus Many-to-Many (see Culnan & Markus, 1987)
One-Way versus Two-Way (see Williams, 1982)
Programming
Reliability (see Boorstin, 1973)
Similarities to Humans
Similarities to Other Technologies (see Form)
Size

[handwritten margin note: I'd a real idea... which all variables need to be perfectly...]

via task-oriented variables will reveal how the technology fits into organizational behaviors (including the production process) and attitudes.

A key difference between the box variables and the task variables is their applicability to workers. The box variables tend to highlight characteristics of technology that are not generally applied to workers (cost and integration are expceptions), because when one studies a worker as a box, one generally focuses on psychological rather than physical characteristics (Mayo, 1945). However, both workers and technologies perform tasks; therefore, the task variables allow direct comparisons of workers and machines. That is, for the task variables, workers and machines are part of the same domain of analysis; for the box variables, they are not (Nass & Reeves, 1989).

Table 3.1 presents the list of variables for technologies as boxes; Table 3.2 presents the list of variables for technologies as sets of tasks. We make no claims that these lists are all-inclusive; limitations of space and a desire for parsimony lead to our presentation of only those variables that we consider to be particularly important or interesting. After presenting the list, we briefly discuss those variables on the list that have not received a great deal of attention in previous studies of technology.

Variables for Technology as Box

Analog or Digital. A crucial feature of most new information technologies is a reliance on digitalization (coding into discontinuous values) of "what even a few years before would have been an analog (continuous values) signal

Table 3.2
Variables for Technology as Set of Tasks

Communication versus Information Processing versus Both (see Beniger, 1986; Nora & Minc, 1981).

Complexity (see Babbage, 1833; Winner, 1977)

Control Focus

Fidelity

Flow Relationship

Goods-Producing versus Service Producing (Compaine, 1984, 1986)

Input Type

Interactivity, Level of (see Rafaeli, 1986)

Regularity

Speed (see Boorstin, 1973; Braverman, 1974)

Space, Permanence Across (see Boorstin, 1973, Pt. 5; Innis, 1951)

Synchronous/Asynchronous (see Culnan & Markus, 1987)

Time, Permanence Across (see Innis, 1951; Jahandarie, 1987, pp. 130-166; McLuhan, 1962)

---

varying continuously across time" (Beniger, 1986, p. 25). Beniger (1986) suggests that the implications of digitalization may be as profound for organizations as the institution of money, because digitalization permits the transformation of "currently diverse forms of information into a generalized medium for processing and exchange by the social system" (p. 25).

Although the processing of information has become increasingly digitalized, the inputs to and outputs from communication technologies have become increasingly analog. For example, one places a picture (analog) into a fax machine; the picture is digitized and transmitted as zeros and ones (digital) over a telephone line; the digits are then reconstructed back into a facsimile of the original picture (analog). Interactions with personal computers have also become increasingly analog (even though the internal processing is digital) with the advent of windows, icons, and the mouse.

McLuhan (1962) argues that digitalization has led to linear thinking and a rejection of metaphoric richness, the same argument he made regarding print (versus audiovisual media). Bolter (1984) suggests instead that digitalization has simply changed our metaphors about the world and our social expectations.

Complexity (of Box). Complexity reflects the extent to which individuals can understand how the technology links inputs and outputs. Complexity has traditionally been used as an independent variable. Winner (1977, chap. 7), for example, argues that as a technology, particularly a computer-driven technology, becomes increasingly complex, individuals increasingly ascribe "soul-like" features to the technology. This has led individuals to assume that technologies are fundamentally autonomous from human control (see also

Barley, 1988). He suggests that the resolution to this problem is for individuals, organizations, and society as a whole to reject technologies that cannot be understood. Beniger (1986), on the other hand, suggests that the appropriate organizational response to complex technologies is to develop and adopt advanced information-processing technologies to facilitate control.

However, complexity of technology can also be dependent on social and cultural forces. For example, organizations may be seen as legitimate if they adopt "state-of-the-art" technologies, even if those technologies are not technically necessary (Meyer & Rowan, 1977). Similarly, managers may attempt to adopt and control complex technologies to achieve power through ambiguity (Pfeffer, 1981).

As Babbage (1833) notes, complexity of a technology is not a necessary correlate of complexity of tasks. Almost any complex information-processing task can be performed by a few complex processors or many simple processors (Babbage, 1833, chap. 18).

Controller Type. Control involves the matching of a present state to a desired goal and the altering of a behavior when the present state seems inconsistent with the goal. Prior to the Industrial Revolution, almost all technologies were controlled by humans or animals, because technologies were not equipped with the information-processing capacity to adequately control behavior (Beniger, 1986). Beginning with the steam governor, the theory of self-regulating systems—cybernetics—became developed to the point that many technologies were built to control themselves independent of human intervention (Beniger, 1986; Wiener, 1961). With the advent of computers and improved communication technologies, external regulation of machines by other machines became possible and has become increasingly common (Forester, 1980). Some have argued that the move away from human control of technology to technological control of technology should lead to de-skilling. However, Noble (1984) provides convincing evidence that production technologies tend not to be truly self-regulating; instead, sophisticated human intervention is a constant necessity.

Cost. Despite its obvious importance, cost has been a frequently neglected variable in the study of communication technology (Vale, 1988). Cost of technology is a complex variable to measure because one must include initial cost, maintenance costs, costs per use (further complicated because communication technologies are frequently regulated by the government), and cost relative to other alternatives. In general, across all these types of costs, information-processing technologies have dropped in cost faster than have communication technologies (although the distinctions are increasingly blurred, as noted by Oettinger, 1971, and Nora & Minc, 1981), and both have dropped in cost significantly faster than matter-energy technologies (Forester, 1980). Similarly, capital costs of technology have tended to decline faster than output and use costs, as in the case of the fax machine. Recently, Vale (1988) has shown that although cost can be an important determinant of both information-seeking in general and relative use of media, the relationship is conditioned by individual and organizational variables.

Form. Form refers to all aspects of the shape and style of a given technology; that is, "form" comprises a number of variables, such as shape and style. Boorstin (1973) suggests that the form of a technology, independent of functional requirements, began to be important in the late stages of the Industrial Revolution. However, Douglas and Isherwood (1979) suggest that the form of *any* technology, like any other social artifact, has always been determined by cultural, rather than technical, considerations.

One of the most important aspects of form determined by social characteristics is that new technologies tend to retain features of old technologies that are irrelevant to the new technology. For example, the first passenger trains had cars that were shaped like stagecoaches, including spaces for the (nonexistent) wagon wheels.

The "QWERTY" keyboard on typewriters represents another complex mix of technological and social variables determining form. The "QWERTY" keyboard, an inefficient design in terms of typing speed, originated with the early upstrike mechanism that easily jammed when neighboring keys were swiftly struck (Adler, 1973). With better mechanisms and word-processors, typing speed need not be limited. However, the legitimacy (Meyer & Rowan, 1977) and training costs (Machlup, 1962) of more technically efficient keyboards have limited their adoption.

Integration. Integration of multiple technologies into a single technology seems to be one of the key legacies of the Industrial Revolution (Chandler, 1977). In the case of information-processing and communication technologies, integration provides significant improvements in speed and quality because it reduces the movement of information, thus reducing opportunities for bottlenecks and noise. Perhaps the most notable trend in integration is the combining of information-processing and communication technologies, called *compunications* (Oettinger, 1971) or *telematics* (Nora & Minc, 1981).

Because integration makes the relationship between inputs and outputs more complex, integration can foster the notion of autonomous technology (Winner, 1977). Integrated technologies may also lead to greater economic power for the firms that produce the technologies (because of switching costs) just as the integration of tasks into professions led to increasing economic power for certain social groups (Weber, 1977; Nass, 1986).

Programming. Programming is "any prearranged information that guides subsequent behavior" (Beniger, 1986, p. 39). Some information technologies have programming built into their physical structure; for example, a record player that has only one means of translating the movements of the tone arm into sounds. This programming is *closed* to the external environment. Other information technologies, such as computer music systems, have programming that is *open*, or responsive, to the environment. Open programming leads the technology to act differently under different external circumstances. Although all technologies that perform autonomous acts are programmed, information technologies such as pencils have *no* programming.

As communication technologies become more sophisticated, technologies with closed programming can perform more complex tasks and technologies with open programming can respond to more external demands. There is no *a priori* reason to prefer open programming to closed programming, or vice versa; for example, early Macintosh computers opted for highly closed architectures, while early IBM personal computers opted for relatively open architectures. It had been traditionally thought that open programming would provide users with more autonomy in work (Bell, 1973), but many now argue that workers can become even more trapped by technologies with open programs than with closed programs (Greenbaum, 1976), because the former are more sensitive to the precise actions of their users.

Similarities to Humans. With the advent of computers, one of the most important characteristics of technologies is the extent to which they mimic human-like behaviors. Similarity to humans has been conceptualized as a set of variables in recent writings. For example, Bolter (1984) suggests that technologies that perform information-processing tasks have become the basis for Western society's metaphor for self. Turkle (1984) argues that language is the key humanlike feature, noting the parasocial relationship that develops between airline personnel and the interactive computers with which they work. Weizenbaum (1976) and Nass (1989) contend that the ways in which computers fill social roles is the key cause and consequence of social change. Beniger (1987) claims that information-processing technologies have become so sophisticated that they can provide a sense of Gemeinschafft.

Size. As miniaturization has become one of the key features of modern information-processing and communication technology, size has become a key variable for understanding the relationships between technology and organizations. During the Industrial Revolution, with its emphasis on mass production, distribution, and consumption (Beniger, 1986), the push was to make technologies as large as possible, because size was positively related to output. In the cultural realm, larger items were more desirable and more expensive, *ceteris paribus*. In the present information society, the goal is to make technologies as small as possible. Smaller technologies, as in the case of watches and calculators, are now more desirable and more expensive. To assume that this desire for smallness will extend to other aspects of the organization, such as office size, would be to fall into a subtle version of the impact-imprint fallacy (Fischer, 1985); that is, the assumption that individual, organizational, or societal attitudes about technology will be transferred to or "imprinted" on all aspects of daily life.

Smaller technologies tend to be more difficult to control and centralize (Dertouzos & Moses, 1979) because they can be placed into individuals' offices rather than in large (and therefore centralized) areas of the firm. This fact should lead to increasing decentralization of communication and information-processing technologies in organizations. Other features of modern communication technologies, including asynchronicity and distance-independence (Hiltz & Turoff, 1978), have also been suggested to lead to decentralization. However, as Simon (1979) notes, although one aspect of a technology, such as size, may lead to decentralization, other aspects of the technology, such as integration, may lead to centralization (for a more detailed discussion of the relationship between centralization and aspects of communication technology, see Swanson, 1987; Markus & Robey, 1988). Of course, management can choose to centralize small technologies even if decentralization is possible or even technically optimal (Edwards, 1979; Noble, 1984).

Variables for Technology as Task

Control Focus. Each task that an information technology performs in an organization is directed toward control (Beniger, 1986). In general, one can distinguish between three categories of activities that organizations wish to control (Beniger, 1986). Both historically and currently within organizations, control is first brought to bear on the *production* of goods, then control is exercised on the *distribution* of the produced goods, and finally control is exerted on the market to encourage *consumption* of the products (Boorstin, 1973; Beniger, 1986).

Because information is the basis of control, information tasks are frequently easier to monitor than are comparable matter-energy tasks. Some have argued that this has led to lower levels of autonomy for workers who operate and use information machines than for workers who operate and use comparable matter-energy technologies (Braverman, 1974; Zuboff, 1988). Others have argued that information tasks primarily foster greater self-monitoring and hence higher levels of autonomy (e.g., Bell, 1973), and yet others have suggested that level of autonomy is determined more by industry type than by worker tasks (Beniger, 1986; Nass & Witten, 1987).

It is important to note that because *all* forms of control are based on information-processing and feedback, virtually no information technology is inherently designed for control of just production, just distribution, or just consumption, and in fact even the same machine may be exercising different types of control over different parts of the organization at different times.

Fidelity. Fidelity is the extent to which an input must match or an output can match a target output. On the input side, information-processing technologies have become increasingly robust against deviations from standard inputs. This is reflected in computer languages (such as PL/C) that make guesses as to what command was intended, word-processing packages that can correct relatively severe spelling errors and make grammatical suggestions, language-recognition systems that can understand people with different accents, and audio systems that can separate out noise from true signal when presenting music. As information-processing and communication technologies become increasingly tolerant of diverse inputs, we should see a decrease in the number and extent of standardized forms and formats (Beniger & Nass, 1986), perhaps weakening the "iron cage" of rationalization (Weber, 1985).

Just as technologies are becoming increasingly flexible relative to inputs, they are demanding less forgiveness relative to outputs. That is, there is a general trend to higher fidelity in output, as represented by high-definition television and compact-disc players, although there is an open question as to whether this trend is primarily demand-driven or supply-driven. Benjamin (1968) provides a brilliant account of the implications of increasing fidelity of information for societal norms and values.

Flow Relationship. Most information-processing and communication tasks in organizations are part of a *flow* of information, such that each task that a technology performs can be defined in terms of its relationship to other tasks along the flow. Nass (1987, 1988) argues that there are six basic information tasks: command, routinized input, creative input, preprocessing, processing, and output. Command tasks include all managing, coordinating, and directing activities; these are tasks that are rarely performed by machines. Routinized input, such as seeing, smelling, listening, observing, and inspecting, creates data through examination of matter-energy inputs or through the arbitrary assignment of information to matter-energy inputs. Creative input tasks, such as inventing, designing, and original work in the arts, produce information that has no clear relationship to prior inputs. Both types of input tasks, which bring information into the economy (Nass, 1987), have been increasingly performed by information technologies as a result of advances in artificial intelligence. Preprocessing (Beniger & Nass, 1986; Nass & Witten, 1987), including summarizing, classifying, and sorting, is that class of activities that limits and/or organizes information to be manipulated in order to increase the speed or reduce the complexity of the later information manipulation. Processing, such as copying, transmitting, translating, calculating, computing, includes the entire range of (non-preprocessing) information transformation activities that, like preprocessing, use information to produce information (other than commands) that will remain within the economy. Preprocessing and processing tasks have been the primary tasks of information and communication technology since the Industrial Revolution. Finally, output tasks, such as lecturing and selling, take information in the economy and remove it from the economy by providing it to consumers.

Previous work by Nass (1986) has highlighted some of the key relationships between these categories. For example, the ratio of routinized to creative inputting and the level of preprocessing have both been shown to lead to decreased complexity of processing across industries (Nass, 1987, 1988). Preprocessing, which is argued to be the key means of indirect control in organizations, has been shown to be inversely related to managerial command activity. Preliminary analysis further suggests that the growth in demand for informational final products has been supported by intensified processing of information that is already in the economy rather than by increased input activity.

One of the advantages of the flow-related approach to task analysis is that one can draw direct comparisons between workers and technologies. As Nass (1987) has demonstrated, one can classify both workers and machines in terms of the amount of time spent on each of the categories of information tasks. One can then draw conclusions about the relationship between increased machine functionality in a given task domain and the effect on workers. For example, through the early part of the twentieth century, the growth in preprocessing and processing technologies greatly exceeded the growth in inputting technologies (primarily because of technical limitations; see Beniger, 1986). However, the number of workers performing preprocessing and processing tasks also grew much faster than the number of workers performing inputting tasks, suggesting (despite the ecological nature of the data) that information technologies do not directly replace workers.

Input Type. It has become traditional to define information technologies by their internal processing or by their output. Using these definitions, one can find variance across the types of inputs the technology receives, depending on the task. Until the widespread use of microprocessors, most information technologies required informational inputs (e.g., typing) or a mix of informational and matter-energy input (e.g., paper, ink, and type to produce newspaper). However, given advances in pattern recognition, information-processing technologies increasingly can accept matter-energy inputs and "draw out" the relevant informational content. At first glance, this new ability might seem to be a significant threat to the labor force, as the ability to use the senses seems to be something that was particularly human. However, as Nass (1987, 1988) has demonstrated, only about six percent of the human work force performs tasks that draw information from non-informational products for output, and that fraction is the highest it has been since 1900.

Regularity. Regularity is the extent to which activities are performed on a fixed schedule. Regularity, according to Beniger (1986), was one of three key technical changes of the Industrial Revolution (the other two were speed and volume). Although the initiator of regularity was the steam engine, by the late 1800s communication technologies, particularly the telegraph, had become an essential part of ensuring that "the trains ran on time."

Regularity has led to at least two critical organizational changes. First, regularity is the key to planning (Beniger, 1986); without knowing when a given amount of goods will be produced, there would be too many contingencies to process and analyze the requisite information successfully. This ability to plan led to the emergence of bureaucracy (beginning with the ancient Egyptians' development of a bureaucracy associated with the regular flooding of the Nile; Innis, 1951), the information infrastructure (Beniger, 1986), and the "planning system" of the military-industrial complex (Galbraith, 1967).

A second consequence of regularity is that time became a critical dimension along which people organized their lives (Boorstin, 1973). The effective use of time in production, distribution, and consumption became an organizational obsession during the Industrial Revolution (Boorstin, 1973).

60

Conclusion

Researchers interested in the study of technology, from e
centered or social-actor-centered approach, traditionally beg.
particular technology, necessarily one that has already been   ...u
generally one that is unique or new. Having chosen the technology, they
either perform a case study or sample across organizations, finding some
organizations that have the technology and some that do not or gathering
information about organizations before and after they have adopted the
technology. After running the study, one could make conclusions that will
apply to a wide range of organizations. However, the researcher could not
make any conclusions about technologies, the subject in which he or she was
interested. That is, a researcher interested in technologies would end up
learning only about organizations!

A variable-centered approach to the study of technology and organizations permits researchers who care about technology to learn about organizations *and* technologies. The researcher begins by choosing variables from
the list of technological variables presented here (or extensions of the list)
and from previous lists of organizational variables (e.g., Blau, 1957; Danowski, 1988; Hall & Tittle, 1966; Scott, 1981), deciding which from each set
are independent variables, which are intervening variables, and which are
dependent variables. Having chosen the variables, researchers have a number of options. First, they can perform a case study of a particular technology
(sampling across individuals or organizations), a technology chosen because
it takes on particularly interesting values on one or more of the variables.
The results of the study will have implications for all technologies that have
the particular value (and possibly other values) for the particular variable.
Second, they can perform a case study of an organization with interesting
values on one or more organizational variables, sampling across technologies
that have different values on the technological variables of interest. By
examining the causes and consequences of the technology variables in terms
of the special characteristics of the organization, one can derive general
theories of how all technologies are affected by that characteristic. Finally,
the researcher can sample across both organizations and technologies, looking at covariation between and among the organizational and technological
variables. This provides the greatest opportunities for external validity and
rich theories of the technology/organization relationship. Whichever approach is adopted, the researcher can make conclusions that will apply to a

wide range of technologies (and organizations), including technologies (and organizations) that the researcher has never seen and including technologies (and organizations) that do not even exist yet.

Two objections might be raised concerning the present approach. First, the variable-centered view proposed here seems to imply that technological characteristics demand specific individual and organizational responses, whether as cause or effect. Organizations of course make their own choices, but they make those choices in a technological environment that, for the most part, they have not created (to paraphrase Marx). The variables proposed here permit the researcher to understand the technological environment in which organizations and individuals in organizations choose and act, a critical step in understanding the causes and effects of information technologies.

A second objection to the present approach is that variables cannot inform organizational practice, because "organizations buy telephones, not analog, keyboard and receiver input, high fidelity, two-way, processing technologies." This objection is only half correct; in buying a telephone, the organization has adopted all the features of the telephone, not just the features that were intended by the purchaser. One of the key rules in understanding the relationship between any technology and any social system is that the adoption of a technology inevitably leads to unexpected consequences (Ogburn, 1957). The literature is filled with unexpected disasters related to organizational adoption of technologies (Adler, 1986; Levitt & March, 1988; Perrow, 1984; Pool, 1983). By considering *all* the dimensions of a technology, not just the dimensions which one intended to purchase, managers can predict the net effect of a technological change on organizational behavior. Thus, there is nothing more practical than a good theoretical paradigm.

In sum, scholars and managers who are concerned with the antecedents and consequences of information technology should pay particular attention to the variables that describe information technologies in general and the values on those variables that define particular information technologies. By making reference to both static and dynamic aspects of technologies, one can generate and test general and precise theories of the relationships between organizations and *all* information technologies.

Notes

1. Studies that traditionally have been viewed as combining the two perspectives, such as Lawrence & Lorsch (1967), Perrow (1967), Thompson (1967), and Woodward (1965), actually relate organization variables to the production process as a whole (the

way economists use the term "technology") rather than to particular technological objects or machines.

2. Compaine's (1984, 1986) characterizations of industries in terms of two technological variables—form/substance and products/services—is a noteworthy exception.

References

Adler, M. (1973). *The writing machine*. London: Allen & Unwin.

Adler, P. (1986). New technologies, new skills. *California Mangement Review*, XXIX (1), 9-28.

Babbage, C. (1833). *On the economy of machinery and manufacturers* (3rd ed.). London: Charles Knight.

Barley, S. R. (1988). The social construction of a machine: Ritual, superstition, magical thinking, and other pragmatic responses to running a CT Scanner. In M. Lock & D. Gordon (Ed.), *Knowledge and practice in medicine: Social, cultural, and historical approaches*. Hingham, MA: Reidel.

Baum, L. F. (1966). *The wonderful wizard of Oz*. New York: Dover.

Bell, Daniel. (1973). *The coming of post-industrial society*. New York: Basic Books.

Bendix, R. (1963). *Work and authority in industry: Ideologies of management in the course of industrialization*. New York: Harper.

Beniger, J. R. (1986). *The control revolution: Technological and economic origins of the information economy*. Cambridge: Harvard University Press.

Beniger, J. R. (1987). Personalization of mass media and the growth of pseudo-community. *Communication Research*, *14*, 352-371.

Beniger, J. R., & Nass, C. I. (1986). Preprocessing: The neglected component in sociocybernetic models. In R. F. Geyer & J. van der Zouwen (Eds.), *Sociocybernetic paradoxes* (pp. 119-130). London: Sage.

Benjamin, W. (1968). The work of art in the age of mechanical reproduction. *Illuminations*. New York: Harcourt, Brace, & World.

Blau, P. (1957). Formal organization: Dimensions of analysis. *American Journal of Sociology*, *63*, 58-69.

Bolter, J. D. (1984). *Turing's man: Western culture in the computer age*. Chapel Hill, NC: University of North Carolina Press.

Boorstin, D. J. (1973). *The Americans: The democratic experience*. New York: Vintage.

Braverman, H. (1974). *Labor and monopoly capital: The degradation of work in the twentieth century*. New York: Monthly Review Press.

Chandler, A. D., Jr. (1977). *The visible hand: The managerial revolution in American business*. Cambridge, MA: Belknap Press.

Compaine, B. M. (Ed.). (1984). *Understanding new media*. Cambridge, MA: Ballinger.

Compaine, B. M. (1986). *Fresh perspectives on the information business*. Unpublished manuscript, Gannett Center for Media Studies, New York.

Culnan, M. J., & Markus, M. L. (1987). Information technologies. In F. M. Jablin et al. (Eds.), *Handbook of organizational communication: An interdisciplinary perspective* (pp. 420-443). Newbury Park CA: Sage.

Danowski, J. A. (1988). Organizational infographics and automated auditing: Using computers to unobtrusively gather as well as analyze communication. In G. M. Goldhaber & G. A. Barnett (Eds.), *Handbook of organizational communication: An interdisciplinary perspective* (pp. 385-433). Newbury Park CA: Sage.

Dertouzos, M. L., & Moses, J. (Eds.). (1979). *The computer age: A twenty-five year view*. Cambridge: MIT Press.

Dickson, K. (1980). Petfoods by computer: A case study of automation. In T. Forester (Ed.), *The microelectronics revolution* (pp. 174-183). Cambridge: MIT Press.

Douglas, M., & Isherwood, B. (1979). *The world of goods*. New York: Basic Books.

Edwards, R. C. (1979). *Contested terrain: The transformation of the workplace in the twentieth century*. New York: Basic Books.

Ellul, J. (1964). *The technological society* (J. Wilkinson, Trans.). New York: Alfred Knopf.

Feller, I., & Menzel, D. C. (1977). Diffusion milieus as a focus of research on innovation in the public sector. *Policy Science, 8*, 49-68.

Fischer, C. (1985). Studying technology and social life. In M. Castells (Ed.), *High technology, space, and society*. Beverly Hills, CA: Sage.

Forester, T. (Ed.). (1980). *The microelectronics revolution*. Cambridge: MIT Press.

Form, W., & McMillen, D. B. (1983). Women, men, and machines. *Work and Occupations, 10*(2), 147-178.

Galbraith, J. K. (1967). *The new industrial state*. Boston: Houghton-Miflin.

Gallo, D. D. (1986). Expectancy theory as a predictor of individual response to computer technology. *Computers in Human Behavior, 2*(1), 31-41.

Greenbaum, J. (1976). Division of labor in the computer field. *Monthly Review, 28*(3), 40-55.

Hage, J. (1972). *Techniques and problems of theory construction in sociology*. New York: John Wiley.

Hall, R. H., & Tittle, C. R. (1966). Bureaucracy and its correlates. *American Journal of Sociology, 72*, 267-272.

Hiltz, S. R., & Turoff, M. (1978). *The network nation: Human communication via computer*. Reading, MA: Addison-Wesley.

Innis, H. (1951). *The bias of communication*. Toronto: University of Toronto Press.

Jahandarie, K. (1987). *The modality effect*. Unpublished doctoral dissertation, Stanford University, Stanford, CA.

Johansen, R., Vallee, J., & Spangler, K. (1979). *Electronic meetings: Technical alternatives and social choices*. Reading, MA: Addison-Wesley.

Kleeman, W. B. (1982). The future of the office. *Environment and Behavior, 14*(5), 593-610.

Lawrence, P. R., & Lorsch, J. W. (1967). *Organization and environment.* Cambridge: Harvard University Press.

Levitt, B., & March, J. G. (1988). Organizational learning. *Annual review of sociology, 14,* 319-340.

Levitt, B., & Nass, C. I. (1989). The lid on the garbage can: Institutional constraints on decision making in the textbook publishing industry. *Administrative Science Quarterly,* 34, 190-207.

Machlup, F. (1962). *The production and distribution of knowledge in the United States.* Princeton: Princeton University Press.

March, J. G., & Simon, H. (1958). *Organizations.* New York: John Wiley.

Markus, M. L., & Robey, D. (1988). Information technology and organizational change: Causal structure in theory and research. *Management Science, 34*(5), 583-598.

Margulies, N., & Colflesh, L. (1982). A socio-technical approach to planning and implementing new technology. *Training and Development Journal, 36*(12), 16-29.

Mayo, E. (1945). *The social problems of an industrial civilization.* Boston: Graduate School of Business Administration, Harvard University.

McLuhan, M. (1962). *Gutenberg galaxy: The making of typographic man.* Toronto: University of Toronto Press.

Meyer, J. W., & Rowan, B. (1977). Institutionalized organizations: Formal structure as myth and ceremony. *American Journal of Sociology, 83,* 340-363.

Meyer, J., & Scott, W. R. (1983). *Organizational environments: Ritual and rationality.* Beverly Hills, CA: Sage.

Morgall, J. (1983). Typing our way to freedom: Is it true that new office technology can liberate women? *Behaviour and Information Technology, 2*(3), 215-226.

Mumford, L. (1935). *Technics and civilization.* New York: Harcourt Brace.

Nass, C. I. (1986). Bureaucracy, technical expertise, and professionals: A Weberian approach. *Sociological Theory, 4,* 61-70.

Nass, C. I. (1987). *Work in an information economy: An information processing model of trends in the past century.* Paper presented at the annual meeting of the International Communication Association. New Orleans, LA.

Nass, C. I. (1988). Work, information, and information work: A retrospective and prospective framework. In I. H. Simpson & R. L. Simpson (Eds.), *Research in the sociology of work: Vol. 4. High tech work* (pp. 311-333). Greenwich, CT: JAI.

Nass, C. I. (1989). *The computer as social actor: Implications of social categorization for the human-computer interface.* Unpublished manuscript, Stanford University, Department of Communication, Stanford, CA.

Nass, C. I., & Reeves, B. (1989). *Domains of analysis in communication research.* Paper presented at the annual meeting of the International Communication Association, San Francisco, California.

Nass, C. I., & Witten, M. (1987). *The relationship between direct and indirect organizational control in the United States, 1960-1970.* Paper presented at the annual meeting of the International Communication Association, Montreal.

Noble, D. F. (1984). *Forces of production: A social history of industrial automation.* New York: Knopf.

Nora, S., & Minc, A. (1981). *The computerization of society.* Cambridge: MIT Press.

Oettinger, A. G. (1971). Compunications in the national decision-making process. In M. Greenberger (Ed.), *Computers, communication, and the public interest* (pp. 73-114). Baltimore: Johns Hopkins Press.

Ogburn, W. F. (1957). How technology causes social change. In A. Allen et al. (Eds.), *Technology and social change* (pp. 12-26). New York: Appelton-Century-Crofts.

Parcel, T. L., Wallace, M., Kaufman, R., & Grant, D. (1988). *Looking forward again: Occupational variation in worker response to employment within an ultra-high technology firm.* Paper presented at the annual meeting of the American Sociological Association.

Patrickson, M. (1986). Adaptation by employees to new technology. *Journal of Occupational Psychology, 59*(1), 1-11.

Perrow, C. (1967). A framework for the comparative analysis of organizations. *American Sociological Review, 32,* 194-208.

Perrow, C. (1984). *Normal accidents: Living with high-risk technologies.* New York: Basic Books.

Pfeffer, J. (1981). *Power in organizations.* Marshfield, MA: Pittman.

Pool, I. deS. (Ed.). (1977). *The social impact of the telephone.* Cambridge: MIT Press.

Pool, I. deS. (1983). *Forecasting the telephone: A retrospective technology assessment of the telephone.* Norwood, NJ: Ablex.

Rafaeli, S. (1986). *Interactivity and the human-computer relationship.* Unpublished doctoral dissertation, Stanford University, Stanford, CA.

Reese, S. D. (1988). Relations of occupations to uses of information technologies. In F. Williams (Ed.), *Measuring the information economy* (pp. 207-214). Newbury Park, CA: Sage.

Rice, R. E., & Bair, J. H. (1984). New organizational media and productivity. In R. E. Rice (Ed.), *The new media: Communication, research, and technology* (pp. 185-216). Beverly Hills, CA: Sage.

Rosenberg, N. (1976). *Perspectives on technology.* Cambridge: Cambridge University Press.

Rostow, W. W. (1971). *Politics and the stages of growth.* New York: Cambridge University Press.

Scott, W. R. (1981). *Organizations: Rational, natural, and open systems.* Englewood Cliffs, NJ: Prentice-Hall.

Simon, H. (1979). The consequences of computers for centralization and decentralization. In M. L. Dertouzos & J. Moses (Eds.), *The computer age: A twenty-five year view.* Cambridge: MIT Press.

Swanson, E. B. (1987). Information systems and organization theory: A review. In R. J. Boland & R. A. Hirschheim (Eds.), *Critical issues in information systems research* (pp. 181-204). Chichester, NY: John Wiley.

Taylor, F. W. (1911). The principles of scientific management. New York: Harper.

Taylor, F. W. (1947). *Scientific management*. New York: Harper.

Thompson, J. D. (1967). *Organizations in action*. New York: McGraw-Hill.

Tikhomirov, O. K., & Gur'yeva, L. P. (1986). Psychological analysis of computer-mediated labor activity. *Psikologicheskii Zhurnal, 7*(5), 13-25.

Turkle, S. (1984). *The second self: Computers and the human spirit*. New York: Simon & Schuster.

Vale, M. E. (1988). *Information structure and the information-seeking behavior of lawyers*. Unpublished doctoral dissertation, Stanford University Stanford, CA.

Vallas, S. P., & Yarrow, M. (1987). Advanced technology and worker alienation: Comments on the Blauner/Marxism debate. *Work and Occupations, 14*(1), 126-142.

Weber, M. (1977). *Economy and society* (G. Roth & C. Wittich, Eds.). Berkeley: University of California Press.

Weber, M. (1985). *Protestant ethic and the spirit of capitalism* (A. Giddens, Trans.). London: Unwin Paperback.

Weikle, R. D. (1986). *The attitude and preferences of local union leaders for adjustment to technological change*. Unpublished doctoral dissertation, University of South Carolina, Columbia.

Weizenbaum, J. (1976). *Computer power and human reason: From judgment to calculation*. San Francisco: W. H. Freeman.

Wiener, N. (1961). *Cybernetics* (2nd ed.). New York: MIT Press.

Williams, F. (1982). *The communications revolution*. Beverly Hills, CA: Sage.

Williams, R. (1974). *Television: Technology and cultural form*. New York: Schocken Books.

Winner, L. (1977). *Autonomous technology: Technics-out-of-control as a theme in political thought*. Cambridge: MIT Press.

Woodward, J. (1965). *Industrial organization: Theory and practice*. New York: Oxford University Press.

Zuboff, S. (1988). *In the age of the smart machine: The future of work and power*. Oxford: Oxford University Press.

PART III

Individual Interactions with Information Technology in the Organizational Context

Many concerns about the adoption, use, and impacts of information technologies focus on cognition and behavior of users, as tempered by constraints and pressures emanating from the organizational context. The outcomes of interest are at the individual level, although the forces influencing individual action are found in the broader context as well. The three chapters in this section all focus upon outcomes at the individual level, while recognizing that processes that produce these outcomes arise from multiple levels within the organization.

Linda Trevino, Richard Daft, and Robert Lengel explicate the process of managerial media choice. Their model extends information richness theory, which posits that effective managers select among communication media by maximizing the fit between the ambiguity of the communication task and the inherent richness of the medium selected. The theory proposes that highly ambiguous messages are best handled via rich media such as a personal visit, rather than via lean media such as written mail. Similarly, routine, unambiguous messages are more efficiently handled via lean media. Drawing on the tenets of structural symbolic interactionism, Trevino et al. expand this model to incorporate two major factors that lead to non-optimal media choices. First, contextual determinants such as the physical distance between parties and pressures to communicate rapidly may constrain media choice. Second, symbolic aspects of media such as the formality of written documents may have value in certain situations that exceeds the benefits of a maximal media/message fit.

Managerial use of information technology is also the concern of the second chapter in this section. Robert Zmud's focus, however, is on "strategic information behaviors." These behaviors involve control or manipulation of information in order to influence other persons. Zmud begins by presenting a model of organizational information systems. Then, he draws on this model to pinpoint the critical points at which strategic information behaviors can occur. He concludes with a set of propositions articulating the specific strategic information behaviors that are most likely to occur with new information technologies.

Janet Fulk, Joseph Schmitz, and Charles Steinfield contrast rational models of media/task match with an alternative social influence model. The social influence model attends to the organizational context and to past behavior in explaining seemingly irrational media selection behavior. This approach postulates that statements and behaviors of coworkers, behavioral norms, and social definitions of rational behavior are key influences on communication technology usage. Furthermore, these social influences may counteract the pressures for rational choice of media. The net effect is that media use behavior is not consistently predictable, based on rational choice assumptions. Media-related behavior is more effectively predicted by attending to the influence of subjective rationality and social information.

LINDA KLEBE TREVINO
RICHARD L. DAFT
ROBERT H. LENGEL

4. Understanding Managers' Media Choices: A Symbolic Interactionist Perspective

Communication is the primary process through which managers do their work. Managers must communicate to motivate and lead employees, to learn about and manage the environment, and to make decisions. Communication is also integral to the roles managers play as figureheads, monitors, spokespersons, and disseminators of information. Communication is so central to the managerial role that managers spend approximately 80% of their time communicating.

In recent years organizational scientists have become interested in understanding a particular aspect of managerial communication—managers' choice of communication media. Mintzberg (1973) noted that most managerial time was spent in verbal communication—in meetings, on the telephone, and during tours. His research suggested that managers seemed to prefer verbal, face-to-face communication. However, until recently, the available research offered little understanding of these apparent preferences.

Today managers have more communication options than ever before. New communication technologies are increasingly available. Electronic mail allows managers to instantly send messages to their distant communication partners without the frustration of telephone tag. Teleconferencing offers the possibility of group meetings without the need for long-distance travel to meet face-to-face. However, all of these options can create confusion. How are managers to choose? Media choice is not the simple, intuitively obvious process it may appear to be at first glance. Appropriate media choice can make the difference between effective and ineffective communication. And, media choice mistakes can seriously impede successful communication—in some cases with disastrous consequences.

Harold Geneen was CEO of ITT from 1959 to 1977. He created ITT-Europe to serve as headquarters for his European operations. One of

71

Geneen's most difficult problems was how to get French, German, Italian, and American managers to go along with central decisions. He discovered that he needed to rely upon face-to-face communication to handle difficult communications among managers from different countries. For 17 years Geneen and his senior staff traveled to Europe for one week each month to deal in person with the European managers' requests and needs.

> One of the first things I learned in those early days was that when I responded to a question or request from Europe while sitting in New York, my decision was often different from what it would have been had I been in Europe. In New York, I might read a request and say no. But in Europe, I could see the man's face, hear his voice, understand the intensity of his conviction, and the answer to the same question might be yes. So, early on, I decided that if I and my headquarters' team intended to monitor and oversee the European operations, I owed it to the European managers to be there on the spot....It became our policy to deal with problems on the spot, face-to-face. (Geneen, 1984)

Traveling to Europe once a month is an expensive way to communicate. However, in the case of Geneen and his European managers, it was probably necessary and appropriate. Face-to-face meetings allowed them to work out complex issues and understand each others' positions. In addition, Geneen's commitment of time and resources to these trips conveyed the importance of the topics discussed and the need for the managers to work as a team.

A single medium is not appropriate for all communications. In one example of a communication media choice mistake, a senior insurance company executive insisted that his managers use a new electronic mail system for nearly all communications. It proved to be a quick and efficient way to transmit many routine messages. However, after only a few weeks, managers began to complain that many issues were being left unresolved. They surreptitiously began making telephone calls and having meetings to solve problems.

Another example of a media choice mistake was the use of teleconferencing to make the decision to launch the Challenger space shuttle in January, 1986. Engineers had strong feelings that the Challenger should not be launched. It is possible that the teleconference medium was incapable of communicating the strength of the engineers' emotions and gut feelings to the managers who had to make the decision. The Challenger was launched and exploded with seven astronauts on board.

In order to be better able to make decisions about when to travel to Europe, when to pick up the telephone, when to send a memo or electronic mail message, or when to arrange a teleconference, managers need to understand media choice processes and their relation to communication effectiveness. Recent research has provided new ways of thinking about managers' media choices. This chapter will present a conceptual framework for understanding the managerial media choice process based upon symbolic interactionism. In addition, research linking appropriate media choice with managerial effectiveness will be presented.

A Symbolic Interactionist Perspective[1]

Symbolic interactionism (Blumer, 1969; Mead, 1934) is a theoretical framework that can be used to explain sociological and social psychological phenomena. In the imagery of symbolic interactionism, we view society as a dynamic web of communication. Thus, society *is* interaction. And, interaction is symbolic because, through their interactions, people assign meaning to things.

This symbolic interactionism imagery can be applied to understanding managerial communication in organizations. Think of the organization as a dynamic web of interaction and communication. The basis for interaction among organization members is a shared system of meaning. People have developed many shared assumptions and understandings about the meaning of words, actions, and events. However, organization members look to each other for help in interpreting ill-defined situations. In ill-defined situations, they must create a common understanding (Weick, 1979; Daft & Weick, 1984) before they can make decisions that others will comprehend, agree upon, and accept. In this type of situation, organization members proactively shape reality together. Through negotiation and feedback they decrease ambiguity and create symbols that establish new organizational meanings. An example of this kind of symbol creation is the communication required to decide upon a new business strategy. Managers may disagree about the meaning of information obtained from the environment. Thus, multiple interpretations of the situation are likely. Negotiation and feedback are necessary for managers to agree about the meaning of the available information so that a common interpretation can be established and a strategy decision can be made.

Over time many symbols evolve within the organization and take on agreed upon meaning. Once that meaning is established, organization members can act from a basis of mutual understanding. Because consensus about meaning exists, negotiation is no longer necessary. Symbols that have already been created and agreed upon simply need to be transmitted. They are automatically understood. An example is a well-defined organizational occurrence such as a regularly scheduled meeting. Shared meaning regarding the meeting means that the individuals involved know what it means. A communication to announce the meeting is routine and can be transmitted in a straightforward manner without negotiation.

The symbolic interactionism framework can provide a basis for understanding managers' media choices. Based upon the symbolic interactionism framework, three types of variables can be expected to influence managerial media choices: (1) the equivocality of the message, (2) contextual determinants, and (3) the symbolic cues conveyed by the medium itself above and beyond the literal message. These three influences on managerial media choice are discussed below.

Message Equivocality and Media Choice

The symbolic interactionism framework proposes that the basis for interaction among organization members is a shared system of meaning. The equivocality of the message provides an important key to selecting the communication medium that is most appropriate for delivering a full and complete message.

Equivocality means the existence of multiple and conflicting interpretations about an organizational situation (Daft & Macintosh, 1981; Daft & Lengel, 1986; Weick, 1979). An equivocal message is like a Rorschach inkblot—multiple individuals may interpret it differently depending upon their unique needs, backgrounds, and perspectives. Therefore, for shared meaning to be created, negotiation and feedback are required. The communicating individuals must rely upon each other to create a shared definition through language and other social cues.

Equivocality may be high when the situation or message is ambiguous. Managers may not even be sure what questions to ask, and simple, objective answers are not available. Thus, confusion, lack of understanding, and differing interpretations are likely to arise. Most high level organizational decisions are made under conditions of ambiguity. Managers have to interpret the situation from vague cues and enact a solution (Mintzberg, Raisinghani, & Theoret, 1976).

Equivocality is also high when managers' frames of reference differ, a common organizational occurrence. A manufacturing manager may have difficulty understanding the perspective of an R&D engineer. Problems may be perceived differently by managers from different functional areas. In addition, emotional messages are subjective and open to multiple interpretations. In these cases, a common perspective does not exist, and shared meaning must be established for mutual understanding to occur.

Equivocality can be reduced by pooling opinions, discussing interpretations, and overcoming disagreement. Managers exchange subjective views to define the problem and resolve ambiguous issues. This leads to a shared understanding and social agreement about the definition of the problem and the correct response.

However, with unequivocal messages, consensus about meaning has already been established. These pre-existing meanings can guide behavior. Little negotiation or feedback is required. Established symbols can be simply communicated among organization members. Information whose meaning is clear can be transmitted without concern about misunderstandings or confusion.

The above ideas have implications for media choice and are related to the recent proposal (Daft & Lengel, 1984) that communication media have varying capacities for resolving ambiguity, bringing multiple interpretations together, and facilitating understanding. Communication media (e.g., memos, telephone, electronic mail, computer printout, face-to-face) can be characterized as "rich" or "lean" based upon their capacity to facilitate shared meaning. Rich media have the highest capacity to facilitate shared meaning. Lean media have the lowest capacity.

Media typically available to managers can be organized into a richness hierarchy (see Figure 4.1). The media richness hierarchy ranks media in terms of their capacity for processing equivocal information. The richness of each medium is based upon a blend of four criteria: (1) the availability of *instant feedback*, making it possible for communicators to converge quickly upon a common interpretation or understanding; (2) the capacity of the medium to transmit *multiple cues* such as body language, voice tone, and inflection, to convey interpretations; (3) the use of *natural language*, rather than numbers, to convey subtleties; and (4) the *personal focus* of the medium. A message will be conveyed more fully when personal feelings and emotions infuse the communication. Some media allow the message to be tailored to the frame of reference, needs, and current situation of the receiver.

According to the hierarchy, face-to-face is considered to be the richest communication medium, followed by the telephone, electronic mail (Steinfield & Fulk, 1986; Trevino, Lengel, Bodensteiner, & Gerloff, 1988), personal written documents such as letters, notes and memos, and impersonal written documents such as fliers, bulletins, and reports. Face-to-face is the richest medium because it allows immediate feedback, has the capacity to provide multiple cues, communicates in natural language, and can be

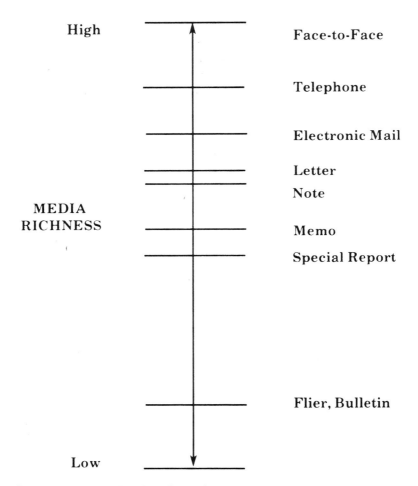

Figure 4.1 Hierarchy of Media Richness

highly personal. A message can be adjusted, clarified, and reinforced instantly.

Telephone conversations are less rich than face-to-face. They provide rapid feedback, are personal, and use natural language, but provide fewer cues than face-to-face. For example, eye contact and body language are missing from telephone communications.

Electronic mail systems vary somewhat in terms of media richness. Most electronic mail systems have the capacity to provide rapid, although not immediate feedback. One individual sends an electronic mail message. The message is read when the receiver decides to turn on the computer and ask for his or her mail. Electronic mail uses natural language. However, it lacks cues such as voice inflection and tone. Some systems allow communicators to interact in real time producing an electronic conversation. Thus, feedback is immediate, but the voice cues are still missing. More recently, voice mail systems are being introduced. These provide voice cues but are not interactive.

Written media may use natural language, but provide limited cues and are particularly slow to generate feedback. Addressed written communications such as letters, notes, and memos convey only written communication. Voice and visual cues are limited to those on paper. A few cues can be conveyed by choice of stationery and the formality of the language. In addition, addressed documents can be tailored to the individual recipient and personalized. For example, a personal note can be added to the bottom of a formal letter.

Formal, unaddressed documents are the leanest communication media. Examples are fliers, bulletins, and standard quantitative reports. They often communicate via numbers that convey quantifiable information but do not have the information-carrying capacity of natural language. Fliers and bulletins fall into this category because they communicate simple, objective information to a wide audience. They are not personalized toward any individual. They provide few cues and feedback is slow.

Several studies have found that managers choose media based upon the equivocality of the communication incident. For example, in an exploratory study (Trevino, Lengel, & Daft, 1987), researchers interviewed 65 managers representing all hierarchical levels in 11 organizations. Managers were asked to describe a recent communication incident in which they used face-to-face, telephone, electronic mail, and written media. For each incident, the manager was asked to discuss reasons why the specific medium was selected. The reasons managers offered for media choice fell into three broad classifications. One of these classifications was *message content* and was related to the ideas outlined above. (The other two classifications will be discussed below.) Managers said that they were more likely to process ambiguous, equivocal communications through rich media such as face-to-face, while unambiguous communications were more likely to be sent via written or electronic media. The reasons managers offered for using face-to-face communication included nonroutine (ambiguous) messages, the need for auxiliary cues, the ability to discuss, and the desire to express emotions. These reasons were given for face-to-face far more often than for other media. In addition, reasons such as immediate feedback and the ability to persuade others were important for both face-to-face and telephone communications. The multiple cues, natural language, and rapid feedback associated with face-to-face (and to some extent, telephone) give these rich media a greater capacity for "symbol creation"—establishing a common grammar for the reduction of equivocality.

Lean media such as electronic mail and written documents were preferred for unambiguous, routine communications where little or no feedback was required. This is consistent with the notion that written and electronic media can be effectively used for simple "symbol transmission" when pre-established meaning already exists between managers. Face-to-face discussion is less necessary when shared meaning exists.

Another study (Daft, Lengel, & Trevino, 1987) also found that managers choose media based upon the equivocality of the communication incident. In this study, 95 managers in a petrochemical company were asked to select the medium of communication they would use for each of 60 communication incidents. The incidents had been developed from interviews with managers and were rated for equivocality. Recall that the concept of equivocality means differing interpretations that arise from ambiguous content or different frames of reference. Low equivocality messages have clear content that suggests a single interpretation. The communicators agree about the meaning.

For communications rated low in equivocality, only 13.5% of the managers in the study chose the face-to-face medium. This percentage increased to 84.1% for communications rated high in equivocality. Compare the following two situations. In the first situation, a senior manager is working out a personality conflict between two subordinates. In the second situation, a manager must remind her supervisors that attendance at their weekly meeting is required. In the first case, the content of the message is emotional and difficult to communicate. Each person has beliefs, values, and feelings that create a unique frame of reference. To communicate effectively, a major change in understanding must take place between the communicators. A rich communication medium allows this to occur. In the second instance, the topic is simple and clear-cut. The message is simply a reminder of a pre-established meeting. A lean communication medium suffices for this exchange.

The research described above supports the idea that a relationship exists between the equivocality of the message and the medium managers select. However, in addition to suggesting a pattern for managers' media choices, the equivocality/richness match idea is prescriptive. Because only rich media are capable of handling equivocal messages, an equivocality/richness match should mean more effective communication. For effective communication to occur, managers should choose media that have the capacity to handle the equivocality of the message. When the communication concerns well-defined issues, equivocality is low. Precise written and quantified data should be communicated through lean media. On the other hand, highly equivocal messages demand rich media to facilitate understanding and the emergence of a common perspective.

A mismatch may explain communication failures. Standard computer reports sent to resolve equivocal problems will not accommodate the subjective, ambiguous nature of these problems. The data oversimplify the problem, and crucial cues may be lost. Moreover, face-to-face media may be ill-suited to objective, well-understood problems. Face-to-face discussion may contain unnecessary, surplus meaning. Multiple cues can over-complicate the communication and distract the receiver's attention from the routine message.

To find support for this prescriptive hypothesis, the researchers (Daft, Lengel, & Trevino, 1987) wanted to determine if managerial effectiveness was related to managers' ability to match media richness to message equivocality. Managers who selected the medium appropriate to the message (i.e., face-to-face for highly equivocal messages) were expected to also be higher performing managers. To investigate this idea, the media selection pattern for each manager in the study was analyzed. The 15 managers who displayed the strongest match between media richness and message equivocality were called "media sensitive." These managers correctly matched rich media to highly equivocal messages and chose lean media for messages rated low in equivocality. Alternatively, the 15 managers showing the weakest matching ability between media richness and message equivocality were assigned to a "media insensitive" group. These managers seemed to select media almost at random. They did not match the richness of the medium to the message content. Members of the media insensitive group often used media completely counter to the richness matching perspective. For a difficult, emotional issue such as telling a subordinate about a demotion, media insensitive managers often selected memos. For routine matters, they often selected face-to-face communication.

The researchers compared the two groups in terms of overall managerial performance. The results provided powerful support for a relationship between media sensitivity and managerial effectiveness. In the media sensitive group, 87% of the managers were rated as high performers on an internal corporate performance rating scale. In the media insensitive group, only 47%

Figure 4.2 Media Sensitivity and Manager Performance

80

MESSAGE

	Unequivocal	Equivocal
Rich	Communication Failure Rich media's excess cues cause confusion and surplus meaning.	Effective Communication Rich media match equivocal message.
Lean	Effective Communication Media low in richness match unequivocal routine message.	Communication Failure Lean media used for equivocal messages provide too few cues to capture message complexity.

MEDIA RICHNESS

Figure 4.3 Message Equivocality/Media Richness Matching Framework for Communication Effectiveness

were considered high performers. Knowledge of managers' message/media matching patterns allowed the researchers to predict whether managers were high performers. These findings are illustrated in Figure 4.2.

Explaining differences in manager performance has been difficult in the past. However, these findings suggest that managers' media sensitivity may be an important component of effective managerial performance. It appears that high performing managers know how to communicate more effectively than low performing managers. They are able to match the equivocality of the message with the richness of the communication medium. Thus, communication effectiveness is not simply a matter of choosing the right words or developing good listening skills. Effective managerial communication also involves selecting the medium with the capacity to create mutual understanding of the message. Effective communicators use written or electronic memos for routine messages to save time and prevent information overkill. More equivocal issues are communicated personally through telephone or face-to-face discussion.

Figure 4.3 outlines a framework for deciding when communication will be effective and ineffective. For example, for equivocal messages, rich media are most appropriate. These media are capable of creating meaning through the use of immediate feedback, multiple cues, personal focus, and natural language. However, if lean media are used to communicate equivocal messages, communication problems result. The medium does not allow for the multiple cues and immediate feedback that are needed to capture the complexity of the message. A memo that attempts to explain an impending organizational merger cannot deal with employee fears and concerns about what the merger means for them.

For routine, unequivocal messages, lean media are effective. They can efficiently transmit the message. However, if rich media are used in these situations, they may provide excess cues that simply cause confusion and provide unnecessary surplus meaning. Consider the example of the manager who needs to remind subordinates of required meeting attendance. If the manager makes a special trip to deliver the message face-to-face, the subordinate may get anxious and wonder if there is more to the message.

Recall Mintzberg's (1973) finding that managers seemed to prefer verbal, face-to-face communication. Based upon the research reported above, this explanation of managers' media preferences appears to be incomplete. It is true that good managers prefer verbal, face-to-face media for equivocal communications. But, they will also readily use lean media for more routine, unequivocal messages. Perhaps Mintzberg found what seemed to be a general preference for verbal face-to-face media because he studied senior managers. Their communications are more likely to involve the resolution of equivocal issues. Executives spend much time dealing with difficult, ambiguous issues and putting out organizational fires. Large changes in understanding must be achieved quickly to deal with these issues. More routine matters are often delegated to subordinates. Therefore, senior managers can be expected to use rich media more frequently. They don't necessarily prefer it. But, the kind of equivocal communication they are most often involved in demands the use of rich media to be effective.

An understanding of media selection based upon message equivocality also provides some understanding of Harold Geneen's need to travel to Europe once a month with his senior staff to meet face-to-face with the European managers. The problems these managers were facing and the decisions they had to make were not routine or clear-cut. The ambiguity of the problems and the managers' different frames of reference required the richness that only face-to-face communication could provide. The group could wrestle with problems, providing each other with immediate feedback. They could see and feel each others' strength of emotion through eye contact, body language, voice tone, and inflection. In these meetings, Geneen, his senior staff, and the European managers were creating symbols, mutual understanding and meaning. It is likely that the decision to invest in face-to-face communication in this situation contributed to ITT's success.

Contextual Determinants and Media Choice

Message equivocality is not the only factor influencing managerial media choices. Although we might like to think that managers are totally free to make the prescribed choice based upon message equivocality, this is not realistic, especially for lower level managers who are often constrained by resource availability. For example, they may not have the funds to make a cross-country trip so that a face-to-face meeting can occur. In addition, past research has characterized managerial work as fast-paced, varied, and fragmented (Mintzberg, 1973). Managers often work under time pressure. Therefore, they may not always have the luxury of time to use the theoretically "best" medium.

Recently, Stryker and Statham (1985) proposed an integrative theoretical framework called *structural symbolic interactionism* (SSI). This framework accommodates the interpretive symbolic interactionism approach described above as well as a more traditional sociology in which behavior is thought to be determined by external forces. Therefore, within this framework, media choice behavior can be viewed as determined at times by contextual influences that either constrain or enable specific media choices. Individual behavior in organizations is often constrained by contextual factors. For example, media choice might be constrained by distance, expediency, time pressure, or simply the accessibility of a particular communication technology.

Distance and Time Pressure. A number of research studies have supported the idea that characteristics of the situation determine media choice. For example, one study (Steinfield & Fulk, 1986) found that geographical distance and time pressure significantly influenced media choice. Managers who were acting under time pressure were more likely to use the telephone regardless of the relative ambiguity of the message. In addition, managers who were geographically distant from their communication partners showed an increased tendency to use electronic mail, again despite message ambiguity. Message content played a less important role when managers were faced with these constraints.

Accessibility and Critical Mass of Users. In addition to distance and time pressure, others have proposed that access to the technology and a critical mass of willing users (Thorn & Connolly, 1987) are important determinants of media choice especially with new communication technologies. This notion has been supported in several studies. One study (Steinfield, 1986) found that access to an electronic mail system was an important determinant of media choice. Without system access, a manager's ability to choose electronic mail is out of the question.

In addition, the effective use of an interactive medium like electronic mail has been linked to the development of a critical mass of users (Markus, 1987). A user cannot achieve the efficiency benefits of new interactive media independently. One's communication partners must also have access to the system. You can imagine how much you would use the telephone if you were the only one to have one! Without a critical mass of users, use of a medium will not spread and may stop entirely (Hiltz, 1984; Uhlig, Farber, & Bair, 1979).

When interviewed managers described their reasons for media choice (Trevino, Lengel, & Daft, 1987), many of the reasons fell into a contextual determinant classification. Managers said that they chose face-to-face when the receiver was close by, such as in the next office. But, they chose the telephone to span long distances and to accomplish communications quickly and efficiently. Both electronic mail and written media were chosen for their ability to reach many receivers at once.

The reality of contextual determinants is evident in the research findings. Managers are busy people with limited resources who select communication media, especially the telephone, written media, and electronic mail for their convenience, efficiency, and accessibility.

Consider Harold Geneen's situation again. He had the resources to travel to Europe quite frequently. However, good managers are interested in the efficient use of resources. Therefore, he probably reserved those expensive and time-consuming European trips for the more equivocal issues that could not be handled successfully via leaner communication media.

Symbolic Meaning and Media Choice

In the past the medium of communication has been conceptualized as a simple pipeline, a carrier of messages. According to the above arguments, this pipeline is selected for convenience, availability, or for its capacity to transmit a certain kind of message (i.e., an equivocal message). However, it is also possible that the medium of communication may be selected for symbolic meaning that transcends the explicit message. In this way, the medium itself becomes a message (Trevino, Lengel, & Daft, 1987). Consider that putting a message in writing may suggest commitment to an idea. A savvy manager may choose to meet face-to-face to convey a willingness to be open to the ideas of others and to allow the option of altering the idea in light of what others say.

The idea that communication media are symbols themselves is consistent with the interpretive approach to organizational communication (Putnam & Pacanowsky, 1983) that emphasizes the importance of symbolic processes and subjective meaning. Communication behavior is largely based upon perceptions, the use of language and symbols to create shared meaning (Feldman & March, 1981; Pfeffer, 1981; Pondy & Mitroff, 1979).

According to symbolic interactionism, anything can be considered a symbol and a carrier of meaning. Therefore, it is possible that the media choice itself may carry symbolic cues beyond the literal message content. When we discuss media richness or leanness, we are making a relatively objective statement about the properties of the medium (Fulk, Steinfield, Schmitz, & Power, 1987). We are considering the capacity of the medium to handle a particular kind of message. But, symbolic cues have nothing to do with the objective characteristics or capabilities of the medium. They are interpretations based upon the subjective norms in the situation. Norms for media use and the meaning of media choice are developed over time. For example, a formal bureaucratic organizational culture may define written memos as appropriate for most communications. Managers may request that even a decision made in a brief informal hallway exchange be put in writing. On the other hand, an informal culture may find written memos to be justified only when a record of the exchange is absolutely necessary. In this organizational culture, a new organizational member who sends memos will be chided for being too formal and discouraged from future memo writing.

Feldman and March (1981) argued persuasively that managerial communication behavior represents ritualistic responses to the need to appear competent, intelligent, legitimate, and rational. For example, if it is necessary to legitimize a decision, decision makers may use a conspicuous consumption strategy. They may request more data than needed and send out professional looking written reports to symbolize the legitimacy and rationality of the decision. Similarly, the face-to-face medium may symbolize concern or caring. The manager who congratulates a subordinate on 25 years of service with an electronic mail message may be sending a symbolic message about lack of concern. A manager wishing to symbolize his or her authority over a particular matter may use a formal written communication to transmit that message. Computer use is facilitated by a network of supportive relationships. Therefore, choosing to send a message via computer may convey the message that one is a member of a particular group (Fulk et. al., 1987).

Trevino, Lengel, and Daft (1987) found support for the symbolic role of media in their research. When interviewed about reasons for their media choices, managers referred to many symbolic reasons. They said that they chose the face-to-face medium to signal a desire for teamwork, to build trust, goodwill, or to convey informality. Both face-to-face and telephone communications symbolized urgency, showed personal concern, and signaled deference to the receiver who preferred that medium. By contrast, written media were thought to show authority, make a strong impression, and be legitimate and official. Written media were also used to get attention and to comply with protocol.

This third factor, the symbolic meaning conveyed by the medium itself, can provide additional understanding of Harold Geneen's media choice situation. By investing in monthly travel and meeting face-to-face with his European managers, Geneen was not only able to effectively handle equivocal situations and solve nonroutine problems. He was also symbolically conveying to these managers his desire for teamwork and his personal caring about them and what they were able to accomplish as a group.

Thus, the research has suggested three factors that influence managers' media choices. These are illustrated in the model presented in Figure 4.4. The first factor is the *equivocality of the message*. For highly equivocal messages, richer media such as face-to-face are required to negotiate meaning and create solutions. For unequivocal or more routine communications, leaner media are capable of handling the message. Electronic media or written media are more likely to be selected and to be effective.

The second factor was called *contextual determinants*. Managers are busy people, working under time pressure. They communicate with other individuals in many geographical locations, from their own building to foreign countries. In addition, depending on the organization, they may or may not have access to all communication media, and there may or may not be a critical mass of users of a particular communication technology. Thus, these external factors influence their media choices. For example, managers who are under extreme time pressure or who are geographically distant from their communication partners are more likely to select the telephone, electronic mail, or written forms of communication. The research suggests that contextual determinants may influence media choice before the other factors (Steinfield & Fulk, 1986). This means that managers are probably influenced first by the contextual factors that constrain and enable them to make media

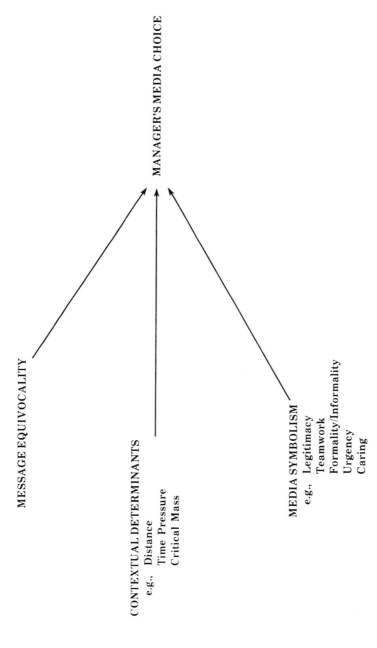

MESSAGE EQUIVOCALITY

MANAGER'S MEDIA CHOICE

CONTEXTUAL DETERMINANTS
e.g., Distance
Time Pressure
Critical Mass

MEDIA SYMBOLISM
e.g., Legitimacy
Teamwork
Formality/Informality
Urgency
Caring

Figure 4.4 Influences on Managers' Media Choice Processes

choices. For example, when confronted with the need to communicate with someone far away, the manager will try a medium that is efficient for that purpose such as the telephone or mail. However, if the message is highly equivocal, the communicators will eventually find that they need to schedule a face-to-face meeting to work out an understanding.

The third factor was the *symbolic meaning* conveyed by the choice of a particular medium. Media choice is not based solely on objective task and contextual characteristics. In organizations, the choice of a particular medium often carries with it symbolic meaning beyond the explicit message being transmitted. Organizational and subgroup norms for media usage create pressure to choose or not choose a particular medium. These norms can have a powerful influence on media choice behavior.

Practical Guidelines for Managers[2]

The research and conclusions described above have practical implications for managers. The following set of guidelines should be considered practical tools to hone the manager's media selection skills (Lengel & Daft, 1988).

1. Send Equivocal Messages Through a Rich Medium

A rich medium is perfect for equivocal communications. For example, face-to-face conveys emotion and strength of feeling through facial expressions, gestures, and eye contact. It is as important for a manager to know that participants are satisfied, angry, cooperative, or resistant, as it is to have accurate production data. Face-to-face also allows differing interpretations of the problem to be resolved through immediate exchange of ideas and opinions. If a leaner medium is used for equivocal communications, important issues and disagreements may remain hidden. Memos and other written directives convey a predefined, literal description that can hide important issues and convey a false sense that everyone understands and agrees. Behind this smoke screen, problems can simmer until they become major fires that are difficult to put out.

However, managers must also be aware of the barriers that can impede perfect matching of media to message. Distance and time pressure are probably the most important ones. They may dictate media choice in many situations. It is up to the manager to decide when these barriers must be overcome—when a face-to-face visit is essential to working out the problem at hand.

2. Send Unequivocal Messages Through a Lean Medium

Time management is important to managers. Therefore, it is essential for them to know when face-to-face discussions are unnecessary. Lean media are perfect for conveying unequivocal messages. They are efficient and precise. Unequivocal messages typically are impersonal and logical. Lean media can clearly convey hard data, obvious conclusions, statistical analyses, or official requests or directives. For example, managers may use a follow-up memo to document an agreement. A note or memo is quick and efficient. It does not require the extra time to contend with the surplus cues associated with a face-to-face meeting. Unless the manager needs to send a symbolic message about issues like caring, trust, or teamwork, a lean medium is perfectly matched to many routine issues.

Guidelines 1 and 2 suggest that by selecting the appropriate medium, the manager can help shape the receiver's reality. By choosing face-to-face, the manager may add emotion to the message, perhaps where it is not needed. By choosing a memo, the manager may mask emotion or disagreement that needs to be addressed. Choosing the medium appropriate to the equivocality of the message will more likely lead to communication effectiveness.

3. Be a Critical Receiver

Guidelines 1 and 2 address the sender. However, managers also receive many messages. They should realize that the messages they receive can color their understanding of the issues because of the medium that was selected. For example, lean media can filter out information about critical issues. Top managers are responsible for interpreting the internal and external corporate environment. However, if they rely solely on written and formal sources of information, the images of corporate reality they receive are oversimplified and insulated from the messy realities. The use of multiple media can help. In addition to formal reports, managers should seek rich face-to-face encounters with customers, suppliers, and subordinates. Their viewpoints will provide alternate views of corporate reality that can be combined with the more rational images generated on paper.

Senior managers rely on their subordinates for much of the information they use for decision making. Therefore, it is also appropriate for top managers to train those who work for them in the importance of using multiple sources of information. Managers should be encouraged to take the time to interact with customers, suppliers, and other organizational stakeholders so that when they write a report or represent a point of view, that report or viewpoint is enriched by the multiple sources that have been used to generate it.

4. Use the Medium for Its Symbolic Message

Organizations have distinctive cultures that guide behavior and create understanding among members. This understanding extends to how media are used and the meaning they convey in the particular organization. Managers who are sensitive to the organization's media culture will consciously choose a particular medium for the meaning it conveys above and beyond the explicit message. Modern managers should be aware of the importance of symbols in their work (Pfeffer, 1981). Media choice presents an opportunity to manage symbols creatively. For example, a manager who makes a special effort to meet with a subordinate is sending a message about personal caring and goodwill. On the other hand, a manager who creates a formal, professional looking report is sending a message about the importance and legitimacy of the topic. Once again, the manager is creating reality through a particular media choice.

Media choices may also create a particular kind of corporate culture. If senior managers promote the frequent use of face-to-face discussions throughout the organization, they may be contributing to the creation of an organizational culture that values informality, teamwork, participation, trust, goodwill, and caring. Alternatively, if senior managers promote the use of written communications, they may create a corporate culture that is efficiency-oriented, bureaucratic, formal, and concerned with status and authority. It is important that managers are consciously aware of the profound impact these symbols can have on their day-to-day communications as well as the creation of a specific kind of organizational culture.

5. Evaluate New Communication Technology Carefully

The astonishing advances in electronic communication technology appeal to the modern executive who wants to be up on the latest and most efficient ways to communicate and process information. Promises of greater efficiency and productivity motivate major corporate investments in computerized management information systems, electronic mail, and teleconferencing systems. The manager as media critic must decide whether these promises are reasonable and if the investment is a wise one.

The manager should evaluate these systems carefully, taking into account their capabilities and their limitations. For example, computer-based systems enable the accumulation and transmission of voluminous objective data about corporate performance, internal activities, and environmental events. However, they can not substitute for the power of the face-to-face medium for transferring multiple cues, enabling rapid feedback among several managers, and attaining social support for enacting solutions to equivocal problems. One solution may be to acknowledge managers' need for both types of information by combining media. Huber (1984) proposed that group decision support systems (GDSSs) offer a way to apply new media to highly equivocal situations. These systems provide face-to-face discussion and access to databases. Each participant in a group meeting has an individual CRT along with the public display screen visible to all members of the group. Each member can work individually with extant databases while exchanging ideas with others through verbal discussions and the public display screen. Feedback among members is fast, and social support can be obtained. This information exchange design is ideal for decision situations that are complex, require data formulations and reformulations, but also require equivocality reduction and social support.

Electronic mail has many characteristics similar to the telephone or written memos because it also has the capacity for rapid feedback and it can quickly reach a large, geographically dispersed audience (Steinfield & Fulk, 1985). However, cues such as eye contact, voice and body language are filtered out. Electronic mail is considered most appropriate for the routine exchange of unequivocal information. It is considered inappropriate for exchanging confidential information, resolving disagreements, getting to know someone, or negotiating (Rice & Case, 1983; Steinfield, 1985).

The early proponents of teleconferencing believed that it would replace much business travel and substitute for face-to-face meetings. However, teleconferencing now appears to be more like a conference telephone call than it is like a face-to-face meeting. Similar to the telephone, voice cues and immediate feedback are available. In addition, visual images such as graphs and charts can be displayed for all to see and discuss. However, the visual image of people on a television screen can not be compared to the exchange that occurs when individuals are physically present together in a room. Much of the body language and other subtle cues are lost as are the important regulating features of mutual gaze (Argyle & Cook, 1975). In addition, managers who think of themselves as being "on television" often become stiff and formal. The informality of the face-to-face medium is lost (Johansen,

Vallee, & Spangler, 1979). Therefore, teleconferencing is appropriate for the presentation and discussion of relatively unequivocal issues among a number of people in several locations. It is an inappropriate medium for the resolution of highly emotional issues or for the discussion of issues about which there is much disagreement—such as the decision to launch the Challenger space shuttle.

Conclusion

Media choice involves more than simple common sense. It is a complex process that is influenced by the interplay of messages, symbols and contextual influences. This chapter has presented three important factors that influence managers' media choices: message equivocality, contextual determinants, and media symbolism. One of these factors, message equivocality, has been related to overall managerial effectiveness. Higher performing managers match the equivocality of the message with the richness of the communication medium. These factors provide a greater understanding of managers' media choice processes and suggest guidelines managers can follow if they wish to be more effective communicators.

Notes

1. This section was adapted from Trevino, Lengel, & Daft (1987).
2. This section was adapted from Lengel & Daft (1988).

References

Argyle, M., & Cook, M. (1975). *Gaze and mutual gaze*. Cambridge, MA: Cambridge University Press.

Blumer, H. (1969). *Symbolic interactionism: Perspective and method*. Englewood Cliffs, NJ: Prentice-Hall.

Daft, R. L., & Lengel, R. H. (1984). Information richness: A new approach to managerial information processing and organization design. In L. L. Cummings & B. M. Staw (Eds.), *Research in organizational behavior* (Vol. 6, pp. 191-234). Greenwich, CT: JAI Press.

Daft, R. L., & Lengel, R. H. (1986). Organizational information requirements, media richness and structural determinants. *Management Science 32*(5), 554-571.

Daft, R. L., Lengel, R. H., & Trevino, L. K. (1987). Message equivocality, media selection, and manager performance: Implications for information systems. *MIS Quarterly, 11*, 355-366.

Daft, R. L., & Macintosh, N. B. (1981). A tentative exploration into the amount and equivocality of information processing in organizational work units. *Administrative Science Quarterly, 26*(2), 207-224.

Daft, R. L., & Weick, K. E. (1984). Toward a model of organizations as interpretation systems. *Academy of Management Review, 9*(2), 284-295.

Feldman, M. S., & March, J. G. (1981). Information in organizations as signal and symbol. *Administrative Science Quarterly, 26*. 171-186.

Fulk, J., Steinfield, C., Schmitz, J., & Power, J. G. (1987). A social information processing model of media use in organizations. *Communication Research, 14*(5), 529-552.

Geneen, H., with Moscow, A. (1984). *Managing*. Garden City, NY: Doubleday.

Hiltz, S. R. (1984). *Online communities: A case study of the office of the future*. Norwood, NJ: Ablex.

Huber, G. P. (1984). Issues in the design of group decision support systems. *MIS Quarterly, 8*(3), 194-204.

Johansen, R., Vallee, J., & Spangler, K. (1979). *Electronic meetings: Technical alternatives and social choices*. Menlo Park, CA: Addison-Wesley.

Lengel, R. H., & Daft, R. L. (1988). The selection of communication media as an executive skill. *Academy of Management Executive, 2*(3), 225-232.

Markus, M. L. (1987). Toward a "critical mass" theory of interactive media: Universal access, interdependence, and diffusion. *Communication Research, 14*(5), 491-511.

Mead, G. H. (1934). *Mind, self, and society*. Chicago: University of Chicago.

Mintzberg, H. (1973), *The nature of managerial work*. New York: Harper & Row.

Mintzberg, H., Raisinghani, D., & Theoret, A. (1976). The structure of unstructured decision processes. *Administrative Science Quarterly, 21*(2), 246-275.

Pfeffer, J. (1981). Management as symbolic action: The creation and maintenance of organizational paradigms. In L. L. Cummings & B. M. Staw (Eds.), *Research in organizational behavior* (Vol. 3, pp. 1-52). Greenwich, CT: JAI Press.

Pondy, L., & Mitroff, I. (1979) Beyond open systems models of organization. In L. L. Cummings & B. M. Staw (Ed.) *Research in organizational behavior* (Vol. 1, pp. 3-40). Greenwich, CT: JAI Press.

Putnam, L., & Pacanowsky, M. E. (Eds.). (1983). *Communication and organizations: An interpretive approach*. Beverly Hills, CA: Sage.

Rice, R. E., & Case, D. (1983). Electronic message systems in the university: A description of use and utility. *Journal of Communication, 33*(1), 131-152.

Steinfield, C. (1985). Dimensions of electronic mail use in an organizational setting. *Proceedings of the Academy of Management* (pp. 239-243). San Diego, California.

Steinfield, C. E., & Fulk, J. (1986). *Task demands and managers' use of communication media: An informational processing view*. Paper presented at the meeting of the Academy of Management, Organization Communication Division, Chicago, Illinois.

Steinfield, C. W. (1986). Computer-mediated communication in an orgaizational setting: Explaining task-related and socioemotional uses. In M. McLaughlin, *Communication yearbook 9*. Beverly Hills: Sage.

Stryker, S., & Statham, A. (1985) Symbolic interaction and role theory. In Lindsay & Aronson (Eds.), *New handbook of social psychology* (3rd ed.). New York: Random House.

Thorn, B. K., & Connolly, T. (1987) Discretionary databases: A theory and some experimental findings. *Communication Research, 14*(5), 512-528.

Trevino, L. K., Lengel, R., Bodensteiner, W., & Gerloff, E. (1988). *Managerial media choice: The interactive influences of cognitive style and message equivocality*. Paper presented at the meeting of the Academy of Management, Anaheim, California.

Trevino, L. K., Lengel, R., & Daft, R. L. (1987). Media symbolism, media richness, and media choice in organizations: A symbolic interactionist perspective. *Communication Research, 14* 553-574.

Uhlig, R. P., Farber, D. J., & Bair, J. H. (1979). *The office of the future: Communication and computers*. Amsterdam: North-Holland Publishing.

Weick, K. E. (1979). *The social psychology of organizing* (2nd ed.). Reading, MA: Addison-Wesley.

ROBERT W. ZMUD

5. Opportunities for Strategic Information Manipulation Through New Information Technology

After 20 years of study, we are just beginning to understand the forces that underlie the organizational impacts of information technology (Attewell & Rule, 1984; Weber, 1988). Here, *information technology* (IT) refers to the application of computer and communications technologies in the acquisition, storage, analysis, distribution, and presentation of information. Those who are pro technologists see the application of IT as a means for both increasing organizational efficiency and effectiveness and improving the quality of work life. Most often, this is achieved by providing an organization's members useful information-based tools and by automating routine, repetitive work tasks. Those who are anti technologists, on the other hand, tend to see the application of IT as a management tool for gaining increased power over employees and as a means for reducing the work force.

Rather than viewing the organizational consequences of IT as being inherently positive or negative, IT is perhaps best viewed as neutral regarding its organizational consequences (Markus & Robey, 1988). The nature of an organization's IT use emerges through complex interactions among the intentions of key actors, attributes of the technology involved, and dynamic organizational processes. If used well, IT can beneficially affect an organization and its members. If used inappropriately, the same technology may very well be associated with negative consequences.

A neglected, but nonetheless important, set of organizational consequences involves the strategic information behaviors of an organization's members. As discussed by Pettigrew (1972), Feldman and March (1981), and Pfeffer (1981), individuals do engage in the deliberate misrepresentation of information or restriction of access to information in order to influence the behaviors of others. A situation in which such behaviors commonly occur is

Author's Note: This paper was initially prepared for presentation at the Academy of Management's 1988 National Meeting, Anaheim, August 1988.

that involving investment decisions. It is quite possible for a knowledgeable individual, through the application of creative statistical or graphical techniques, to present convincing cases for both accepting or rejecting an investment alternative *from the same set of data*. This chapter argues that recent advances with information technology, which are drastically changing organizations' information landscapes, is dramatically increasing the potential scope and impact of strategic information behaviors.

The chapter begins by developing a simple yet robust model of an organizational information system (OIS). This model is then applied in analyzing the literature on managerial information behaviors in order to identify "critical influence points," that is, those OIS functions particularly vulnerable to strategic information behaviors. An analysis of the influence of new information technology on these critical influence points is then undertaken in order to project their potential impact on strategic information behaviors. The chapter concludes with suggested research directions for better understanding these phenomena.

A Modular Perspective on Organizational Information Systems

An organization's members are consumers, managers, and purveyors of information. *Information* refers to the *meaning* human actors assign to items or collections of data. Information is sought from internal and external sources in deciding:

- what to do (setting work goals and objectives, and identifying the tasks to be performed);
- how to do it (identifying resource requirements, situational constraints, and task procedures);
- when it is to be done (determining resource availabilities and the status of antecedent or subsequent tasks); and
- how it was done (assessing work volumes, rates and exceptions as well as the extent to which objectives were met).

Acquired information is maintained along with that created in the process of doing work in order that questions about the past, the present, and the future can be explored. These questions are raised by workers, coworkers, and superiors, and by individuals from outside the organization (e.g., customers, suppliers, stockholders).

The paramount "information problem" faced by most managers is not the lack of data but its overabundance. As work environments become more complex, turbulent, and hostile (Huber, 1984), this problem will only intensify. Without the information processing support provided by artifacts (computer- and communications-based information systems) or by support staff (who themselves utilize artifacts), most managers would experience severe information overload. As a result, pertinent information would be (1) overlooked or not sought; (2) gathered or transmitted in a hurried or incomplete manner; (3) analyzed through hurried, incomplete or inappropriate procedures; and (4) incorrectly or inappropriately incorporated or neglected within the mental models used to represent work situations.

It may be helpful to conceptualize an organization as a communication system consisting of interconnected networks of *processing nodes* and *information buffers*. Processing nodes transport or transform *messages*, which can be stored in temporary or permanent buffers (Kmetz, 1984). A few examples of information buffers include a file cabinet, an in-box on a manager's desk, a finished-goods inventory, a manager's memory, and a computer database.

Many of these nodes and buffers are also linked to nodes and buffers in other organizations. A clear example of both such links and the use of information technology involves electronic data interchange (EDI) technology, or the fully electronic transfer of business documents (orders, shipping lists, invoices, payments) between organizations. This is illustrated in Figure 5.1. These business documents are the "messages" being processed. A computer program (TN2) operated by a provider of EDI services obtains electronic copies of invoices (the messages) from a data file (VB) stored on the vendor's computer. Program TN2 then stores these invoices in a data file (TB) maintained on the third-part supplier's computer system. At some later time, a program (MN2) maintained on a computer system operated by the manufacturer reads these invoices off data file TB and stores them within a data file maintained by the manufacturer (MB). Processor nodes labeled "-N2" represent computer programs, nodes labeled "-N3" represent accounts payable/accounts receivable clerks, and nodes labeled "-N1" represent EDI analysts at each organization responsible for ensuring compatible information flows. An EDI task force, established to coordinate EDI exchanges across these three organizations, is represented by the dotted line.

It is important to recognize that OIS message handling is always subject to errors and delays. Errors are the result of imperfect processor node behaviors. Finite time delays arise in four ways: node processing time; buffer storage and retrieval time; time lost while a message sits in a node's or buffer's wait-queue as the node or buffer attends to other tasks; and, time lapse while a message is held in a buffer (Huber, 1982).

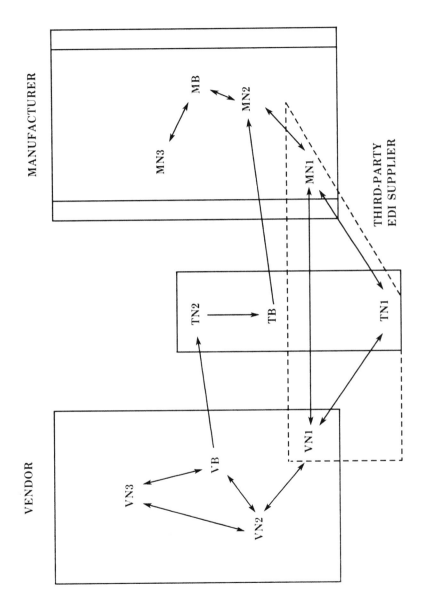

Figure 5.1 Networks Supporting and EDI Exchange

The messages conveyed within and through an OIS cover a wide variety of items, including but not limited to facts, observations, projections, beliefs, opinions, guides-for-action, score-cards, triggers-for-action, and contexts-for-action. As mentioned above, the invoices in the EDI example are examples of fact messages. Guides-for-action represent norms, policies, plans, instructions, rules, or procedures indicating "what to do" and "how to do it." Score-cards represent measures of task performance—what was accomplished and how well it was accomplished. Triggers-for-action represent signals to commence a certain action. Contexts-for-action represent the provision of data on the nature, history, and objectives that invoke a particular schema for a work situation.

Most OIS can be characterized by seven types of processing nodes:

sensor
: Sensor nodes detect environmental *signals* and transform these into messages. Sensor nodes can exhibit distinct types of behavior (Huber, 1984; El Sawy & Pauchant, 1988): as scanners (gathering information that has no immediate use), as trackers (routine monitoring of issues, events, or entities), and as probers (one-time exploration of a specific issue, event, or entity).

filter
: Filter nodes operate on input messages in order to screen out those which are irrelevant (Daft & Weick, 1984). Relevant messages are maintained within the OIS; irrelevant messages are lost.

router
: Router nodes distribute an input message to particular nodes and to particular information buffers (Huber, 1982).

carrier
: Carrier nodes move, or "carry," messages to and from processing nodes and information buffers.

interpreter
: Interpreter nodes apply existent guides-for-action and contexts-for-action to input messages to enhance the information value of a message. As a result, uncertain or equivocal messages are interpreted (Daft & Weick, 1984), i.e., made more meaningful.

learner
: Learner nodes apply existent guides-for-action and contexts-for-action to uncertain or equivocal input messages in order to create new score-cards, triggers-for-action, guides-for-action, or contexts-for-action. Without these new schema, the input message would remain uncertain or equivocal. When learning occurs, a new reality is enacted within an OIS (Weick, 1977; Daft & Weick, 1984).

modifier
: Modifier nodes transform input messages but do not add value to these messages. The information potential of an output message is at best equivalent to that of its associated input message. In most cases, a message's information potential is

Table 5.1
OIS Model of a Parts-Clerk Situation

SITUATION: Handling a Parts Transaction

Processing Nodes	Human Information Processing System Component	Description
sensor	eyes	Recognize that a requisition form has been received.
filter	automatic response maintained in short-term memory	Embedded actions that identify the nature of a transaction and assign it a handling priority.
router	standard operation rules maintained in working memory	Set of rules retrieved from long term memory that initiate a handling procedure based on a transaction's nature and priority
carrier	nervous system	Carries signals between sensory organs, muscles, and brain.
interpreter	substitution procedures maintained in working memory	Algorithm retrieved from long term memory to locate a substitute part for an out-of-stock requisitioned part.
learner	development of substitution procedures	Algorithm retrieved from long term memory to construct a new set of substitution procedures as new car models are introduced.
modifier	part identifier reduction rules	Rules maintained in working memory that both reduce the length of part identifiers and insure a fit with the *ad hoc* coding maintained in the short, working and long term memory.

reduced through summarization or distortion (Huber, 1982). Summarizing a message reduces its size while faithfully reproducing its meaning; distortion (conscious or unconscious, well-intended or malicious) changes the meaning of the message.

Illustrations of these different types of nodes, using the example of a retail automobile supply store, are provided in Tables 5.1 and 5.2.

The examples given in Tables 5.1 and 5.2 illustrate the dual roles served by messages. Not only are messages operated on by processor nodes, but they also direct these operations. Sensor, filter, router, carrier, interpreter, learner, and modifier nodes all function through embedded score-cards, triggers-for-action, guides-for-action, and contexts-for-action. And, not only are messages stored in information buffers, but they constitute the structure by which storage areas are organized.

Table 5.2
OIS Model of a Parts-Department Situation

SITUATION: Assigning Inventory Storage Locations of New Parts

Processing Nodes	Departmental OIS Component	Description
sensor	parts manager	Signs contract with salesman for shipments of new parts.
filter	parts clerk	Identifies possible locations through walking tour.
router	none	
carrier	paper memos	Messages between actors are sent via written notes.
interpreter	parts managers	Assigns each new part to a "parts family" (through knowledge of common part attributes maintained in long term memory); each new part will be stored in the available bin closest to others in its "family"
learner	parts manager and parts clerk	Identifying new "parts family" when existing families are insufficient via a discussion of attributes of a "problem" part (applying knowledge of common part attributes maintained in each person's long term memory)
modifier	bin location code	Coding system maintained in procedures manual that provides a short code for each storage bin; codes are based on physical location of each bin.

This OIS model possesses a number of useful attributes. First, its simplicity results in its being a good vehicle to describe complex organizational processes. For example, Figure 5.1 should communicate the basic ideas behind EDI to an individual unfamiliar with this technology. Second, its modular nature—nodes and buffers can be interconnected in an infinite variety of ways—results in it being extremely flexible. A particular OIS element can be represented as a node (VN3, the vendor's account receivables clerk in Figure 5.1), a buffer (TB, the "invoice mail box" maintained on the third-party supplier's computer system in Figure 5.1), a cluster of nodes (the EDI tasks force, comprised of VN1, TN1 and MN1 in Figure 5.1), a cluster of buffers (all the "invoice mail boxes" maintained on the third-party supplier's computer system in Figure 5.1), or a cluster of nodes and buffers (the manufacturer's computer system, comprised of MN2 and MB in Figure 5.1). Any information processing situation or phenomenon can be represented via the model. Third, the model can be applied at any level of organizational analysis: subindividual, individual, group, organization, industry). This is illustrated by the processor node examples given earlier in Tables 5.1 and

5.2. Here, the processor nodes of an OIS model of a "parts clerk" are described in Table 5.1 and those of a "parts department" are described in Table 5.2. Fourth, these levels of analysis can easily be intermixed.

Finally, it is important to note that the OIS model makes no assumptions about the nature of these processing nodes or information buffers. They can represent humans or artifacts and can reflect formal or informal behaviors, restricted or unrestricted behaviors, mandatory or discretionary behaviors, and automatic or directed behaviors. As a result, the OIS model can depict information processing activities that only involve humans (e.g., a top management team developing an organization's mission statement), that only involve artifacts (e.g., an automated command and control center at a nuclear power plant), or that involve human-artifact teams (e.g., operations activities transpiring within an air traffic control tower).

Critical Influence Points Regarding Strategic Information Behaviors

While a considerable body of literature exists on human information processing behaviors (see Ungson, Braunstein, & Hall, 1981; Kiesler & Sproull, 1982, for representative literature reviews), the topic of managerial information processing behaviors has recently experienced a resurgence in interest (Isenberg, 1986; Boynton, 1987; Bourgeois & Eisenhardt, 1988; El Sawy & Pauchant, 1988). Likely explanations for such a resurgence include transformations in the nature of organizational environments, the development and general availability of new technologies for supporting managerial information processing, an increased interest in strategic organizational processes, and a recognition that managerial information-processing behaviors are far more complex than earlier believed. In this section, literature related to these issues are examined in order to identify those elements of the modular OIS model most sensitive to strategic information behaviors.

Sensor Nodes

The dominant ideas that underlie most views of managers' efforts to scan, probe or track their environments are reflected in Huber's (1984) essay on the nature of postindustrial organizations: organizations (and, hence, managers) in information-rich, complex, and turbulent environments will engage in continuous, wide-ranging, and directed information acquisition. Recent findings, however, suggest that managers engage in far less information acquisition than would be expected. Not only is information acquisition often "cut short" (Isenberg, 1986), but much of what does occur is likely to be both bounded in scope and delegated to others (El Sawy & Pauchant, 1988). Further, recently acquired evidence (Boynton, 1987) indicates that managers in information-rich environments, for example, an environment for which high quality and easily accessible information is available, actually spend less time scanning than those in information-poor environments.

While the nature of the information ultimately retained from managerial sensing is largely a function of the filters that are applied, certain features of environmental situations are often unconsciously gathered and retained (Kiesler & Sproull, 1982; Schwenk, 1986). Signals that appear frequently tend to be automatically captured, as are the spatial and temporal attributes of captured signals. Further, signals sensed together, regardless of their "true relationship," tend to be associated with one another; the more frequent these occurrences, the stronger this association.

Filter Nodes

A considerable amount of research has been directed at exploring managerial information filters (Staw, Sandelands, & Dutton, 1981; Kiesler & Sproull, 1982; Schwenk, 1986). What emerges is consistent and convincing: these filters (1) serve a dominating role in managerial information processing as information acquisition "triggers, guides, and contexts," and (2) are based on historical rather than current representations of an organization's environment. Further, these filters tend to be simple, supportive of existing cause-effect beliefs and expectations, and self-enhancing. And, the more threatening a work situation, the more likely it is than a manager will apply an existent filter rather than engage in efforts to revise an old filter or construct a new one (Staw, Sandelands, & Dutton, 1981).

Router Nodes

Managerial routing behaviors have received relatively little attention from OIS researchers. Huber (1982) summarizes the factors believed to affect the likelihood that a specific message will be routed to particular OIS nodes: the costs associated with routing, the work-load of the router node, the relevance of the message to a receiving node, repercussions to the router node from communication "bad news," the relative power and status of the router node and receiving nodes, and the history of prior routings to the receiving nodes.

An examination of organizational members' motivations to contribute information to discretionary data bases is a recent addition to the research on routing behaviors (Connolly & Thorn, 1987). A discretionary data base is a "public" information buffer; that is, one that is freely available and of potential benefit to all of an organization's members and that contains information contributed by any of the organization's members. Applying the results of a laboratory study, Connolly and Thorn suggest that less information is likely to be contributed to discretionary data bases than either its proponents or participants would desire. If contribution costs are significant, it is not clear how users repay contributors. If contribution costs are subsidized to the point where it is profitable to do so, information will be contributed without regard to its value to potential users. Interestingly, the larger the discretionary database, the more diluted are contributor/user reciprocities.

Carrier Nodes

Aside from naturally occurring, unintended effects regarding message delay and modification via transmission errors (Huber, 1982), little is known about carrier nodes.

Interpreter and Learner Nodes

As with filters, a large body of literature exists on the nature of managerial sense-making; that is, interpreting and learning (Staw, Sandelands, & Dutton, 1981; Kiesler & Sproull, 1982). Three facets of these behaviors have been examined: the schema (triggers, guides, and contexts), information, and processes that are applied. The schema used to direct managerial sense-making and learning, like those used to direct managerial filtering, are heavily influenced by an individual's experiences and expectations. And, it is these schema, rather than current information, that most influence managerial responses to stimuli (Isenberg, 1986). When current information is integrated along with these schema, it is likely (Schwenk, 1986) to be that which is vivid, personal, anecdotal, and received most frequently. Finally, the sense-making processes that combine schema and current information are best characterized as being simple, structured (even if the face of complex and dynamic situations), information-poor (information search is cut-off early; input messages are partially interpreted), and quick (Ungson, Braunstein, & Hall, 1981; Isenberg, 1986; Bourgeois & Eisenhardt, 1988). And, as with filtering, incidents of illusory correlation and illusory causation, that is, the inappropriate association of information elements because of their fortuitous pairing, are commonly observed (Kiesler & Sproull, 1982).

Modifier Nodes

It is well-recognized that managers often modify input information prior to its being routed elsewhere (Feldman & March, 1981; Huber, 1982). Summarization, operationalized as abstraction or filtering, is applied to ease the information-processing burden of carrier nodes and of the nodes or buffers to which a message is routed (Huber, 1982). Given the dysfunctional consequences of information overload on information processing behaviors (Hiltz & Turoff, 1985), another motivation may be to increase the likelihood that receiving nodes or buffers will, in fact, attend to the message. Distortion occurs for one of two major reasons (Feldman & March, 1981; Huber, 1982): to increase the likelihood a receiving node will attend to a message in a manner that (1) beneficially affects goal attainment of the receiving node and (2) beneficially affects goal attainment of the modifier node. That OIS researchers have emphasized examinations of the first reason should not be surprising given this literature's emphasis on rational models of organizational behavior. Recognition that message modification does occur and awareness of its motivations, however, are far removed from understanding how it is best accomplished. The vast literature that examines these issues is fraught with inconsistencies (Hogarth, 1987), which are now being addressed through more comprehensive research models and designs.

Information Buffers

Information buffers, while omnipresent and critically important to all organizational processes (Kmetz, 1984), have largely been ignored by OIS researchers. Heimer (1985) has shown that the nature of the information held in buffers and the establishment of maintenance responsibilities and access rights to these buffers depend on the relative power of the actors involved in negotiating these issues. Very little is known, however, about information buffers aside from efficiency concerns regarding how best to organize information within one or more buffers in order to optimize storage, maintenance, and access costs.

Summary and Implications to Strategic Information Behavior

The behaviors of OIS processor nodes is largely directed by schema in the form of score-cards, triggers-for-action, guides-for-action, and contexts-for-action. For the most part, these schema are relatively simple, reflect historical rather than current environments, and are self-enhancing. Far less sensing occurs than might be expected: much is delegated, and that which does occur is very bounded in scope. Automatic sensing does occur, but it is heavily influenced by the frequency by which stimuli are sensed, by spurious associations among these stimuli, and by temporal and spatial attributes of the phenomena being sensed. Filtering, which is also driven by existing schema, is perhaps the most active, most common, and most dominant process within an OIS. Message routing and modifying appear to be active, common, and important OIS processes. Interpreting and learning, which clearly serve crucial OIS roles, tend to be driven by relatively simple, well-structured schema (even in the face of complex, dynamic stimuli), are often completed prior to all available information having been explored, and are prone to apply more weight to information that is vivid, personal, and anecdotal, and that appears in a large number of messages. Carrier nodes and information buffers, while active and widely evident throughout an OIS, appear to primarily serve "enabling" rather than proactive roles; that is, they facilitate and are under the direction of other processor nodes.

In their essay on organizations as interpretation systems, Daft and Weick (1984) conclude that sensing, interpreting, and learning are the most critical OIS behaviors. However, an examination of the OIS literature via the modular OIS model suggests that message filtering, routing, and modifying may actually dominate sensing, interpreting, and learning. Filtering, routing, and modifying behaviors dictate, at least in the short run, the nature of the messages input into sense-making, interpreting, and learning processes. Such a difference in emphasis likely reflects a "single-loop" versus a "double-loop" orientation. A single-loop context reflects behaviors that are driven by current schema, while a double-loop context reflects behaviors to devise new schema when it is recognized that current schema are not appropriate for the work situation being addressed. It seems intuitive that the rules embedded within filtering, routing, and modifying processes are fabricated and evolved via sensing, interpreting, and learning (which, in turn, are triggered through filtering, routing, and modifying behaviors). It is precisely this intertwined set of relationships among OIS processes that subjects organizational information to the threat of misrepresentation. And, with most organizational members delegating much of their information processing to others, opportunities for strategic misrepresentation repeatedly arise. The more that is known about a potential "victim's" information-processing behaviors (e.g., operative filters, schema, memory structures) and about general managerial information-processing tendencies, the more likely it is that a misrepresentation effort will be successful.

New Information Technologies and Their Potential Impacts on Strategic Information Behavior

Until recently, the nature of available information technologies served to inhibit rather than facilitate strategic information behaviors. Four reasons support this position:

1. Only a minor portion of the information used by managers was maintained in or obtained through computer- or communication-based information buffers.
2. Most technology-based information systems followed an organization's formal authority structure.
3. Because of their cost, their complexity, or both, most technology-based information systems were not accessible by a majority of an organization's members.
4. When access did occur it often was through technical intermediaries, for example, staff or clerical assistants. When the receiver is not directly reached, the misrepresentation of information becomes either much more complex or requires the collaboration of more than one individual.

Today's organizational information processing landscape is no longer subject to such constraints. (See Tables 5.3 and 5.4 descriptions of relevant new technologies and their combined impact on organizational information processing.) As a result, the potential scope and impact of strategic information behavior is being refashioned. These changes are explored by examining the influences of new technology on each of the elements of the modular OIS model.

Messages

New technology is increasing the absolute number of messages (Culnan & Markus, 1987) and message sources (Keen, 1987; Huber, 1988) within an

Table 5.3
Selective New Information Technologies

Technology	Description
end-user computing	Enables members provided with little technical training to quickly and easily access, manipulate and distribute information items
computer-mediated communication	Enables members to transmit, route and receive messages quickly and inexpensively
groupware	Supports collaborative interactions among members of a social group
expert systems	Embed relatively complex decision rules, which handle or direct the handling of information, within technology-based information systems
intra-organizational systems	Support information flows that cross departmental boundaries
inter-organizational systems	Support information flows that cross organizational boundaries

Table 5.4
Joint Impacts of New Information Technologies

- increasingly favorable economics and ease-of-use
- capability to handle numeric, text, image, and audio data
- greatly expanded user community
- horizontally extended information flows
- removal of geographic and temporal barriers
- capability to embed "intelligence" within applications
- capability to support informal and global information processing tasks as well as formal, local tasks.

OIS. Additionally, while message contents available overall in an OIS are less rich (being more "rationalized") (Huber, 1988), the content of messages available through artifacts are increasingly rich (Child, 1987). Finally, certain message attributes, such as its source (Culnan & Markus, 1987) and social context (Sproull & Kiesler, 1986), can "disappear."

Such changes can increase the potential for strategic information behaviors in at least four ways. First, information overload is likely to intensify, reducing managers' capabilities to manage their own information environments and thus increasing their susceptibility to information misrepresentation by others. Second, as the marginal value of a single message is less, the motivation for proactive information behaviors by managers is reduced (thereby intensifying the aforementioned tendency for delegation). Together, these two trends lead to the following prediction:

Proposition 1: Organizational members will increasingly relinquish individual responsibilities for information processing.

The more that responsibilities for information processing are delegated, the more susceptible an individual is to the strategic information behaviors of others.

Schema

New technology is increasing the number and apparent rationality of the schema being embedded in artifact nodes (Hiltz & Turoff, 1985; Malone, Grant, Turbak, Brobst, & Cohen, 1987) and promoting the indirect use, that is, more distant delegation, of processor nodes (Huber, 1984; Child, 1987). Perhaps the clearest illustration of such phenomena is the recent increase in installed operations-level expert systems throughout the "value chains" (Porter & Millar, 1985) of many organizations (Leonard-Barton & Sviokla, 1988).

Such changes by themselves have little direct impact on strategic information behaviors. However, when they are combined with message changes, significant impacts materialize. Managers are becoming more willing to access artifacts for messages. Further, as messages tend to be accompanied with less information regarding their sources or their social context and since messages from artifacts are usually perceived to be characterized by a high degree of "rationality," message contents are more likely to be taken at their face value. Together, these findings suggest two additional propositions:

Proposition 2: Organizational members will become increasingly dependent on artifacts as information sources.

Proposition 3: Organizational members will place increasing confidence in messages obtained from artifacts.

As artifacts are not conscious entities, they do not possess ethical codes of behavior. Consequently, a perpetrator of a strategic information behavior who gains access to a receiver through an artifact does not first have to coopt the artifact. Thus, it becomes easier for an individual skilled in manipulating artifacts to exhibit strategic information behavior.

Processor Nodes

Through the elimination of the need for information intermediaries, new technology will reduce the absolute number of nodes in an OIS (Keen, 1987; Huber, 1988). In relative terms, the proportion of carrier or modifier nodes will decrease (Keen, 1987) and the proportion of sensing, filtering, and routing nodes will increase (Huber, 1984; Hiltz & Turoff, 1985). Added nodes are most likely to be artifacts and narrowly focused human specialists (Huber, 1984). Such changes are likely to further increase a manager's dependence on artifact nodes and to further increase the ease with which individuals possessing the ability to manipulate processor nodes or the schema embedded within these nodes are able to undertake strategic information behaviors. Considerable evidence supporting such effects in the public sector does exist (Dutton & Kraemer, 1985; Gulley & Mei, 1985; Kraemer, Dickhoven, Tierney, & King, 1987).

Information Buffers

New technology will increase the use of information buffers, relative to the use of processing nodes, as message sources (Huber, 1984, 1988). An increasing proportion of these buffers will be artifacts and will be characterized as being both public and discretionary (Culnan & Markus, 1987). Finally, richer messages will be stored in these buffers (Culnan & Markus, 1987) as also might be the histories of managers' information processing behaviors (access and flow patterns, schema, etc.).

Such changes are likely to increase the potential for strategic information behaviors in at least three ways. First, managers' dependence on artifact information buffers (e.g., computerized databases and bulletin boards) as a primary source of information will increase their potential susceptibility to others' efforts to misrepresent information. Second, both the scope and potential effect of strategic information behaviors are heightened when misrepresented messages are placed within public information buffers— such messages are a costless public good, subject to rapid diffusion throughout an organization. Third, if accessible, the stored histories of managers' information processing behaviors provide exceptional guides as to how best to present misrepresented information to a particular individual. This reasoning leads to a fourth proposition:

Proposition 4: Strategic information behaviors will increasingly occur indirectly via artifacts rather than through direct perpetrator-victim interactions.

It will thus become much easier for perpetrators to "cover their tracks" and remain unknown. It is unlikely that substantial efforts to audit or otherwise control the messages being input to public information buffers since such actions would likely reduce the influx of messages and significantly lessen the value of such public goods. A fifth proposition is thus stated:

Proposition 5: Strategic information behaviors and their perpetrators will be increasingly difficult to identify.

Message Flows

Through the relaxation of economic, geographic and temporal constraints (Child, 1987; Huber, 1988), new technology will expand the variety of message sources and receivers available to individuals. In particular, sources and receivers external to formal work groups, and the organization itself will become increasingly prevalent in OIS. Further, the density of links among sources and receivers will also increase (Culnan & Markus, 1987; Keen, 1987). Even so, the average number of nodes and buffers involved in routing a message to a specific receiver will decrease (Huber, 1988). Finally, sender (via routing processes) control rather than receiver (via filtering processes) will drive OIS traffic patterns (Hiltz & Turoff, 1985).

Such changes are likely to increase the potential for strategic information behaviors in at least four ways. First, a wider and denser OIS network will further increase both managers' willingness to delegate their personal information management activities and the reach of those individuals engaged in information misrepresentation. Second, the reduced cost of message flows and the fewer delays and modifications associated with these flows should increase the effectiveness of strategic information behaviors. Put simply, it will be more likely that misrepresented information will be received "accurately" within a "strategic time frame." Third, misrepresented messages can be routed to a target through multiple "sources," thus amplifying a message's perceived importance, value, and credibility. These ideas as well as all previous trends suggest a final proposition:

Proposition 6: The incidence of strategic information behaviors will increase.

Table 5.5 summarizes the likely effects of new information technologies on the constituent elements of the modular OIS model and, hence, on the incidence of strategic information behavior. It is important to recognize that

Table 5.5

Expected Effects of New Technology on Strategic Information Behaviors

OIS Element	Impact
Messages	• information overload increases managers' dependence on other OIS nodes and buffers
	• decreasing marginal value of messages reduces motivation for proactive information behavior thus increases managers' dependence on other OIS nodes and buffers
	• message contents more likely to be taken at their face value
Schema	• apparent rationality of OIS filters
	• apparent rationality of the OIS filters embedded in artifacts increases managers' willingness to delegate critical information processing behaviors to artifacts
Processor Nodes	• increase dependence of managers on artifact nodes
	• greater potential for individuals with capability to influence artifact nodes and buffers to misrepresent information
	• fewer intermediate nodes lessens likelihood that attempted strategic information behaviors will be thwarted
Information Buffers	• increased dependence of managers on artifact nodes
	• increased use of public buffers heightens scope and effect of strategic information behaviors
	• capability to retrieve managers' information processing histories from buffers will provide guides as to how best to present misrepresented information
Message Flows	• wider and denser OIS networks will increase managers' willingness to delegate critical information management activities
	• wider and denser OIS networks will extend the reach of individuals engaged in information misrepresentation
	• reduced cost and fewer unintended modifications increases effectiveness of information misrepresentation
	• capabilities to rout messages through numerous other buffers and individuals increases effectiveness of information misrepresentation

new technology *by itself* does not lead to an increased incidence of strategic information behavior. The forces for such behaviors are rooted deep within the psyches of organizational members and triggered by complex interactions among environmental forces, individual motivations, situational contingencies, an organization's existing portfolio of information technologies, the configuration of these technologies, and each individual's understanding of the capabilities of these technologies. Additionally, the direct effect of new technology on the incidence of strategic information behaviors is likely to involve rather indirect paths: relaxing the constraints that otherwise inhibit motivations to misrepresent information, increasing the potential scope of misrepresentations, and increasing the perceived meaningfulness of misrepresented information.

Future Research Directions

This examination of the likely effects of new information technologies on strategic information behaviors is based far more on informed speculation than on an empirical understanding of these issues. Both the need and opportunity exist for research directed toward confirming and disconfirming the propositions developed in this essay's preceding section as well as the speculations that led to these propositions.

An even greater need involves research that provides a firmer basis on which to develop the research models and designs used in assessing this essay's propositions. This more basic research falls into three categories. First, more comprehensive examinations of managers' *personal information behaviors* are desirable. Of particular importance are studies aimed at understanding which of these behaviors tend to be delegated, the extent they are delegated, and why they are delegated. One exploratory study, for example, has found a sample of managers willing to delegate a majority of their communications-related behaviors to others (Flatterly, 1981). Second, in-depth examinations of the components of the modular OIS model *across all levels of analysis* are desirable. While fairly extensive literature exist regarding certain of these components (e.g., sensing, filtering, and interpreting nodes), this research has been primarily undertaken at an individual level of analysis; much less is known about these processes at group and organizational levels of analysis. And, very little at all is known about the remaining components: routing nodes, carrier nodes, learning nodes, modifier nodes, and information buffers. Third, examinations of the role of artifacts within OIS are also desirable. While much research does exist on computer-based artifacts, it tends to be devoid of empirically grounded OIS implications. Exactly how extensive are artifacts within OIS? Which OIS components, if any, tend to be handled through artifacts. How "intelligent" are these artifacts. How are the schema embedded within artifacts specified and adjusted?

Conclusion

Strategic information behavior is an integral aspect of organizational life. While organizational actions are influenced by many factors, the personal interests and objectives of an organization's members are clearly a dominant factor in explaining why particular actions are observed. Thus, it is only natural to expect information misrepresentation to occur in organizations— and only natural that new information technologies, as with any organizational tool, would be applied in furthering such behaviors.

Traditionally, an organization member's zone of information influence has been limited by a number of constraints, most of which reflect task designs, authority relationships, and physical, geographic, and temporal boundaries. New information technologies are relaxing many, if not most, of these constraints. This essay has argued, as a consequence, that the incidence of strategic behavior will increase, precisely because of this enlarging of individuals' zone of information influence and an increasing willingness of many of an organization's members to delegate important information processing behaviors. If true, this essay's implications might be extended to suggest that disparate levels of technological understanding and facility among an organization's members may promote realignments in the *real* influence that particular individuals hold in their organizations. That is, knowledgeable individuals may be able to gain increased organizational leverage through their abilities to route messages through OIS networks, into information buffers, and into the schema that direct processor nodes and information buffers. Over time, exposure to and interaction with these OIS artifacts is likely to effect the schema directing the behaviors of human OIS processors.

Even though most of these ideas are speculative, their potential organizational implications are significant. As mentioned at the beginning of this essay, the study of strategic information behaviors has been neglected by most organizational scholars. It is hoped that this essay will renew interest in efforts to understand this important facet of organizational life.

References

Attewell, P., & Rule, J. (1984). Computing and organizations: What we know and what we don't know. *Communications of the ACM*, 27(12), 1184-1192.

Bourgeois, L. J., III, & Eisenhardt, K. M. (1988). Strategic decision processes in high velocity environments: Four cases in the microcomputer industry. *Management Science*, 34(7), 816-835.

Boynton, A. C. (1987). *Predictors of managerial scanning.* Unpublished Ph.D. dissertation, University of North Carolina.

Child, J. (1987). Information technology, organization, and the response to strategic challenges. *California Management Review, 30*(1), 33-50.

Connolly, T., & Thorn, B. K. (1987). Discretionary data bases: A theory and some experimental findings. *Communications Research, 14*(5), 512-528.

Culnan, M. J., & Markus, L. M. (1987). Information technologies. In F. M. Jablin, L. L. Putnam, K. H. Roberts, & L. W. Porter (Eds.), *Handbook of organizational communication.* Newbury Park, CA: Sage.

Daft, R. L., & Weick, K. E. (1984). Toward a model of organizations as interpretation systems. *Academy of Management Review, 9*(2), 284-295.

Dutton, W. H., & Kraemer, K. L. (1985). *Modeling as negotating.* Norwood, NJ: Ablex.

El Sawy, O. A., & Pauchant, T. C. (1988). Triggers, templates, and twiches in the tracking of emerging strategic issues. *Strategic Management Journal, 9*(5), 455-473.

Feldman, M. S., & March, J. G. (1981). Information in organizations as signal and symbol. *Administrative Science Quarterly, 26,* 171-186.

Flatterly, M. E. (1981). A comparative analysis of the written communication of managers at various organizational levels in the private business sector. *The Journal of Business Communication, 19*(3), 33-49.

Gulley, D. A., & Mei, D. M. (1985). The impact of decision models on federal coal leasing. *Management Science, 32*(12), 1547-1568.

Heimer, C. A. (1985). Allocating information costs in a negotiated information order: Interorganizational constraints on decision-making in Norwegian oil insurance. *Administrative Science Quarterly, 30,* 395-417.

Hiltz, S. R., & Turoff, M. (1985). Structuring computer-mediated communication systems to avoid information overload. *Communications of the ACM, 28*(7), 680-689.

Hogarth, R. M. (1987). *Judgment and choice.* Chichester, England: John Wiley.

Huber, G. (1982). Organizational information systems: Determinants of their performance and behavior. *Management Science, 28*(2), 138-155.

Huber, G. (1984). The nature and design of post-industrial organizations. *Management Science, 30*(6), 928-951.

Huber, G. (1988). Effects of decision and communication support technologies on organizational decision processes and structures. In R. M. Lee, A. M. McCosh & P. Migliarese (Eds.), *Organizational decision support systems.* Amsterdam, North-Holland.

Isenberg, D. J. (1986). Thinking and managing: A verbal protocal analysis of managerial problem solving. *Academy of Management Journal, 29*(4), 775-788.

Keen, P. G. W. (1987). Telecommunications and organizational choice. *Communications Research, 14*(5), 588-606.

Kiesler, S., & Sproull, L. (1982). Managerial response to changing environments: Perspectives on problem sensing from social cognition. *Administrative Science Quarterly, 27,* 548-570.

Kmetz, J. L. (1984). An information processing study of a complex workflow in aircraft electronics repair. *Administrative Science Quarterly, 29,* 255-280.

Kraemer, K. L., Dickhoven, S., Tierney, S. F., & King, J. L. (1987). *Datawars: The politics of modeling in federal policymaking.* New York: Columbia University Press.

Leonard-Barton, D., & Sviokla, J. J. (1988). Putting expert systems to work. *Harvard Business Review, 66*(2), 91-98.

Malone, T. W., Grant, K. R., Turbak, F. A., Brobst, S. A., & Cohen, M. D. (1987). Intelligent information-sharing systems. *Communications of the ACM, 30*(5), 390-402.

Markus, M. L., & Robey, D. (1988). Information technology and organizational change: Causal structure in theory and research. *Management Science, 34*(5), 583-598.

Mintzberg, H. (1973). *The nature of managerial work.* New York: Harper & Row.

Pettigrew, A. (1972). Information control as a power resource. *American Sociological Review, 32,* 187-204.

Pfeffer, J. (1981). Management as symbolic action. In L. L. Cummings & B. M. Staw (Eds.), *Research in organizational behavior.* Greenwich, CT: JAI Press.

Porter, M. E., & Millar, V. C. (1985). How information gives you competitive advantage. *Harvard Business Review, 63*(4), 149-160.

Schwenk, C. R. (1986). Information, cognitive bias, and commitment to a course of action. *Academy of Management Review, 11*(2), 298-310.

Sproull, L., & Kiesler, S. (1986). Reducing social context cues: Electronic mail in organizational communication. *Management Science, 32*(11), 1492-1512.

Staw, B. M., Sandelands, L. E., & Dutton, J. E. (1981). Threat-rigidity effects in organizational behavior: A multilevel analysis. *Administrative Science Quarterly, 26,* 501-524.

Ungson, G. R., Braunstein, D. N., & Hall, P. D. (1981). Managerial information processing: A research review. *Administrative Science Quarterly, 26,* 116-134.

Weber, R. (1988). Computer technology and jobs: An impact assessment model. *Communications of the ACM, 31*(1), 68-77.

Weick, K. E. (1977). Enactment processes in organization. In B. M. Staw & G. R. Salancik (Eds.), *New directions in organizational behavior.* Chicago: St. Clair.

JANET FULK
JOSEPH SCHMITZ
CHARLES W. STEINFIELD

6. A Social Influence Model of Technology Use

The explosion of new communication technologies has generated widespread controversy over their potential effects on the workplace. Accurate claims of effects must be rooted in valid assumptions about just *how the technologies are used*. Consequently, media-use behavior has resurfaced as a vibrant area of inquiry. In this chapter, we take a close look at current media-use theories. We argue that they rest on some very unrealistic assumptions about human behavior in organizations. In particular, we take issue with the rationalist bias and technological determinism that pervades these approaches. Current media-use theories fail to recognize a central premise of current organization theory: Behavior occurs in a very social world which is far from neutral in its effects.

Once we assume an active and influential social context of media use, we then face the problem of specifying the social processes more precisely. An appropriate starting point is to examine existing theories of social relations in organizations with an eye to how their premises apply to media-use behavior. This chapter presents a model of media use that is derived from such an examination.

We begin by summarizing traditional models of media use. Then, we show how these theories are incapable of adequately explaining a whole range of findings on media use in real-life organizations. As a promising alternative, we develop a model of social influences on media-related attitudes and behavior in organizations. Then, we review research results that shed light on the validity of the new model compared to traditional theory. Finally, we

Author's Note: We would like to thank George Huber, Lynne Markus, and Ron Rice for their helpful comments. We are indebted to Peter Monge and Ev Rogers for their insightful discussions over the course of this work. Gerry Power provided important contributions during the initial stages of conceptual development.

outline the implications of the social influence perspective for management practice, and provide suggestions to guide research on communication technologies in organizations.

Rational Choice Models

Media use is known to be a function of a number of facilitating factors, such as media accessibility, availability of communication partners, experience with the medium, personal style in using media, time and cost advantages, and communication task requirements (for reviews see Culnan & Markus, 1987; Rice, 1980, 1984; Steinfield, 1986b; Svenning & Ruchinskas, 1984). Media use theory proposes that individuals choose media through a matching process. This matching involves assessing the requirements of the particular communication task at hand and selecting a medium with communication capabilities that match these requirements. Efficient communication takes place when the match is perfect: the medium has neither more nor less communication capability than the task requires. This rational choice approach is described using two illustrative theories. Note, however, that this perspective is not the hallmark of any single theoretical model, but rather a general tradition characterizing the study of media choice processes (Williams, 1977).

Social Presence Theory. Short, Williams, and Christie (1976) conceptualized communication media as falling along a single continuum of "social presence." *Social presence* is the degree to which the medium facilitates awareness of the other person and interpersonal relationships during the interaction. Face-to-face communication has the greatest social presence, followed by audio plus video (e.g., videoconferencing), audio-only (e.g., telephone), and print.

Communication is efficient when the medium selected has a social presence level that matches the level of interpersonal involvement required for the task. Highly involving tasks (e.g., conflict and negotiation) are best completed using high social presence media (e.g., face-to-face). Similarly, media with less social presence (e.g., written letters) are optimally efficient for simple information exchange tasks.

Tests of the social presence model primarily have been conducted in the laboratory using cooperative versus competitive tasks. The model received moderate support in these contexts, but explained only a small proportion of the variance in media-related behavior. However, results have limited generalizability beyond the laboratory setting (for reviews see Albertson, 1980; Fowler & Wackerbarth, 1980; Short et al., 1976; Williams, 1977).

Information Richness Theory. An alternative view is provided by Information Richness Theory (Daft & Macintosh, 1981; Daft & Lengel, 1984, 1986; Daft, Lengel, & Trevino, 1987). From this perspective, communication media are arrayed along a continuum of "information richness" based on four criteria: speed of feedback, types of channels employed, personalness of source, and richness of language carried. Face-to-face is the richest medium followed in decreasing order of richness by telephone, electronic mail, written personal, written formal, and then numeric formal media.

The key criterion for media choice is message ambiguity. Ambiguous tasks should be completed using rich media, while unambiguous tasks require lean media. Efficient managers select media whose richness matches the ambiguity of the communication task. Recent statements of the model (Trevino, Lengel, & Daft, 1987) include two additional factors. First, contextual determinants such as geographical separation between communication partners may constrain which media can employed. Second, the symbolic character of formal written media may serve to increase its appropriateness in certain situations in which the user wants to convey an impression of authority.

Direct tests of this newer model are as yet scarce. Trevino et al. (1987) and Daft, Lengel, and Trevino (1987) found support for the basic information richness proposition, although Steinfield and Fulk (1986) and Markus (1988) found only weak support. Trevino, Daft, and Lengel (Chapter 4 of this volume) present evidence that links rational media choice to performance ratings.

Social Presence Theory and Information Richness Theory are the best known rational choice models of media use. They share with most other media use perspectives a number of key assumptions about media and about choice-making processes.

Assumptions of Rational Choice Models

Media. Each communication medium has fixed, inherent properties. A medium's social presence or information richness is *invariant* regardless of who is using it or what the context is. Task requirements, as well, are largely based on objective features such as ambiguity. As Albertson (1980, p. 389) noted about social presence theory, "people are regarded as 'black boxes'."

Differences among media in their objective features are *salient* to users. That is, people are aware of inherent differences among media and they are "differences that make a difference." Similarly, users also perceive variations across tasks in such features as social presence requirements.

Choice-Making Processes. Individuals make *independent choices.* The interpersonal setting in which choice occurs does not intrude directly upon the decision process. The only exception occurs if the sender wants to symbolically convey impressions of formality or authority, as specified in information richness theory.

Choice-making is a *cognitive* process. Attitudes and behaviors follow from cognitive evaluations of media attributes and message requirements. Choice is also *prospective* in that it depends upon assessments of current needs and future goals. Purpose is posited to occur before action.

Choice-making is *objectively rational.* The user objectively evaluates the characteristics of tasks and media, and then chooses that combination that most closely matches task requirements with media capabilities. Rational choices are based upon inherent features of media and tasks; little place is accorded for individual variation in deciding what is an optimal match.

Behavior is *efficiency-motivated.* Use of overly rich media for unambiguous tasks is inefficient. The efficient user treats media capacity as a resource not to be squandered. At the same time, insufficient media capacity is ineffective. Exact matches are optimally efficient (Williams, 1977).

Evidence for Social Context Effects

Recent investigations of new information technologies cast doubt on the overarching importance of inherent media characteristics and objectively rational choice processes in predicting media use:

- Highly interpersonally involving interactions such as conflict resolution and negotiation consistently occur over electronic mail, a low social presence medium (Hiltz & Turoff, 1978; Kiesler, Siegel, & McGuire, 1984; Rice & Love, 1987; A. Phillips, 1983; S. Phillips, 1988; Steinfield, 1985; Markus, 1988).
- Use of personal computers and computer-mediated communication systems is facilitated by a network of supportive relationships (Kling & Gerson, 1977), such that "being a member of one group (or subculture) rather than another seems to shape the experiences of the members and the quality of their (electronic) life" (Hiltz, 1984, p. 90).
- Recent investigations in a large office products firm (Steinfield, 1986a) and a city government (Schmitz, 1987) discovered that a potent predictor of electronic mail use was the extent of use by relevant coworkers, including supervisors. A similar (but less strong) relationship was reported for voice mail use in a large insurance firm (Shook, 1988).
- Research in a major petrochemical firm found that a significant predictor of attitudes toward videoconferencing was an individual's percep-

tions of the opinions of coworkers and supervisors about videoconferencing (Svenning, 1982).

Rational choice models cannot account for these findings.

Where do we search for explanations of the apparent influence of the social context on media use behavior? A logical source is theory that focuses on the dynamics of social influence. In the next section we develop a model and predictions of media use that has roots in various approaches known as *symbolic interactionism* (Mead, 1934; Cooley, 1902; Dewey, 1922), *attribution theory* (Bem, 1972), *cognitive dissonance theory* (Festinger, 1954), *social learning theory* (Bandura, 1977, 1986), and *social information processing* (Salancik & Pfeffer, 1978). The latter work is particularly helpful because it focuses specifically on the work environment.

A Social Influence Model of Media Use

The social influence model starts with the same basic assumption that individuals cognitively process stimuli. However, it departs substantially from rational choice models in positing how cognitions develop and change.

Media perceptions are, in part, *subjective and socially constructed*. Clearly, they are determined to some degree by objective features such as ability to provide a permanent record, asynchroneity and the like (see Culnan & Markus, 1987 for a review of these features). However, they are also determined to a substantial degree by the attitudes, statements, and behaviors of coworkers.

How do coworkers exert social influence? The most direct way is by *overt statements* about characteristics of media or tasks that individuals assimilate into their own evaluations (Salancik & Pfeffer, 1978). These direct statements also have an indirect effect. By discussing particular features, coworkers increase the saliency of those features. Coworkers also voice judgments and interpretations of events that may be accepted by the individual (Bandura, 1986; Salancik & Pfeffer, 1978). The net effect is that media perceptions are not fixed and objective; instead they will *vary* across individuals and situations.

One example of this cuing occurred in the production research division of a large petrochemical company. An R&D manager reported to a division manager that rapid information exchange with field sites via PROFS electronic mail helped to speed up the product development cycle. This social cue had at least three points of potential influence on media evaluations. First, it highlighted speed of feedback as an important criterion for media assessment. Second, it described one feature of electronic mail (ability to rapidly convey messages to a remote site) as particularly salient. Third, it provided an interpretation of the shortened product development cycle as resulting from electronic mail rather than other potential causes. Thus, it implied a very favorable evaluation of the medium's effect on a key organizational goal.

Statements by coworkers also directly affect choice making. Remarks may cue an individual about the requirements of a communication task. They may also help define the individual's media options in relation to the task requirements. More explicit statements may make specific recommendations about media choice.

An example of this overt cuing occurred at an electrical equipment manufacturer. An engineer needed to inform the manufacturing manager about a last-minute product design modification. Another engineer advised against using a written memo for what she saw as a politically sensitive issue. She recommended that the engineer personally visit the manufacturing manager's shop as soon as possible. She believed the personal visit would get the changes made quickly and not damage relations between the two units.

Of course, sources of influence may conflict in their statements. In the previous example, a third engineer recommended using a written memo. He believed that the use of proper channels and established procedures would show the most respect for the manufacturing group and would also protect the design modifications. A fourth person even got involved by telling a story of what happened with manufacturing several years ago when an engineer sent last-minute product design changes in a written note. The last element of the story is particularly instructive because it illustrates that choice occurs in a rich historical context as well.

Social influence also may take the form of *vicarious learning* from observing the experiences of others (Bandura, 1986). When the choices have lead to positive consequences, behavior modeling may occur. Thus, effective behavior by one person may well be repeated by others through a process of observational learning. Similarly, choices that lead to undesirable consequences may be avoided by others.

An example of vicarious learning occurred in an advertising agency. An account representative lost a major client because the client misinterpreted a brief electronic mail message. One consequence was that other account reps used the telephone more frequently for similar transactions because they wanted to avoid that same fate. The opposite could easily have occurred as well: An account rep gaining a prized client presumably because of a well-timed electronic mail message. Electronic mail use for courting clients might then increase throughout the agency in the hope of achieving a similar outcome.

Thus far, we have said that media perceptions are subjective and socially constructed. Two processes of social influence were described: (1) overt statements by coworkers about media characteristics, task features, and choice making; and (2) vicarious learning.

Rationality

Assumptions about rationality are quite different when viewed from a social influence perspective. *Rationality is subjective, retrospective, and influenced by information provided by others.* Cognitions are used for rationalizing and giving meaning to behavior. However, cognitions may arise from prior history of social interaction. That is, sense-making may well be created *after* the occurrence of the behavior. In this case, it is used to interpret the behavior retrospectively rather than to direct the choice prospectively. Individuals observe their own present and past behavior and develop explanations for it. In the process, goals and intentions may be created after the fact to make sense of what has occurred (Weick, 1979). The inferred goals are sensible and rational in the current interpretation, whether or not they were at the time the behavior occurred. One outcome of retrospective sense-making is the reconciliation of goals with current and past behavior. A simple form of this process is the classic response to failure: "Well, I wasn't really trying anyway."

Interpretation also involves a process of attribution in which past behavior serves as a source of current attitudes (Bem, 1972). Thus, people make assumptions about what their attitudes are about an issue, event, or person by recalling their own behavior surrounding the issue, event, or person. "I did it so I must like it" is an only slightly exaggerated view of the attribution process. Like goals, attitudes are used to interpret and make sense of behavior that has already occurred. Salancik and Conway (1975) note that inferences about attitudes are based not on one's actual behavior, but rather upon what someone actually knows or remembers about his or her behavior. As Pfeffer (1982) indicates, this means that different attitudes can be created by altering the information provided about past behavior.

A key point is *both sense-making and behavior are subject to social influence.* One form of direct influence is group norms. Social psychologists (e.g., Asch, 1952) have shown that group norms have powerful effects on individual cognitions and behaviors. Social cues regarding appropriate media use may well be embedded within the norms of a particular group.

For example, in one work unit of an employment agency, members exerted pressure against using written memos within the group—memos were viewed as too impersonal for almost any kind of group interaction. In this group, a simple information exchange frequently required face-to-face interaction. The choices that individuals made to adhere to social pressures were rational from their own subjective view, even though they did not meet efficiency criteria (March, 1974). Thus, although choice-making may be supported by norms favoring prospective and objectively rational choice, it need not be. It can equally well be subject to normative pressures to behave in a nonefficient manner. The key implication is that behavior is subjectively rational.

The social environment also influences retrospective sense-making. Social contexts embody requirements for "meaningful and justifiable behavior." They also provide "norms and expectations that constrain their rationalization or justification of those activities" (Salancik & Pfeffer, 1978, pp. 232, 233). In essence, the social environment creates requirements for sense-making but also constrains the types of sense-making that are acceptable. What is sensible in one social environment may not be in another.

For example, a rationale of "don't fix what ain't broken" may support resistance to experimenting with new communication technologies in one unit. At the same time, another unit may support this experimentation with the axiom "you don't get anywhere by standing still." In each case, the justification is framed to reflect what appears to be quite sensible behavior.

One key constraint in social environments is that people are typically expected to be consistent over time in their statements and behaviors. Deviations require justifications that are sensible within social definitions of rational behavior. This may lead to commitment to courses of action beyond the point when those actions are sensible from other points of view (Becker, 1960).

For example, an executive in the auto industry initially opposed the installation of terminals for a computer-based integrated office system for his level of management. He continued to maintain resistance to the system, even after it had become considerably more user-friendly. His rationale for opposing the innovation was consistent with social definitions of rational behavior in that context—"a manager is paid a lot of money to make tough decisions, not to sit at a keyboard and type." To overcome this opposition, the manager must perceive a reason to change, but he also needs a socially acceptable rationale that defines *both* past resistance and current acceptance as appropriate.

Table 6.1
Comparison of Assumptions

RATIONAL CHOICE MODELS	SOCIAL INFLUENCE MODEL
Media and Task Features	
• Fixed	• Variable
• Objective	• Subjective; socially constructed
• Uniformly salient	• Variably salient
Choice-Making	
• Cognitive	• Cognitive
• Independent	• Subject to social influence
• Prospectively rational	• Can be retrospectively rational
• Objectively rational	• Subjectively rational
• Efficiency-motivated	• Can be efficiency-motivated but need not be

Summary. Media-use behavior is, at its core, subjectively rational. Behavior need not meet efficiency criteria in order to be considered rational within the particular social context. Behavior is subject to social influence in the form of widespread norms and pressure for sense-making. Although sense-making may be prospectively rational, it is often better described as retrospectively rational. Thus, the social influence perspective starts from an assumption of cognitive processing of stimuli, then departs radically from rational choice theories. A comparison summarizing the contrasting assumptions of the two approaches is provided in Table 6.1.

Under what conditions are social influence processes strongest? One consistent finding is that individuals rely more strongly on social comparison processes in ambiguous situations (Festinger, 1954; Salancik & Pfeffer, 1978). In fact, Thomas and Griffin (1983) found that greater experience with a task reduces the influence of social information about that task. In a parallel fashion, we may expect that social information regarding a particular medium will be more influential for individuals who have less experience and knowledge of that medium. Experienced users will have longer histories of their own behavior upon which to base attributions. Also, greater mastery of the skills necessary to employ the newer communication technologies such as electronic mail or computer conferencing is likely to directly facilitate use of those media. Evidence from four studies shows electronic mail use to be directly linked to experience with the medium and knowledge mastery (Kerr & Hiltz, 1982; Johansen, 1988; Schmitz, 1988; Fulk, Schmitz, & Steinfield, 1988).

Situational Factors

A host of factors beyond those described above come into play in any organizational context. A detailed treatment of these factors necessarily would complicate the social influence model to the point where it becomes the proverbial "Indian war," with causal arrows flying in every direction. Then, the model would lose its unique value as a guide for highlighting the social influence process as applied to media use. For purposes of simplicity, we simply label these other contextual features *situational factors*. This section briefly describes several categories of more obvious situational influences on media use.

One set of factors is *individual differences*. Perceptions of computing have been found to relate to an individual's cognitive style (Aydin, 1987) and to individual media style (Rice & Case, 1983). Although this latter moderator is defined behaviorally, it is intended to reflect a psychological factor that predisposes individuals to select certain media over others.

A second group are the *facilitating* factors mentioned earlier. This would include such variables as accessibility of the medium, training support for new media, critical mass of users, protection of documents, nonpunitive budget and pricing policies, reliability and flexibility of the technology, compatibility of the technology with current values, and organizational support for the medium, as well as specific hardware and software features.

A final category is *direct constraints* on media use. This includes such considerations as barriers of geography and time that prevent utilization of certain media (Steinfield & Fulk, 1986; Trevino et al., 1987).

A Caveat

The social influence perspective does not imply that socially constructed reality is idiosyncratic or random. Social construction of reality entails some degree of agreement on the nature of past events and on appropriate future behavior (Rose, 1962). The process of developing understandings is ongoing and somewhat self-correcting. Over time, people come to share similar interpretations and parallel realities which vary as a function of their group membership and of their personal interaction history. The net effect is this: Although it is unlikely that perceptions of media and tasks will be invariant across individuals, neither will they be random. There will be patterns of systematic variation which are reliably linked to the social context.

The perspective articulated here in no way excludes objectively rational media choices as one outcome. Rather, it subsumes rational choice as simply one of many options that may emerge from the social influence process in organizations. The limitation of traditional media use theories is their over-reliance on rational processes to explain the entire range of media-choice situations. A realistic understanding of behavior requires knowledge not simply of objective features of the environment, but also the social milieu that alters and adjusts perceptions of that environment. The advantage of the social influence model is its potential to explain a much wider range of media-use behavior across a greater variety of situations.

Figure 6.1 provides a schematic that indicates the pivotal role of social influence in media evaluations and behavior. Formally stated, the propositions supporting Figure 6.1 are:

Proposition 1: *Media evaluations* (perceptions and attitudes) are a function of: (a) objective media features; (b) media experience and skills; (c) social influence, in the form of direct statements by coworkers, vicarious learning, group behavioral norms, and social definitions of rationality; and (d) prior media-use behavior.

Proposition 2: *Task evaluations* are a function of: (a) objective task features; (b) task experience and skills; and (c) social influence, in the form of direct statements by coworkers, vicarious learning, group behavioral norms, and social definitions of rationality.

Proposition 3: For any application, an individual's *media use* is a function of: (a) media evaluations (perceptions and attitudes); (b) media experience and skills; (c) social influence in the form of direct statements by coworkers regarding the application, vicarious learning, group behavioral norms, and social definitions of rationality; (d) task evaluations; and (e) situational factors such as individual differences, facilitating factors, and constraints.

Assessing the Social Information Model

One way to assess how accurate a picture the social influence model paints is to identify specific predictions of the model for real-life organizations. Then we can examine findings from organizational studies to see whether these predictions hold up.

Predictions for Media Evaluations

The social influence model predicts that people will vary in how "rich" they perceive a particular medium to be. It also predicts that this variation will not be random or idiosyncratic. Rather, variation will be systematically

128

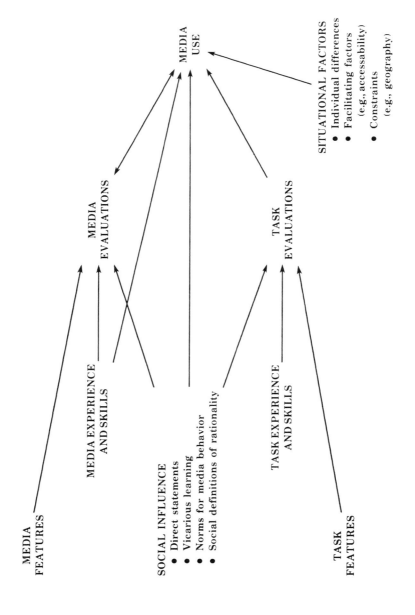

Figure 6.1 A Social Influence Model of Media Use

linked to variation in the social context and media experience/skills. Alternatively, rational choice models predict no variation in media perceptions, except for random variation or errors in measuring media perceptions. In effect, if nonrandom variation exists that is not attributable to measurement error, social influence theory provides explanatory power, while rational media choice models do not.

What evidence exists regarding variation in media perceptions? Several studies have asked respondents to rate different media on perceived information richness. A review of this combined evidence (Steinfield & Fulk, 1989) showed that the rank order of media ratings was consistent across the studies, with one exception. Electronic mail was sometimes ranked above written media, and sometimes below. The rank order of other media was predicted by rational choice models. A rank order, however, may mask considerable variation in people's perceptions of individual media. In some studies, the mean ratings for certain mid-range media were quite close to each other, while in others these same media were much farther apart on the richness scales used. Yet, both patterns produced the same rank order. These results are consistent with earlier findings that individuals varied in their perceptions of the social presence of a medium, but that the rank order of mean ratings stayed the same (Short et al., 1976).

A recent pair of studies provides more direct evidence (Fulk, Schmitz, & Steinfield, 1988; Fulk & Ryu, 1990). Each study used the exact same measure of information richness, one taken directly from written statements of this theory. Both samples were R&D units involved in applied petrochemical research. The researchers found the same pattern as the earlier studies: rankings were similar across studies, although electronic mail was lower in richness than was predicted by information richness theory. More importantly, the mean ratings in each unit were different for the same media.

Was this variation in richness ratings systematically linked to variation in social context and media experience/knowledge? To address this question, the researchers asked each respondent to name the five persons he had most communication with—the respondent's important potential sources of social influence within the organization. For each source of influence plus the supervisor, respondents rated the person's attitudes about electronic mail. The researchers also gathered information on the respondent's experience with electronic mail, computing experience, and training in system use. The findings from both studies were that: (1) People's perceptions of electronic mail were significantly related to the attitudes of both the supervisor and the five frequent communication contacts; and (2) persons with more electronic mail experience and training rated electronic mail as richer than those without such experience and training. These findings are consistent with an earlier study in a large petrochemical company, which found that attitudes toward videoconferencing were positively related to perceptions of the attitudes held by coworkers toward the same system (Svenning, 1982).

In combination, these findings suggest that: (1) richness perceptions vary in a nonrandom fashion, and (2) they are directly linked to social context and media experience factors, as predicted by the social influence model.

Predictions for Media Use

Less explicit evidence exists for media use. An indirect test is the ability of the models to explain existing findings. Below we describe briefly three sets of research findings that demonstrate the enhanced explanatory ability of the social influence model.

Pattern Matching Within Groups. Rational choice models predict that we will find similar patterns of media use across individuals in situations where their tasks are similar. By contrast, the social influence model predicts some similarity of media attitudes and use behavior within groups, even across tasks with different communication requirements.

What evidence exists to date? A study in a large insurance firm found similar patterns of usage of voice mail among coworkers occupying the same structural network position (Shook, 1988). Rice, Grant, Schmitz, and Torobin (1988) found similar patterns of electronic mail adoption among closely connected coworkers. Fulk, Schmitz, Ryu, and Steinfield (1989) found that electronic mail use (number of messages sent and percent of time using the medium) was predicted by the perceptions of the medium's usefulness held by communication network partners. Research in a large office products firm (Steinfield & Fulk, 1989) found that 25% of the variation in electronic mail use could be explained by the proportion of coworkers who used electronic mail, while no variation in use was explained by a global measure of task ambiguity. To make sense of these findings using rational choice models, we would have to assume that the tasks were similar across individuals in the same network. This is a considerably more restrictive assumption than social influence models would require.

Information richness theory also predicts that leaner media will be used relatively less frequently at each higher management level (Daft & Lengel, 1984), because higher level jobs confront greater ambiguity. The social influence model predicts less discrepancy between adjacent levels *if* there is intense social interaction, such as between supervisor and subordinate. It also proposes other factors that influence media selection, so that lean media may be used in spite of a lack of "fit" with task ambiguity.

Some evidence is available. Both survey and computer-captured usage data from a city government showed that 20% of the variation in electronic mail use was explained by organizational level (Schmitz, 1987). However, the direction of the relationship was contrary to predictions from information richness theory: the use of this relatively lean medium increased with organizational level. And, an additional 10% of variation in electronic mail usage was explained by the *supervisor's* usage patterns. Rice, Hart, Torobin, Shook, and Tyler (1989) found that electronic mail was used more heavily by managers than by technicians or clerical staff. These findings are generally consistent with the more robust social influence explanation.

Pattern Mismatching Across Groups. Several studies have found differences in attitudes or patterns of use of the same communication technology across groups with relatively equal access to the technology (e.g., Hiltz & Johnson, 1987; Kerr & Hiltz, 1982; Schmitz, 1987). Without descriptions of task features, the rational-choice and social-influence explanations for these differences cannot be compared conclusively. Theoretically, the social influence model predicts the observed findings from its basic premises. Rational choice theories could explain the findings only by resorting to assumptions of similar levels of task ambiguity or unusual contextual determinants.

Two other studies of similar R&D units did present more information on tasks (Fulk et al., 1988; Fulk & Ryu, 1990). Both samples were engaged in production research for the same corporation, used the same PROFS electronic mail system, and were subject to similar organizational budgets and corporate policies. Levels of experience were relatively similar, as both units had been using PROFS for several years. In this situation, rational choice models predict similar patterns of use. The social influence model predicts that usage will vary between units because their social norms and interaction histories are different. In fact, the patterns of use were different. In Unit A, more time was devoted to using the system, and almost three times the number of electronic mail notes were sent. Also, Unit A members considered this system more effective across the board for all types of communication tasks.

Inefficient Choice-Making. Several investigators have reported that low social presence media are used for high social presence tasks. Studies of electronic mail and computer conferencing have found socioemotional uses such as getting to know someone, maintaining relationships, resolving conflict and disagreements, negotiation and bargaining, and expressing anger or gripes (Hiltz & Turoff, 1978; Kiesler, 1986; Kiesler et al., 1984; Phillips, 1983; Rice & Love, 1987; Steinfield, 1986a). The other type of mismatch is illustrated in the earlier example of the employment agency where people met face-to-face for nearly all communication tasks. Rational choice models cannot readily explain these findings. The social influence model directs us to search for potential explanations in social norms which can develop to encourage experimentation with a wide variety of applications for new media.

A common observation is that old media-use patterns persist even after more efficient communication options become available (Panko, 1984). Rational choice models imply that when a new medium is introduced into the work situation, media-use patterns should change; for example, electronic mail should replace some telephone calls or some written letters for low social presence tasks. Evidence exists to support this media substitution prediction (Picot, Klingenberg, & Kranzle, 1982; Rice & Bair, 1984), but that evidence also suggests that substitution effects are somewhat limited. Retrospective sense-making and the influence of social norms would explain those additional situations in which new and more efficient media continue to be underutilized.

The evidence to date indicates that rational choice models effectively predict some observed patterns of media use in organizations. Nevertheless, these models fall short in their ability to account for behavior patterns that appear nonrational on the surface. From the rational choice perspective, such findings are anomalies that leave the researcher puzzled. The number of such anomalies in the research literature is not small and is rapidly growing. There is clearly a need for a theory which explains more of these anomalies—a theory that solves more of the puzzle. While no theory can solve the whole puzzle, the social influence model takes us further in explaining patterns found in today's organizations. The model also offers one additional advantage. It takes into account the social context of behavior—a factor known by organizational theorists to be an integral part of organizational behavior.

Implications for Management Practice

Given that social influence is a key factor in media use, what does this knowledge offer to management? To illustrate the benefits of a management approach informed by a social influence perspective, we sketch two contrasting situations involving the introduction of a new medium, videoconferencing, into two organizations. Each example is an actual occurrence from a real organization.

Company One: The Costs of Neglecting the Social Network

An aerospace firm decided to try videoconferencing. Engineers in California and Arizona needed to consult frequently about aircraft design. Written reports and letters were slow. Fax was quicker, but the engineers couldn't jointly view and modify documents. The telephone provided a synchronous medium, but not shared text. The company was experiencing delays in the product delivery schedule because of communication lags. The solution was to install a two-way, full-motion videoconferencing system that linked both sites. The system was "almost as good as face-to-face."

After an initial test period, the system fell into disuse. Why would a system specifically designed to meet well-articulated communication needs sit idle? In this case, the answer lay not in the technology, but in the social system. A key engineer, widely recognized as a knowledgeable computer buff, refused to use the system. This engineer claimed that the system was not secure and that competitors might intercept the satellite signal linking the two sites. His opinion quickly diffused throughout the engineering division; no engineer would use the system.

The example is particularly instructive because the conferencing system was among the most secure in the nation; it used scrambled signals and other sophisticated protection procedures. Technical experts on videoconferencing were convinced that the system was secure. Yet, widespread perceptions of security flaws were conveyed by social information communicated among users—by persons who lacked the telecommunications expertise necessary to evaluate the security measures.

Could this innovation have been salvaged? Possibly. Once the opinion leader had communicated his security reservations to others, he made a public commitment to that point of view. To change his position, he would need a socially acceptable reason to act inconsistently with his expressed position. The critical deficiency occurred when system designers and managers failed to anticipate the importance of the security issue for users. Therefore, they failed to inform users, especially opinion leaders, of existing and extensive safeguards. A preimplementation evaluation of user needs should have surfaced the engineers' concern with security, a concern typical in the aerospace industry. In addition, keeping in touch with informal discussions in the social network during the early implementation stages might have made early detection and correction possible.

Company Two: Using a Social Influence Strategy

Several years ago a petrochemical firm introduced a corporate-wide video-conferencing system. Each of seven major locations within the continental United States and Alaska was provided with a completely equipped video-conferencing facility and staff support to operate it. The goal was to provide better communications among corporate locations ranging from Texas to Alaska.

Implementation began with an organization-wide survey of communication needs and attitudes toward videoconferencing. Survey results pinpointed employees who were most likely to have success experiences. This group included persons who met two criteria. First, they had high cross-locational communication needs, and thus were likely to try the new technology. Second, they held positive attitudes toward videoconferencing, and thus were motivated to maintain these positive evaluations. These individuals were enlisted as initial system users during the project's first stage. Opportunities were created for vicarious learning by using individuals who were prominently located. In diffusion of innovations parlance, an attempt was made to increase the "observability" of the innovation (Rogers, 1983). Finally, to the extent that these individuals were opinion leaders, rapid diffusion of positive attitudes toward the system resulted through their overt statements in support of the new medium. The success of this strategy, described in detail by Ruchinskas, Svenning, and Steinfield (1989), is particularly impressive given the relatively poor track record of videoconferencing to date (Olgren & Parker, 1983; Svenning & Ruchinskas, 1984).

These two contrasting situations highlight some of the ways that social influence processes may be harnessed to introduce and/or enhance the use of communication and information technologies on the one hand or lead to expensive but underutilized systems on the other. One other information technology strategy that relies on social influence processes is *informal peer training*. Strassman (1985) contends that informal training in the peer-group is likely to be the most effective and the least costly training method. In contrast, *formal training* conveys an initial but limited competence that is often rapidly forgotten. During interviews, members of an R&D unit using the PROFS electronic mail system often described how they relied on nearby coworkers for assistance in using unfamiliar features of the system. Nearly all members had gone through a formal training process, but lack of regular use of many system features soon eliminated the requisite knowledge from members' repertoires. Sustained usage is more readily achieved if users are members of a group that shares and reinforces the common use of a communication medium. Quite often, secretarial staff who used more advanced features on a regular basis became informal consultants to both R&D professionals and department heads.

Implications for Research on Communication Technologies

The recognition that media use occurs within a web of social relationships has important implications for the conduct of research. Research must broaden methodological repertoires with designs and approaches that are robust enough to capture social influence processes. We briefly highlight a few of the considerations that are suggested by the above review and analysis.

First, although experimental designs are useful starting points for research on social cuing, they lack external validity. The effects of naturally occurring communication among coworkers about media use must be studied in field settings. Actual communication flows also can be modeled using communication network analysis procedures. This procedure will permit us to more directly track the flow of social information throughout the natural social system.

Second, behaviors are responsive to social cuing during prolonged and intense social interaction. This imposes the need for longitudinal research designs. Miller and Monge (1985) point out that little is known about the relative influence of immediate versus accumulated social information. Also, previous research provides little indication of the temporary versus permanent nature of the effects of social influence. This is particularly important for research on new technologies, because patterns identified in the initial phases of an implementation may be substantially different from the equilibrium patterns attained over time (Huber, this volume; Johansen, 1976).

Third, research designs should incorporate measures of group level attitudes and behavior. This could include, for example, perceptions of coworkers sentiments (Svenning, 1982), coworker media use (Fulk et al., 1988), or actual computer-monitored usage of significant others (Rice & Borgman, 1983; Schmitz, 1988). One promising research strategy is to explicitly model relational ties among individuals with communication network models of social influence. Group level measures will also enable comparisons across social or organizational groupings, in addition to comparisons across types of jobs or tasks. A last note on group level measures is that the study of the dispersion of perceptions may be as fruitful as the study of central tendencies (Zalesny & Farace, 1986). Danowski (1980), for example, found lower standard deviations in attitude scores for more highly connected groups, reflecting a social influence that would have gone unnoticed if he had only examined mean group scores.

Fourth, we should treat rationalizations as valuable objects for study. Investigation of the etiology and development of these rationalizations should provide important insights into how individuals learn to make sense of their media environments. Effective social influence research may depend as much upon qualitative methodologies as upon quantitative strategies.

Conclusion

This work was motivated by our perception that although communication scientists are aware of significant social effects on the attitudes and behaviors of individuals, much greater efforts are needed to explicitly specify these factors in models of organizational media use. Accurate predictions of technological effects critically rely on valid assumptions about how individual and organizations interact with the technology. If we are to rest our claims on valid premises, social forces must be incorporated into our knowledge base about new information technology.

References

Albertson, L. A. (1980). Trying to eat an elephant. *Communication Research*, 7, 387-400.

Asch, S. E. (1952). *Social psychology*. Englewood Cliffs, NJ: Prentice-Hall.

Aydin, C. E. (1987). The effects of social information and cognitive style on medical information system attitudes and use. In W. W. Stead (Ed.), *Proceedings of the Eleventh Annual Symposium on Computer Applications in Medical Care* (pp. 601-606). New York: Institute of Electrical and Electronics Engineers.

Bandura, A. (1977). *Social learning theory*. Englewood Cliffs, NJ: Prentice-Hall.

Bandura, A. (1978). The self system in reciprocal determinism. *American Psychologist, 33*, 344-358.

Bandura, A. (1986). *Social foundations of thought and action*. Englewood Cliffs, NJ: Prentice-Hall.

Becker, H. (1960). Notes on the concept of commitment. *American Journal of Sociology, 66*, 32-40.

Bem, D. J. (1972). Self perception theory. In L. Berkowitz (Ed.), *Advances in experimental psychology* (Vol. 6, pp. 1-62). New York: Academic Press.

Cooley, C. H. (1902). *Human nature and the social order*. New York: Charles Scribner's Sons.

Culnan, M. J., & Markus, M. L. (1987). Information technologies. In F. M. Jablin, L. L. Putnam, K. H. Roberts, & L. W. Porter (Eds.), *Handbook of organizational communication* (pp. 420-443). Newbury Park, CA: Sage.

Daft, R. L., & Lengel, R. H. (1984). Information richness: A new approach to managerial behavior and organization design. In L. L. Cummings & B. M. Staw (Eds.), *Research in organizational behavior* (Vol. 6, pp. 191-233). Greenwich, CT: JAI Press.

Daft, R. L., & Lengel, R. H. (1986). Organizational information requirements, media richness and structural design. *Management Science, 32,* 554-571.

Daft, R. L., Lengel, R. H., & Trevino, L. K. (1987). Message equivocality, media selection, and manager performance: Implications for information systems. *MIS Quarterly, September,* 355-366.

Daft, R. L., & Macintosh, N. B. (1981). A tentative exploration into the amount and equivocality of information processing in organizational work units. *Administrative Science Quarterly, 26,* 207-224.

Danowski, J. A. (1980). Group attitude uniformity and connectivity of organizational communication networks for production, innovation and maintenance content. *Human Communication Research, 6,* 299-308.

Dewey, J. (1922). *Human nature and conduct.* New York: Holt.

Festinger, L. (1954). A theory of social comparison processes. *Human Relations, 7,* 114-140.

Fowler, G., & Wackerbarth, M. (1980). Audio teleconferencing versus face-to-face conferencing: A synthesis of the literature. *Western Journal of Speech Communication, 44,* 236-252.

Fulk, J., & Ryu, D. (1990).*Perceiving electronic mail systems: A partial test of the Social Information Processing Model of communication media use in organizations.* Paper presented to International Communication Association, Dublin, Ireland.

Fulk, J., Schmitz, J., & Steinfield, C. W. (1988). *Social information and technology use in organizations.* Paper presented at the Annual Academy of Management Convention. Anaheim, California.

Fulk, J., Schmitz, J., Ryu, D., & Steinfield, C. W. (1989). *Communication in R&D via electronic mail III: Final report.* University of Southern California, Annenberg School of Communications.

Hiltz, S. R. (1984). *Online communities: A case study of the office of the future.* Norwood, NJ.: Ablex.

Hiltz, S. R., & Johnson, K. (1987). *Measuring acceptance of computer-mediated communication systems.* Paper presented at the International Communication Association, Montreal, Canada.

Hiltz, S. R., & Turoff, M. (1978). *The network nation: Human communication via computer.* Reading MA.: Addison-Wesley.

Johansen, R. (1976, May). *Pitfalls in the social evaluation of teleconferencing media.* Paper presented at the meeting of Second Annual International Communications Conference, University of Wisconsin, Madison.

Johansen, R. (1988). *Groupware: Computer support for business teams*. New York: Free Press.

Kerr, E. B., & Hiltz, S. R. (1982). *Computer mediated communication systems*. New York: Academic Press.

Kiesler, S. (1986). Thinking ahead: The hidden messages in computer networks. *Harvard Business Review, 64* (January-February), 46-60.

Kiesler, S., Siegel, J., & McGuire, T. (1984). Social psychological aspects of computer-mediated communication. *American Psychologist, 39,* 1123-1134.

Kling, R., & Gerson, E. M. (1977). The social dynamics of technical innovation in the computing world. *Symbolic Interaction, 1*(11), 132-146.

March, J. G. (1974). Bounded rationality, ambiguity, and the engineering of choice. *Bell Journal of Economics, 9,* 338-353.

Markus, M. L. (1988). *Information richness theory, managers, and electronic mail*. Paper presented at the Annual Academy of Management Convention, Anaheim, California.

Mead, G. H. (1934). *Mind, self and society*. (C. Morris, Ed.). Chicago: University of Chicago Press.

Miller, K. I., & Monge, P. R. (1985). Social information and employee anxiety about organizational change. *Human Communication Research, 11,* 365-386.

Olgren, C. & Parker, L. (1983). Teleconferencing technology and applications. Dedham, MA: Artech House.

Panko, R. (1984). Electronic mail: The alternatives. *Office Administration and Automation, 45*(6), 37-43.

Pfeffer, J. (1982). *Organizations and organization theory*. Boston: Pitman.

Phillips, A. (1983). Computer conferences: Success or failure? In R. Bostrom (Ed.), *Communication yearbook 7* (pp. 837-856). Beverly Hills, CA: Sage.

Phillips, S. R. (1988). *Electronic persuasion: The uses of electronic mail for interpersonal influence in organizations*. Unpublished doctoral dissertation, University of Southern California, Los Angeles.

Picot, A., Klingenberg, H., & Kranzle, H-P. (1982). Organizational communication between technological development and socio-economic needs: Report from field studies in Germany. In M. Burgoon (Ed.), *Communication yearbook 6*. Beverly Hills, CA: Sage.

Rice, R. E. (1980). The impacts of computer-mediated organizational and interpersonal communication. In M. Williams (Ed.), *The annual review of information science and technology* (Vol. 15, pp. 221-249). White Plains, NY.: Knowledge Industry Publications.

Rice, R. E., and Associates. (1984). *The new media: Communication, research, and technology*. Beverly Hills, CA: Sage.

Rice, R. E., & Bair, J. H. (1984). New organizational media and productivity. In R. E. Rice (Ed.), *The new media: Communication, research, and technology* (pp. 185-215). Beverly Hills, CA.: Sage.

Rice, R. E., & Borgman, C. L. (1983). The use of computer-monitored data in information science and communication research. *Journal of the American Society for Information Science, 34,* 247-256.

Rice, R. E., & Case, D. (1983). Electronic message systems in the university: A description of use and utlity. *Journal of Communication, 33*, 131-152.

Rice, R. E., Grant, A., Schmitz, J., & Torobin, J. (1988). *A network approach to predicting the adoption and outcomes of electronic messaging.* Paper presented at the Annual Academy of Management Convention, Anaheim, California.

Rice, R. E., Hart, P., Torobin, J., Shook, D., & Tyler, J. (1989). *Task analyzability, media use and performance: A multi-site test of information richness theory.* Paper presented to International Communication Association, San Francisco.

Rice, R. E., & Love, G. (1987). Electronic emotion. *Communication Research, 14*, 85-108.

Rogers, E. M. (1983). *Diffusion of innovations* (3rd ed.). New York: Free Press.

Rose, A. M. (1962). *Human behavior and social processes: An interactionist approach.* Boston: Houghton Mifflin.

Ruchinskas, J., Svenning, L., & Steinfield, C. (1989). Video comes to organizational communications: The case of ARCOVISION. In B. Sypher (Ed.), *Case studies in organizational communication.* New York: Guilford.

Salancik, G. R., & Conway, M. (1975). Attitude inferences from salient and relevant cognitive content about behavior. *Journal of Personality and Social Psychology, 32*, 829-840.

Salancik, G. R., & Pfeffer, J. (1978). A social information processing approach to job attitudes and task design. *Administrative Science Quarterly, 23*, 224-253.

Schmitz, J. (1987). *Electronic messaging: System use in local governments.* Paper presented at the International Communication Association, Montreal, Canada.

Schmitz, J. (1988). *Electronic communication: A longitudinal view.* Paper presented at the Annual Academy of Management Convention, Anaheim, California.

Shook, D. E. (1988). *A structural equivalence and contingency theory perspective on media usage and communication performance: The case of voice messaging.* Unpublished doctoral dissertation, University of Southern California, Los Angeles.

Short, J., Williams, E., & Christie, B. (1976). *The social psychology of telecommunications.* London: John Wiley.

Steinfield, C. W. (1985). Dimensions of electronic mail use in organizations. In J. Pearce & R. Robinson (Eds.), *Proceedings of the Annual Meeting of the Academy of Management* (pp. 239-243). Mississippi State University: Academy of Management.

Steinfield, C. W. (1986a). Computer-mediated communication in an organizational setting: Explaining task-related and socioemotional uses. In M. McLaughlin (Ed.), *Communication yearbook 9* (pp. 777-804). Beverly Hills, CA: Sage.

Steinfield, C. W. (1986b). Computer-mediated communication systems. In M. Williams (Ed.), *The annual review of information science and technol-*

ogy (vol. 21, pp. 167-202). White Plains, NY: Knowledge Industry Publications.

Steinfield, C. W., & Fulk, J. (1986). *Task demands and managers' use of communication media: An information processing view*. Paper presented at the Academy of Management, Chicago.

Steinfield, C. W., & Fulk, J. (1989). *New information technology and communication media use in organizations: An extension and empirical test of the information richness model*. Manuscript submitted for publication.

Strassman, P. (1985). *Information payoff: The transformation of work in an electronic age*. New York: Free Press.

Svenning, L. (1982). *Explaining predispositions toward telecommunications innovations: The influence of individual, contextual, and innovation factors on attitudes, intentions, and projections toward video-conferencing*. Unpublished doctoral dissertation, University of Southern California, Annenberg School of Communications, Los Angeles.

Svenning, L., & Ruchinskas, J. (1984). Organizational teleconferencing. In R. Rice (Ed.), *The new media: Communication, research, and technology*. (pp. 217-248). Beverly Hills, CA: Sage.

Thomas, J., & Griffin, R. (1983). The social information processing model of task design: A review of the literature. *Academy of Management Review*, *8*, 672-682.

Trevino, L. K., Lengel, R. H., & Daft, R. D. (1987). Media symbolism, media richness, and media choice in organizations: A symbolic interactionist perspective. *Communication Research*, *14*, 553-574.

Weick, K. E. (1979). *The social psychology of organizing* (2nd ed.). Reading, MA.: Addison-Wesley.

Williams, E. (1977). Experimental comparisons of face-to-face and mediated communication: A review. *Psychological Bulletin*, *84*, 963-976.

Zalesny, M. D., & Farace, R. V. (1986). A field study of social information processing: Mean differences and variance differences. *Human Communication Research*, *13*, 268-290.

PART IV

Information Technology and Collective Behaviors

This section examines information technology issues that take shape among collectivities of social actors. Group and community level phenomena can not be addressed adequately by simply aggregating individual responses to information technologies. Structural features of social systems come into play as key independent and dependent variables that interact with information technologies. The chapters in the section directly confront ecological issues and explicitly model multilevel phenomena.

Noshir Contractor and Eric Eisenberg begin this section with a broad look at the interplay between social networks and media usage. Their concerns extend beyond the role of the social network as an influence on communication media use. Drawing on structuration theory, they link media-use models upward to show how social structure is, recursively, influenced by media use. In particular, they posit that media-usage patterns affect social network participation and network structure. Their work touches on individual, dyadic, and group parameters of networks. Their conceptual framework is then used as a backdrop against which to derive expectations about the reciprocal interaction of social structure and new communication technologies.

In a more targeted examination of group process and communication technology, Scott Poole and Gerardine DeSanctis concentrate on group decision support systems (GDSS). The importance of social context continues as a recurring theme, as the authors develop a theory of adaptive structuration to explain the outcomes of group interactions with GDSS technology. Structure is viewed as a dynamic rather than static phenomenon. Information technologies such as GDSSs provide rules, as well as resources, and thus influence the structuration processes of groups. Because structuring occurs through group interaction, there will be divergent interpretations of rules, and consequently, divergent outcomes of group activities. The chapter continues with an analysis of specific features of GDSS and specific contextual factors that are most likely to influence group decision-making activities.

The central focus of Lynne Markus' chapter is the adoption and use of interactive media by communities. Markus points out that interactive media have two characteristics that are not shared by many other innovations. First, use of interactive media involves reciprocal interdependence among adopters. Early adopters of interactive media pay considerable costs because few communication partners are yet available. Over time, if an insufficient number of potential partners adopt the medium, early adopters will discontinue usage. Thus, early adopters of interactive media are interdependent with later adopters in ways that are not true for other types of innovations. Second, widespread usage results in universal access, which can be viewed as a public good in classic economic theory. Individuals may derive benefit from the public good even if they have not contributed the initial cost of obtaining it. Building upon this foundation, Markus employs theories of collective behavior to develop a "critical mass" theory, which predicts the likelihood of widespread diffusion of interactive media. In addition, she isolates the factors that can influence the development of universal access.

In the final chapter, Terry Connolly and Brian Thorn also apply theoretical constructs from the study of public goods to explain information behaviors. Their model focuses on individuals' willingness to contribute information voluntarily to shared databases through such new information technologies as computerized bulletin boards, computer conferences, distribution lists on electronic mail systems, or other organizational information systems. The analysis of public-goods theories leads these authors to predict that such information generally will be undersupplied. Because the enjoyment of benefits for a public good is independent of a focal individual's contribution, his or her best strategy from an economic perspective is not to pay the costs of contributing. These so-called free riders benefit from others' information without incurring any costs of contributing their own information. If everyone takes a low-cost solution and a free ride, no information will be contributed and no one benefits. Connolly and Thorn derive a series of propositions about the likely inducements that might influence rates of contribution, and they report experimental tests of these propositions.

NOSHIR S. CONTRACTOR
ERIC M. EISENBERG

7. Communication Networks and New Media in Organizations

The Street finds its own uses for things—uses the manufacturers never imagined. The microcassette recorder, originally intended for on-the-jump executive dictation, becomes the revolutionary medium of magnizdat, allowing the covert spread of suppressed political speeches in Poland and China. The beeper and the cellular telephone become tools of an increasingly competitive market in illicit drugs. Other technological artifacts unexpectedly become means of communication, either through opportunity or necessity. The aerosol can gives birth to the urban graffiti matrix. Soviet rockers press homemade flexi-discs out of used chest X-rays. (Gibson, 1989, p. 85)

Introduction

There is no such thing as pure technology. To understand technology, one must first understand social relationships. Understanding social relationships requires a grasp of communication. Everything about the adoption and uses of media is social (e.g., Contractor, Fulk, Monge, & Singhal, 1986; Ebadi & Utterback, 1984; Fulk, Steinfield, Schmitz, & Power, 1987; Kling & Scacchi, 1982; Markus & Robey, 1988). Logical expectations for the adoption and use of the new media are rarely met (Kiesler, 1986; Rogers, 1988; Watson, DeSanctis, & Poole, 1988). The pragmatics of technological communication must always be understood in the context of the motives, paradoxes, and contradictions of everyday life.

On the one hand, individuals use media within the framework of their lives, to accomplish their personal goals (i.e., to get ahead, to be liked, to pass the time). On the other, technology shapes individuals' goals and actions, their wishes and behaviors; both the tool and the person using the tool are changed through its application (Barley, 1986; Ochs, 1989; Rice & Contractor, in press).

The aim of this chapter is to explore in detail the interplay between the social environment and the application of communication technologies in organizations. We begin with the well-accepted idea that interaction patterns influence social practices. We add to this a plea for recursivity. When the practices being shaped are themselves communicative (as is the case with communication technologies), changes in these practices directly shape these very same social relations.

A complete discussion of communication and its relationship to technology is beyond the scope of this or any one chapter. Consequently, we choose to focus on what is but one way of articulating or operationalizing the social environment within which technologies are implemented—communication networks, the interaction patterns that surround the adoption and use of media. Specifically, we set our sights on the role emergent communication networks play (Monge & Eisenberg, 1987) in influencing (and being influenced by) new media in formal organizations.

Toward this end, the chapter is divided into two sections. The first section presents our main argument, that the relationship between communication networks and new organizational media is fundamentally emergent and recursive, best understood as part of the "duality of structure" that constitutes organizing. The second section is a more detailed review of the theoretical connections between networks and organizational media.

Technology and the Duality of Structure in Organizations

Prior research addressing the role of technology in organizations has not always proceeded from a strong theoretical basis. In the recent *Handbook of Communication Science*, Chaffee and Berger (1987) comment on the conspicuous absence of a chapter on technology this way:

> Several of our authors consider technological impacts in their particular domains of inquiry. Perhaps this is as it should be for now. While it is obvious that new technologies will have considerable impact . . . this concern is currently devoid of a unique theoretical focus. (p. 893)

This section describes the dominant theoretical approaches that focus on media characteristics; highlights one approach specifically applicable to communication networks, social information processing theory; and offers a new, recursive model of the relationship between communication network participation and media use in organizations.

Media Characteristics

If there is an over-riding theme in past research, it is the ongoing attempt to match media characteristics with task characteristics within organizations. Those theoretical statements that do exist classify the media and the communication requirements of tasks on the basis of social presence (Short, Williams, & Christie, 1976) or media richness (Daft & Lengel, 1986). In other words, media characteristics such as asynchronicity, channel capacity (audio versus visual versus audiovisual), and the opportunities for feedback are catalogued in an attempt to determine the social presence or richness of the media. Likewise, communication tasks are classified on the basis of their characteristics (such as "getting acquainted," "seeking factual information," or "negotiating"). Empirical research tests hypotheses about the effectiveness of specific media to accomplish certain communication tasks. Clearly this model is based on the assumptions that each medium has an "objective" social presence and each communication task a single goal.

Neither assumption is borne out in communicative practice. The idea that specific media or messages can be understood in terms of their ability to simply transmit information has been rejected as an inappropriate, "conduit" metaphor of organizational communication (Axley, 1984). There are at least three problems with this model.

First, it assumes a passive receiver. We believe that audiences actively co-construct the meanings of the messages they receive. This means that when you interact with someone, you don't have everything planned ahead of time—new ideas emerge in the exchange, precisely *because* it is a dialogue. Second, the conduit model of communication does not sufficiently account for the role played by the local context in determining the meaning of any given communication. To suggest that meaning is transferred from "head to head" greatly underestimates the moderating effects of the situation on the meanings that are constructed. Third, and finally, the conduit metaphor is symbolic of an ideology of clarity and openness that equates these qualities of communication with effectiveness. We maintain that communication can be political, strategic, and effective without being open or clear (Eisenberg & Witten, 1987). Furthermore, it is these more subtle instances of strategy that reveal most about the functions of communication in organizations.

Along these lines, then, we question the assumption that the channel which provides the most nonverbal cues (i.e., face-to-face communication) will also by definition be the most effective communication medium. In some instances, a medium that filters cues (such as computer-conferencing) may be *more* effective than face-to-face communication in achieving strategic goals. Most previous research has assumed at least implicitly that the effectiveness of face-to-face communication be used as a benchmark to compare the effectiveness of all mediated communication. We question research based on the notion that media that filter cues may substitute, but cannot supersede and are always in some way inferior to face-to-face communication (Culnan & Markus, 1987).

Our final difficulty with the media characteristics approach has to do with our belief that communicators in organizations always have multiple goals (Eisenberg, 1984). Previous work has assumed that at any given moment, individuals are trying to accomplish just one thing; that is, to "gain compliance," "ingratiate," or "save face." But the general case of organizational communication is significantly more complex, with multiple goals and strategies commonly enacted simultaneously in a single communication situation. Speaking to your subordinate about a work assignment, for example, may require attention to relational goals (such as the subordinate's feelings), as well as more instrumental goals (such as ensuring an effective plan of action). Past research has attempted to identify the most appropriate medium to achieve these goals each taken individually. Since these goals rarely, if ever, occur independently, we advocate studying how combinations of media are used over time to accomplish a complex profile of goals.

Social Information Processing

Echoing broader criticisms of overly rational models of organizational behavior, Fulk et al. (1987) offer a significant theoretical advance over this work. They point out that previous approaches assume "objective" definitions of media and task characteristics, neither of which exist in pure form. Instead, these characteristics are socially constructed through the information people receive about them. Citing a simple example, if a senior manager learns from her peers that the electronic mail system is "too darned complicated" to use interactively, she may in turn develop a similar attitude and pattern of usage reflecting this negative perception.

Fulk et al. (1987) apply Salancik and Pfeffer's (1978) social information processing theory to explicate the influence of the sociocommunicative environment on behavior with new media. This is a novel application of the theory, which had previously been reserved for the study of task characteristics and job attributes (e.g., Miller & Monge, 1985). There are two limitations to the theory as Fulk et al. (1987) have applied it. First, because it is not explicitly a communication theory, social information processing has not articulated the mechanisms by which social information flows to and from individuals. Second, while highlighting the important effects of social information on patterns of media use, Fulk et al. fail to consider influences in the opposite direction; how patterns of media use in turn effect patterns of social interaction and information. We have developed a model that responds in part to both of these concerns.

A Recursive Model of Communication Networks and Media

We propose a simple, recursive model that extends the social information processing approach in two ways (see Figure 7.1). First, we apply communication network concepts as one way of specifying the social mechanisms by which individuals' perceptions and behaviors with new media are shaped. Second, we describe the manner in which individuals' use of the media in turn influences their positions in emergent communication networks. Underlying both of these moves is our contention that the social environment and applications of communication technologies are recursively linked to each other and to other organizing processes through the "duality" of social structure. This duality has well-known roots, three of which are discussed below.

Giddens' Structuration. Antony Giddens (1984) is best known for his metatheory: structuration. Structurationists (Barley, 1986; Ranson, Hinings, & Greenwood, 1980; Poole, Seibold, & McPhee, 1986; Riley, 1983) see social interaction as a kind of prism through which individual and communal ends are refracted to create social reality. Organizing consists of an unresolved dialectic between autonomy and interdependence, agency and constraint. According to Giddens, "Human social activities, like some self-reproducing items in nature, are recursive. That is to say, they are not brought into being by social actors but continually recreated by them via the very means whereby they express themselves as actors. In and through their activities agents reproduce the conditions that make these activities possible" (Giddens, 1984, p. 2). And so it is with the relationships between communication structure and uses of organizational media—each shapes the other in an emergent pattern of mediated and non-mediated social interaction.

Burt's Theory of Structural Action. In the network domain, we trace our argument to Burt's (1982) theory of structural action, which also features the recursive nature of social structures. Burt argues that "social structures constrain actors in their ability to take (purposive) action," but also that

147

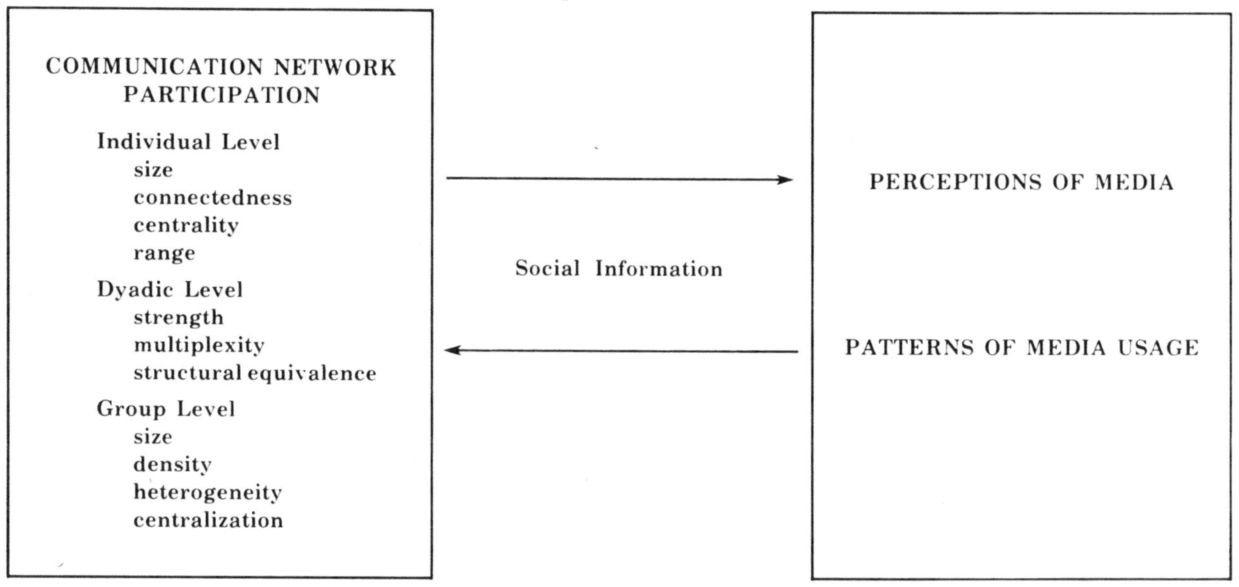

Figure 7.1 A Recursive Model of Network Involvement and Media Use in Organizations

"actions taken under social structural constraint can modify social structure itself and these modifications have the potential to create new constraints to be faced by actors within the structure" (p. 9). Burt's theory echoes Giddens' structuration theory on the processual recursive character of the interaction between agency and structure. There are some important differences, however. Burt (1982) draws his ideas more from a morphogenetic view of recursivity, one which has a decidedly sequential flavor (Archer, 1982). In this way, the dialectical interplay between agency and constraint can be analyzed cycle by cycle. Structuration, on the other hand, focuses more on the nonsequential interpenetration of agency and constraint. For example, when employees use a new communications medium, from this perspective their use at once reflects a history of constraint and opens up a wealth of future possibilities.

Our use of the term *recursive*, then, is meant to encompass both notions of sequentiality *and* simultaneity. In addressing relationships between social structure and media use, we are interested both in cycles and sequences of effects and in the moment-to-moment interpenetration of agency and constraint.

Technology as Tool. Finally, we borrow the tool/container distinction as it has been applied to language and offer it here as a way of understanding technology (Ochs, 1989). A tool-like conception of language sensitizes us to the ways in which people use words to shape their worlds. But the tools themselves are altered in the process. Similarly, communication technologies are not dumb carriers of users' intentions. Technologies are tools with varying capabilities, used by individuals in organizations to define problems, to develop solutions, and to change their environments (Dhar & Olson, 1989).

Computer-mediated communication technologies in particular are remarkably plastic, Rorschach-like symbols—"cultural objects which different people and groups of people can apprehend with very different descriptions and invest with very different attributes" (Turkle, 1984, p. 320). The social context constrains what tools are available (Markus, 1987; Rice, 1988; Robertson, 1988; Rogers, 1988) how these tools are understood and enacted (Bikson, Eveland, & Gutek, 1989; Fulk et al., 1987; Papa & Tracy, 1988), and how the consequences of their use will be received. In turn, the context is ever-evolving partly as a result of the ways in which these new media are used.

Beyond the Technological or Organizational Imperative. The notion of a duality of structure is rarely seen in the literature on organizational media, which has focused instead on either a "technological" or an "organizational" imperative (Markus & Robey, 1988). The technological imperative privileges media characteristics as determining uses and behavior. The organizational imperative privileges the ability of organizational designers and managers to use media in rational ways, to accomplish specific, clearly defined ends.

Neither approach has received much empirical support. Research adopting the technological imperative has been confronted with the "dual effects hypothesis," which states that communication technologies can have opposite impacts simultaneously and in spite of one another (Mesthene, 1981). For example, the introduction of phones fostered both decentralization (the growth of the suburbs) and centralization (the growth of the skyscraper) at the same time (Pool, Decker, Dizard, Israel, Rubin, & Weinstein, 1981). Research based on the organizational imperative has also been inconclusive. Johansen (1977) reviewed 251 articles in an attempt to understand the match between the nature of organizational communication tasks and various configurations of teleconferencing. While exceptionally comprehensive, the review did not reach any unequivocal conclusions for designers of information systems (Culnan & Markus, 1987).

Hence, neither approach alone gives a true picture of the social nature of technology in organizations. This is not that surprising since, generally speaking, neither deterministic theories of social conformity nor radical theories of individual agency have ever, taken individually, provided adequate explanations of human behavior (Wentworth, 1980). We agree with Markus and Robey (1988) that the study of technologies in organizations is best served by what Pfeffer (1982) called the *emergent perspective* on action in organizations. According to this perspective, "the uses and consequences of information technology emerge unpredictably from complex social interactions" (Markus & Robey, 1988, p. 588). It is these interactions that must be examined as where the ongoing tensions between agency and constraint are worked out. This implies full attention to the pragmatics of media usage in organizations, considering at once the reciprocal relationships among goals, technology, actions, and interactions that constitute the emerging situations (Kling & Scacchi, 1982; Weick, 1984). It is therefore critical that our theories and research methods recognize the emergent structural relationships among individuals, rather than focus exclusively on their attributes.

Communication Networks and New Media

The purpose of this section is to describe the various theoretical mechanisms by which the social environment shapes media use—and vice versa—focusing specifically on communication networks as an operationalization of the social environment.

150

Why Apply Communication Networks to the Study of Technology?

Despite both theoretical and methodological challenges, the concept of communication networks has had a positive and important effect on the way we understand organizations. Based in part on systems theory (Buckley, 1967), communication networks are one attempt to operationalize the ways in which the whole is indeed greater than the sum of its parts (i.e., attributable precisely to the relationships between parts). Network explanations move us into the social realm in understanding human behavior, freeing us from the limitation of considering only microscopic or macroscopic factors. Network theories provide us with a vocabulary for identifying and measuring information flow between people, about a variety of topics, using a variety of media (Monge & Contractor, 1987). A working understanding of the networks that may emerge in any given organization goes a long way toward helping us understand individual and aggregate behavior, and the connection between the two (Monge, 1987; Monge & Eisenberg, 1987).

The major difference between network theory and most other social science perspectives is the emphasis placed on the relationship between two or more objects (or individuals) over the attributes of these objects (Monge & Miller, 1985). The objects or "nodes," in network parlance, may be individuals, groups, organizations, even societies. Network researchers have studied a diverse range of phenomena, including the flow of goods, personnel, money, information, social support, power, and kinship (Knoke & Kuklinski, 1982). Network researchers believe that the natural unit of analysis is not an isolated individual but the relationships between individuals. One prominent student of social support networks, Barry Wellman, criticizes individual research as inevitably concluding that "social behavior is the result of the fact that individuals possess common attributes rather than that they are involved in structured social relationships" (1988, p. 31).

Perhaps the central theoretical concern of network studies, however, is the ways in which patterns of interaction (networks) affect and are affected by individuals' behaviors and cognitions. While it is traditional in the technology literature to speak of antecedents and consequences of technological adoption and usage, when networks are involved, the understanding of these terms must change somewhat. Because communication networks are informal, emergent, and hence always changing, they are continually both antecedents and consequents of behavior with and attitudes toward technology. Hence, while in the following discussions we have been faithful to previous work in its use of the terms "antecedents" and "consequents", our conceptualization sees networks as emergent communication processes that both affect and reflect many aspects of human behavior, behavior with media included.

The use of network methodologies to study organizational media is not a new idea. Several researchers have proposed using network methods for this purpose (e.g., Fulk, Power, & Schmitz, 1986; Rice, 1988; Rice & Borgman, 1983; Rogers, 1987; Williams, Rice, & Rogers, 1988). They all claim that networks are well-suited to capture ongoing patterns of communication among a net of individuals interconnected via different media. They note that network methods are desirable for studying technology because they are unobtrusive, they can be automated, they do not neglect weak (i.e., less frequent, but informationally rich) ties, and they provide accurate data.

Others have advocated a network approach because relational-level variables can boost the explained variance in individual-level phenomena. Thus, network methods are proposed as "turbo-chargers" for explaining attribute-level phenomena (e.g., Rogers, 1983; Wellman, 1988). A main consideration of these researchers is the way in which networks shape behaviors and cognitions. Anderson and Jay (1985), for example, examined the adoption of a computerized information system by physicians. They found network variables to be predictive of adoption above and beyond that which was explained by individual attribute variables.

Despite the fact that network methods have been applied to the study of new media, theoretical arguments have been slow in coming (Rogers, 1987). We respond to this criticism by identifying several theoretical mechanisms relating communication networks and media use. Previous usage leads us to organize these unarguably recursive processes as "effects of networks on media attitudes and usage" and "effect of media usage on networks." In each direction we describe these relationships at the individual, dyadic, and group levels.

At the *individual* level, we focus on the role of "key communicators" who have a large number or diverse range of contacts. There are several network metrics that attempt to represent these characteristics. The simplest metric is the size (absolute number of contacts) of a member's network. Other measures frequently used by organizational network researchers include connectedness, centrality, and range (Tichy, 1981). Connectedness (or prominence) refers to the ratio between a member's actual and potential communication links in the network (Alba, 1982). One measure of centrality, betweenness, indicates the extent to which a member communicates with others who do not themselves communicate (Freeman, 1979). These members therefore serve as liaisons between groups. Range (or diversity) is the degree to which a person communicates with heterogeneous groups of others, along some salient dimension (Rogers & Kincaid, 1981).

Next, we discuss the relationship between a *dyad's* network characteristics and their similarity in media use and attitudes. The most frequently studied characteristics of a dyad are its strength, multiplexity, and structural equivalence. The strength of a dyad indicates the time spent communicating or frequency of communication. The multiplexity of the dyad refers to the number of types of relationships (in terms of content or media) that exist between the two members. The structural equivalence of a dyad is the extent to which the two members share similar patterns of communication with others in the network (Burt, 1980).

At the *group* level we examine the relationship between the group's network characteristics and media use. The simplest group characteristic, size, refers to the number of members in the network. Other network characteristics include connectedness, heterogeneity, and centralization. A group's connectedness (or density) is the ratio of actual communication links among group members to the number of potential communication links. A group's heterogeneity is the degree to which group members differ on key attributes. A group's centralization refers to the extent to which some members are more central than others.

Finally, very little is known about the relationship between an organization's environment and its adoption and use of a particular medium. Interorganizational networks provide one operationalization of an organization's environment (Aldrich & Whetten, 1981; Lincoln, 1982; Tichy, 1981; Whetten, 1981). Eisenberg et al. (1985) suggest that interorganizational linkages can be classified on the basis of transactional content (material or information) and level of contact (personal, representative, or institutional). In the following discussion, we propose that the recursive relationship between media usage and networks at the individual, dyadic and group levels can be informed by both the examination of intra- and interorganizational networks.

Effects of Communication Networks on Media Attitudes and Usage

Key Communicators. Individuals differ in the degree to which they are prominent in a given communication or social network. Those who are well connected can play a key role in shaping the behavior and perceptions of others in the social group (Marsden, 1981). One of the earliest demonstrations of this is work on opinion leadership in the diffusion of innovations—key communicators played a major role in shaping the adoption patterns throughout the social system (Parks, 1977; Rogers, 1988). Rogers points out that adoption is facilitated if the administrative head of the group is a key communicator who favors the new medium.

An individual may also serve as an information broker or liaison between individuals who do not communicate with each other. Information brokers are well positioned to maintain the existence of multiple, and possibly conflicting perceptions of the new media. Thus, they can play a key role in helping to define the salience of certain media characteristics and consequently aid (or impede) the diffusion of attitudes and behaviors among diverse groups (Marsden, 1981). In the literature on organizational boundary spanners, Tushman and Scanlan (1981) described effective spanners as both internal and external "stars"; individuals capable of communicating and maintaining the trust of diverse groups can play a key role in the spread of information about new media.

There is considerable research support for the role of prominent communicators in the diffusion and use of new media in the workplace. For example, Rice, Grant, Schmitz, and Torobin (1988) found that prominent individuals were also early adopters of a new information system and facilitated the development of a critical mass of users. Papa and Tracy (1988) report that highly connected individuals in an organization's communication network were also the most productive with the technology, and reported the most positive experiences. There is also some evidence that under certain conditions, the relationship between connectedness and usage is not a simple one. Hiltz (1981) found that scientific researchers of moderate connectedness in their profession were the most frequent users of a computer-mediated conference. "Isolates and sociometric stars do not use the system as much as those with moderate number of professional connections, who seem to have the most motivation to expand their professional networks" (p. 66).

At the interorganizational level, resource dependency theory (Pfeffer & Salancik, 1978) suggests that prominent organizations might influence the adoption patterns of others in their network. According to resource dependency theory, organizational action is in part explained by the conditions and constraints imposed by the environment. Thus, a prominent organization that controls resources sought by other organizations in its environment can play a key role in shaping others' adoption decisions. For example, General Motors recently announced implementation of Machine Automation Protocol (MAP), a communication protocol for their assembly line. Their unilateral announcement forced vendors who made equipment and did most of their business with GM to adopt the communication protocol. In another instance, Chase Manhattan Bank recently became the first major bank to announce an electronic mail gateway that permits 5,000 of its employees to communicate electronically with customers. By giving incentives Chase Manhattan is expecting to encourage adoption of this technology among clients who rely heavily on the bank for financial transactions (Pelton, 1989).

Range or Diversity. In addition to the effect of key communicators, an individual's range of contacts has an impact on his or her attitudes and behaviors toward the new media. Individuals who communicate with a diverse set of people bring new information, alternative perspectives, and often a greater degree of influence to the media perceptions of others in the group. A broad or diverse range of contacts means making novel information available from outside of the focal group (Granovetter, 1973, 1982; Friedkin, 1982). Granovetter's strength of weak ties theory, for example, proposes that people who have diverse, weak ties bring new social resources and information-rich ideas to their networks. In the realm of new media, such individuals provide missing pieces regarding design or application that may facilitate its adoption or redefinition (Rogers, 1988). In interorganizational networks, organizations that scan diverse sectors of the environment are exposed to novel information about the new media and are therefore more likely to introduce these ideas to their networks. In several instances, these ties are formalized by appointing individuals with diverse backgrounds to the corporation's board of directors (Pennings, 1980).

Dyadic Level. Social information processing theory proposes that an individual's attitudes about the media are in large part influenced by the attitudes of others in the communication network (Fulk et al., 1987). The process by which individuals are influenced by the attitudes and behaviors of others in their environment is termed social contagion. There are two network models that are used to study social contagion (Burt, 1987; Erickson, 1988). First, the *relational model*, maintains that people will influence (and be influenced by) those with whom they have direct communication contact (Burt, 1980). Accordingly the relational network model predicts that the strength, multiplexity, or symmetry of a dyad's communication will in part determine the extent to which they are also similar in attitudes toward and experience with the media. Rice et al. (1988) found that dyads who communicated frequently with each other about task-related topics were significantly more likely to either both adopt or not adopt an electronic mail system.

The second, *positional model* maintains that individuals will be most influenced by others who share similar status in the organization. People

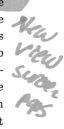

holding similar status often manifest similar patterns of communication and consequently can be considered "structurally equivalent," even though they may not communicate directly (Burt, 1980). According to this model, people's attitudes toward and behaviors with the new media will be similar to those individuals with whom they are structurally equivalent. This is because structurally equivalent individuals are subject to similar constraints, socialization experiences and organizational expectations. Robertson (1988) found that organizational members who are structurally equivalent were significantly more likely to perceive and utilize information systems in similar ways. Likewise, Walker (1985) reports that, in a computer software firm, members who were structurally equivalent were significantly more likely to share their cognitions about product goals and ways to achieve these goals.

At the interorganizational level, the process by which organizations are influenced by the structure and behavior of other organizations in their environment is termed isomorphism (DiMaggio & Powell, 1983). Isomorphism may result from mimetic, normative, or coercive processes in the interorganizational network. Organizations have difficulty making rational decisions in the face of high uncertainty (March & Simon, 1958). Because there is a high degree of uncertainty surrounding new media in organizations, the decision to adopt may have more to do with interorganizational isomorphic processes than rational intraorganizational criteria such as efficiency. For instance, the "bandwagon effect" observed in the adoption of facsimile machines by organizations suggests that mimetic and normative processes may have influenced the decision more than a rational cost-benefit analysis. Galaskiewicz and Wasserman (1988) have demonstrated the ability of network models to articulate and test for the existence of these isomorphic processes across organizations.

Group Characteristics. There has been very limited research studying the impact of group network characteristics on media use. Markus (1987) suggests that the adoption of a particular medium can be explained by theories of collective action (Oliver, Marwell, & Teixeira, 1985). She argues that the adoption of a communication technology by a group requires the existence of a "critical mass" of users. Recent work has shown that a group's network characteristics can be used to predict the prospects of collective action (Bonacich, 1987; Marwell, Oliver, & Prahl, 1988; Oliver & Marwell, 1988). Based on a series of computer simulations, they posit that the density and centralization of a group will be positively related to the likelihood of collective action.

The theory of collective action can be easily extended to the interorganizational realm. A case in point is the aerospace industry. Comprised of only a handful of major manufacturers, this industry is a highly centralized interorganizational network. Recent increase in the volume of subcontracting in the aerospace industry has resulted in increased density of this network. The result is unusually strong pressure to adopt specific kinds of communications media that allow quick communication and the monitoring of subcontracts. For example, in a recent landmark decision by the industry, the 50-member Aerospace Industry Association became the first major U.S. industry consortium to announce a standardized interorganizational electronic mail network (Seghers, Rothfeder, & Hof, 1989).

Hence, we see that individual, dyadic and group level network measures can be used to bring theoretical insight to our understanding of media adoption and use within and across organizations. At the individual level, theories of the diffusion of innovations and resource dependency suggest that prominence in a network influences members' perceptions and use of the new media. At the dyadic level, the relational and positional network models provide alternative mechanisms for understanding social information processing among organizational members. Further, studying the influence of isomorphic processes in interorganizational networks helps explain organizational decisions about new media. At the group level, network characteristics provide ways of testing theories of collective action within and across organizations. The next section focuses on the reverse relationship, how patterns of media use recursively impact communication networks.

Effects of Media Use on Communication Network Participation

Members' perceptions of and behavior with media are based in large part on the information they receive. As this information must also come through some communication channels, it is itself restricted by previous media choices. It follows that changes in patterns of media use will impact members' positions in their social network, and as a result influence and alter the information they receive. This completes the recursive loop between media attitudes and usage and participation in communication networks. The impact of media use on network participation within and across organizations can be analyzed at the individual, dyadic, and group level.

Key Communicators. At the individual level, media use affects network prominence. A number of factors come into play in determining how media use will alter the prominence of individuals. These factors fall into three general categories. Prominence in a network is influenced by: (a) individuals' access to media; (b) individuals' ability to cope with the uncertainty associated with media; and (c) individuals' ability to accentuate their positive-affect cues and mask their negative-affect via these media. These are described in the next three paragraphs.

Several studies have documented how access to media has influenced the prominence of certain individuals in the system (e.g., Leduc, 1979; Rice & Case, 1983; Sproull & Kiesler, 1986). In general, these studies indicate that access to superiors in an organization via technologically mediated channels prompts individuals to dramatically increase their communication. Consequently, in some organizations the implementation of electronic mail has made senior management more prominent. In some cases the increase in prominence for those at the top of the hierarchy undermines the prominence of intermediaries in the hierarchy (Fulk & Dutton, 1985).

In addition to access, individuals' ability to cope with the uncertainty of various media also influence their position in the network. Individuals who are knowledgeable about a medium tend to rise to immediate prominence within the network. Thus, internal consultants are typically very popular throughout adoption and beyond. Aydin's (1989) study of student health services at a university shows that the people who knew most about the system and were formally responsible for helping users become proficient were also the most prominent in the accompanying communication networks. In his study of the Electronic Information Exchange System (EIES), Rice (1982) found that user consultants and personnel monitoring the system emerged as information brokers in the communication network.

Finally, individuals' ability to highlight or shield their positive and negative affect cues influence their prominence in a network. Olgren and Parker (1983) have documented the prevalence of a "Hollywood Syndrome" in videoconferences leading to the emergence of new stars who put on "a slick performance . . . for effect rather than substance" (p. 239). Likewise, Kerr and Hiltz (1982) review several studies where computer-conferencing was especially helpful in expanding opportunity structures for the handicapped. They point out that "the suppression of nonverbal cues means they interact more equally" (p. 138). In addition, researchers have proposed that network involvement is related to organizational commitment (Eisenberg, Monge, & Miller, 1983), turnover (Krackhardt & Porter, 1986), leadership (McElroy & Schrader, 1986), and the socialization process (Jablin & Krone, 1987; Sherman, Smith & Mansfield, 1986). By virtue of its direct influence on the organization's communication network, media usage has the potential to indirectly affect several other key employee reactions.

The effects of media usage can also be observed in interorganizational networks. Organizations often adopt new media to gain a competitive advantage. A well-known example of this strategy was the introduction of Sabre, a computerized airline reservation system developed by American Airlines (Williams, Rice, & Rogers, 1988). In the early 1980s, American Airlines offered travel agents a free desktop terminal and access to the Sabre reservation system. The new system was very attractive to agents who were frustrated with the inefficiency of the telephone. The rapid adoption of the Sabre system by travel agents boosted American Airlines' betweenness (or centrality) among organizations in the travel industry. Further, American Airlines had easier access to fare and schedule information from the other airlines, which was useful in their own scheduling and pricing to make their flights more competitive.

Range or Diversity. Media use can also alter the range and diversity of an individual's communication network. This diversity results from the new media's potential to span geographical and temporal boundaries. Fulk, Power, and Schmitz (1986) reviewed several studies where introduction of technologically-mediated communication served to increase the diversity of communication relationships by linking diverse groups (e.g., Johansen & DeGrasse, 1979).

The use of the media can also have a major impact on the diversity of links across organizations (Huber, 1984; Leduc, 1979). The proliferation of broadcast media such as public electronic bulletin boards and computer conference systems potentially increases the diversity of "weak" interorganizational ties. These "weak" ties can help organizations scan their environments (Huber, 1982) or assist disgruntled employees in seeking new jobs (Granovetter, 1973). In addition, the boom in one-to-one electronic mail systems increases the diversity of "strong" ties across organizations. These ties can be especially influential in creating "invisible colleges" that connect researchers dispersed geographically but who share a common intellectual interest (Allen, 1977; Crane, 1969; Lievrouw, Rogers, Lowe, & Nadel, 1987).

Dyadic Level. Similarities in perceptions and use of the media can result in an increase in dyadic communication. This argument is based on findings that mediated communication reinforces rather than substitutes for face-to-face communication. For instance, studies reviewed by Kraemer (1982) show that organizational teleconferencing *increased* overall communication rather than simply substituting for face-to-face communication. In a longitudinal study, Eveland and Bikson (1988) found that pairs of individuals who had access to electronic mail (in addition to face-to-face contact), interacted more frequently with each other than those who only communicated in person. Further, the adoption of new media in addition to, rather than as a replacement for existing media increases the multiplexity of the dyad.

Studies based on Berger and Calabrese's (1975) uncertainty reduction theory indicate that increased multiplexity helps reduce uncertainty and thus facilitates organizational innovation (Albrecht & Ropp, 1984; Bach, 1989).

Likewise, the adoption of a new medium for interorganizational communication normally serves to increase rather than replace the communication via existing media. For instance, analysts in the aerospace industry predict that the introduction of an industry-wide electronic mail system (discussed earlier) is likely to increase the total amount of interorganizational communication by about 20% (Seghers, Rothfeder, & Hof, 1989). An increase in interorganizational communication can have diverse implications. Monge (1987) points out that more communication can facilitate coordination and cooperation (Van de Ven & Walker, 1981), or competition and control (Aldrich & Whetten, 1981), or both (Zeitz, 1980).

Group Level. At the group level, media use can alter the structure of networks by changing existing boundaries. In general, network studies provide little or no theoretical rationale for their choice of system boundaries. Most organizational network studies specify the limits of the formal organization as the boundary of their network. Thus, a boundary spanner has been traditionally defined as one who communicates with individuals outside of the formal organization (Adams, 1976; 1980; Katz & Kahn, 1978). The introduction of new media in and across organizations makes the specification of organizational boundaries even more difficult.

Further, the use of new communication technologies in organizations can alter access and control over the "means of production" and pose new political challenges that existing structures may not be able to handle (Zuboff, 1988). Burkhardt and Brass (1989) note that the uncertainty accompanying the diffusion of technology (and the new capabilities of the technology itself) can undermine the existing power structure and therefore alter the networks in organizations. Further, the use of certain technologies can result in the reconfiguration of the network. In her study of a major hospital, Aydin (1989) reported that the implementation of a computer information system disturbed traditional status distinctions between nurses, doctors, and pharmacists, resulting in considerable short- and long-term changes in communication patterns.

Organizational Communication Networks and the Structuring of Technology

Having reviewed the current literature on the new media and communication networks in organizations we now return to articulating ways in which networks structure the uses of new media in organizations. The above review indicates that previous work has for the most part taken a limited view of how network structure and individuals' positions in a network might affect their attitudes and utilization of the media.

Returning to the theme of an emergent perspective on organizational action, the "effects" of technology are not always direct, anticipated, or desirable (Rogers, 1983; Kiesler, 1986). In the case of the telephone, Pool et al. (1981) document how society appropriated only a handful of the hundreds of applications that could have been implemented. Clearly, characteristics of the media interact with cultural and social norms to constitute the nature of the implementation.

In addition to reflecting existing social norms, it is important to recognize that employees continually use the media to create new, and to modify existing, norms. Johnson and Rice (1987) document the norms that evolved about the use of word-processing. Watson et al. (1988) identify the gradual emergence of norms for reaching group consensus using group decision support systems. Steinfield (in press) reports that users of a recently implemented electronic mail system used the medium to censure certain forms of communication (such as flaming). Steinfield also describes how the medium was used to structure users' perceptions of "message discipline" including the frequency of checking electronic mail, and the acceptable turnaround time for responses.

We expect that perceptions and use of the media are the outcome of an interplay among actors, context and technology. This interplay is an adaptive process that allows for widely divergent outcomes in different settings. For instance, Barley (1986) described how the introduction of computerized tomography (CT scanners) occasioned similar dynamics but lead to very different structural outcomes in two radiology units.

The idea of studying technology in organizations from an emergent perspective is a novel and, we believe, useful approach. More specifically we believe that an emergent network perspective affords a unique set of conceptual and methodological tools to examine the restructuring of communication technologies in the workplace.

First, the emergent network perspective provides an opportunity to examine how microlevel appropriation processes impact macrolevel adoption by the group. It therefore highlights the potential for mutual influence between human agency and collective action. Thus, the network approach can be made to reflect our assumption about the existence of an autonomy-interdependence dialectic in organizational communication.

Second, using this perspective, we can study communication technologies broadly rather than restrict ourselves to the study of specific goals or media. A network perspective is well-suited to the systemic study of multiplex networks (i.e., with multiple goals and media). Hence, we see that an emergent networks perspective, unlike the media characteristics perspective, can be aligned with our assumption that communication involves multiple goals that cannot be separated from one another.

Third, and finally, the emergent network perspective provides specific ways of examining how the appropriation of technology influences the individual. These characteristics set it apart from the other approaches to the emergent perspective discussed above.

A Hypothetical Scenario

Our discussion so far of the emergent network perspective has been largely abstract and theoretical but with important practical implications. In order to exemplify some of the practical implications we invite you to consider a hypothetical scenario. The scenario, describing the introduction of a voice-mail system in a manufacturing organization, permits us to explicate the recursive processes relating communication networks and media use.

The idea of using a voice mail system was initially championed by the chief executive officer. Voice mail systems were not widely used in the city or in this industry, but the CEO had heard the virtues of such a system extolled at a trade convention. Changes in the organization's environment were forcing the CEO to spend an increasing amount of time away from headquarters. Hence, the CEO proposed the use of voice mail as a "personal," prompt, and accurate way for organizational members to stay abreast of events in the organization and its environment. In other words, the idea of adopting the technology came from one of the CEO's "weak" ties at a convention.

To test the idea, the voice mail system was first introduced as a service for top management. The pilot project was an instant success. The voice mail system was quickly adopted and widely used. Clearly, none of the members of top management could risk being excluded from a system that (a) had the blessings of the CEO (a key communicator who had diverse links both inside and outside the organization), and (b) was being used by others with similar status (i.e., were structurally equivalent).

The success of the pilot project reinforced the CEO's commitment to the idea. The system would provide a personal way to quickly and accurately monitor events throughout the organization. It would also provide an efficient way of instantaneously disseminating information via broadcast messages to several people on a "mailing list". Citing these reasons, the CEO announced the introduction of a voice mail system for the entire organization.

The CEO's rationale made employees more sensitive to certain aspects of communication in the company. The CEO made clear that oral communication was most desirable because it was "personal" (as compared to impersonal memos) and that a premium was placed on speed and accuracy of communication. The members of the organization used these and other criteria to evaluate the voice mail system.

The adoption of the voice mail system by key communicators in top management provided an incentive for others in the organization to follow suit. However, within a short period of time, different constituencies used the system with varying regularity and for diverse purposes. As expected, the system was used by sales representatives who were geographically dispersed. The adoption of the new medium reduced the feeling of isolation among some of these employees. The system was also used extensively by workers on the assembly line. Contrary to expectations, however, they did not use the system to provide reports to superiors. In fact, they only used voice mail to send messages to superiors when they wanted to *avoid* direct contact. They redefined the functionality of voice mail primarily to communicate problems and seek solutions from mechanics on other shifts.

Also unforeseen by the CEO, the voice mail system faced resistance from two other departments. Objections were raised privately and publicly by accountants and engineers. Accountants had problems with the system because it deviated from the traditional ways they were used to communicating using text and numbers. Engineers also failed to see the value of the system, as so much of their communication depended on visual aids. Consequently, the adoption and use of this new medium had differential impacts on the communication networks *within* the organization. Within sales, the introduction of the system resulted in *increased* communication (and cohesiveness) across geographic and formal status divisions. Because of the resistance, however, there was little change in the communication networks either within or between the accounting and engineering departments.

The use of voice mail also influenced communication networks *across* departments. Employees in sales used the system not only to improve coordination within their department, but also to forge closer links with senior management. Further, and much to the chagrin of the accounting department, employees in sales began to send the accountants voice mail messages in lieu of "putting things in writing." The networks in the accounting and engineering departments remained largely inwardly focused and unchanged resulting in their increased isolation in inter-departmental communication networks. More significant was a felt *decrease* by both departments in influence over senior management decision-making. Their text and visual-based proposals were being discounted by the CEO and senior management who began to rely more heavily on the more timely, oral arguments presented by other departments via voice mail. Clearly, the introduction of voice mail was, for separate reasons, undermining the position of the accounting and engineering departments in the organization's communication networks.

To reassert their declining political position, the accounting and engineering departments used different strategies. The accounting department embarked on a campaign to change employee perceptions of the voice mail system. They used the system itself to "broadcast" messages pointing to the steep rise in costs associated with the use of the voice mail. They also forwarded to senior managers examples of voice messages that they argued did not warrant the cost of messaging. These actions generated a debate on the cost-effectiveness of voice mail. In addition, the fact that private messages were "forwarded" (as illustrations) raised questions of privacy that had not surfaced before. These changes in perceptions of voice mail led to the emergence of new norms regarding its usage. Employees cut back on their use of voice mail, avoiding communication of a confidential or sensitive nature. Further, in response to some of the issues raised by the accounting department, the management restricted access of the voice-mail system for certain employees.

The engineering department addressed their growing isolation differently. They capitalized on the euphoria surrounding new communication technologies in the organization to propose the purchase of a broadband local area network (LAN). This system would allow the transmission of high-resolution visual communication within the organization's main location. The information could be accessed via terminals placed on managers' desks. The top management, who viewed this proposal as reinforcing their information-gathering and decision-support capabilities, approved the purchase. Thus, engineering now had direct access to management using a channel that was most appropriate to support their communication requirements. In addition, the fact that top management had invested heavily in this new technology persuaded them to heed more carefully the advice they received via this medium.

To summarize, this scenario provides several examples of the recursive interplay between networks and media use. It was one of the CEO's "weak" inter-organizational ties that suggested the idea of using voice mail. The prominence of the CEO among the top management's communication network contributed to the success of the pilot test. Subsequently, the rationale and adoption by top management contributed to the initial perception and use of the system by various departments in the organization. Over time, however, the system was appropriated differently by individual departments. These differences in turn resulted in changes in the communication networks within and across departments. In particular, it led to the relative isolation of the accounting and engineering departments. Their isolation was for different reasons and they used different strategies to address these problems. These strategies resulted in redefinition of the norms surrounding use of the voice mail system, and the adoption of a new visual communication medium. These changes set the stage for yet another reconfiguration of the emergent communication network.

References

Adams, J. S. (1976). The structure and dynamics of behavior in organizational boundary roles. In M. D. Dunnette (Ed.), *Handbook of industrial and organizational psychology* (pp. 1175-1199). Chicago: Rand McNally.

Adams, J. S. (1980). Interorganizational processes and organizational boundary activities. In L. L. Cummings & B. M. Staw (Eds.), *Research in organizational behavior* (pp. 321-355). Greenwich, CT: JAI Press.

Alba, R. D. (1982). Taking stock of network analysis: A decade's results. In S. B. Bacharach (Ed.), *Research in the sociology of organizations* (pp. 39-74). Greenwich, CT: JAI Press

Albrecht, T. L., & Ropp, V. A. (1984). Communicating about innovation in networks of three U.S. organizations. *Journal of Communication, 34*(3), 78-91.

Aldrich, H., & Whetten, D. (1981). Organization-sets, action-sets, and networks: Making the most of simplicity. In P. Nystrom & W. Starbuck (Eds.), *Handbook of organizational design* (pp. 385-408). New York: Oxford University Press.

Allen, T. (1977). *Managing the flow of technology.* Cambridge: MIT Press.

Anderson, J. G., & Jay, S. J. (1985). Computers and clinical judgment: The role of physician networks. *Social Science of Medicine, 10,* 969-979

Archer, M. S. (1982). Morphogenesis versus structuration: On combining structure and action. *British Journal of Sociology, 33*(4), 455-483.

Axley, S. R. (1984). Managerial and organizational communication in terms of the conduit metaphor. *Academy of Management Review, 9*(3), 428-437.

Aydin, C. (1989). Occupational adaptation to computerized medical information systems. *Journal of Health and Social Behavior, 30*, 163-179.

Bach, B. W. (1989). The effect of multiplex relationships upon innovation adoption: A reconsideration of Rogers' model. *Communication Monographs, 56*(2), 133-150.

Barley, S. R. (1986). Technology as an occasion for structuring: Evidence from observations of CT scanners and the social ordering of radiology departments. *Administrative Science Quarterly, 31*, 78-108.

Berger, C., & Calabrese, R. J. (1975). Some explorations in initial interaction and beyond: Toward a developmental theory of interpersonal communication. *Human Communication Research, 1*, 99-112.

Bikson, T. K., Eveland, J. D., & Gutek, B. J. (1989). Flexible interactive technologies for multi-person tasks: Current problems and future prospects. In M. H. Olson (Ed.), *Technological support for work group collaboration* (pp. 89-112). Hillsdale, NJ: Lawrence Erlbaum.

Bonacich, P. (1987). Communication networks and collective action. *Social Networks, 9*(4), 389-396.

Buckley, S. (1967). *Sociology and modern systems theory.* Englewood Cliffs, NJ: Prentice-Hall.

Burkhardt, M., & Brass, D. (1989, February). *Technology adaptation: Changes in centrality and power in an organization.* Paper presented at the Ninth Sunbelt Social Networks conference, Tampa Bay, Florida.

Burt, R. (1980). Models of network structure. *Annual Review of Sociology, 6*, 79-141.

Burt, R. (1982). *Toward a structural theory of action: Network models of social structure, perception, and action.* New York: Academic Press.

Burt, R. S. (1987). Social contagion and innovation: Cohesion versus structural equivalence. *American Journal of Sociology, 92*, 1287-1335.

Chaffee, S. H., & Berger, C. R. (1987). Epilogue. In C. R. Berger & S. H. Chaffee (Eds.), *Handbook of communication science* (pp. 893-896). Newbury Park, CA: Sage.

Contractor, N. S., Fulk, J., Monge, P. R., & Singhal, A. (1986). Cultural assumptions that influence the implementation of communication technologies. *Vikalpa, 11*(4), 287-300.

Crane, D. (1969). Social structure in a group of scientists: A test of the "invisible college" hypothesis. *American Sociological Review, 34*, 335-352.

Culnan, M. J., & Markus, M. L. (1987). Information technologies. In F. M. Jablin, L. L. Putnam, K. H. Roberts, & L. W. Porter (Eds.), *Handbook of organizational communication: An interdisciplinary perspective* (pp. 420-444). Newbury Park, CA: Sage.

Daft, R., & Lengel, R. (1986). Organizational information requirements, media richness, and structural design. *Management Science, 32*(5), 554-571.

Danowski, J. A., & Rice, R. E. (1989, May). *Correspondence between users' semantic networks and computer-monitored data on uses of voice mail for messaging versus answering.* Paper presented at the annual meeting of the Information Systems Division of the International Communication Association, San Francisco.

Dhar, V., & Olson, M. H. (1989). Assumptions underlying systems that support work group collaboration. In M. H. Olson (Ed.), *Technological support for work group collaboration* (pp. 33-50). Hillsdale, NJ: Lawrence Erlbaum Associates.

DiMaggio, P., & Powell, W. M. (1983). The iron cage revisited: Institutional isomorphism and collective rationality in organizational fields. *American Sociological Review, 48*, 147-160.

Ebadi, Y., & Utterback, J. (1984). The effect of communication on technological innovation. *Management Science, 30*(5), 572-585.

Eisenberg, E. M. (1984). Ambiguity as strategy in organizational communication. *Communication Monographs, 51*, 227-242.

Eisenberg, E. M., Farace, R. V., Monge, P. R., Bettinghaus, E. P., Kurchner-Hawkins, R., Miller, K. I., & Rothman, L. (1985). Communication linkages in interorganizational systems: Review and synthesis. In B. Dervin & M. Voigt (Eds.), *Progress in communication sciences* (pp. 210-261). Norwood, NJ: Ablex.

Eisenberg, E. M., Monge, P. R., & Miller, K. (1983). Involvement in communication networks as a predictor of organizational commitment. *Human Communication Research, 10*(2), 179-201.

Eisenberg, E. M., & Witten, M. G. (1987). Reconsidering openness in organizational communication. *Academy of Management Review, 12*(3), 418-426.

Erickson, B. H. (1988). The relational basis of attitudes. In B. Wellman & S. D. Berkowitz (Eds.), *Social structures: A network approach* (pp. 99-121). Cambridge: Cambridge University Press.

Eveland, J. D., & Bikson, T. K. (1988). Work group structures and computer support: A field experiment. *ACM Transactions on Office Information Systems, 6*(4), 354-379.

Freeman, L. C. (1979). Centrality in social networks: Conceptual clarification. *Social Networks, 1*, 215-239.

Friedkin, N. E. (1982). Information flow through strong and weak ties in intraorganizational social networks. *Social Networks, 3*, 273-285.

Fulk, J., & Dutton, W. (1985). Videoconferencing as an organizational information system: Assessing the role of electronic meetings. *Systems, Objectives, Solutions, 4*, 105-118.

Fulk, J., Power, J. G., & Schmitz, J. (1986, March). *Communication in organizations via electronic mail: An analysis of behavioral and relational issues.* Paper presented at the meeting of the American Institute of Decision Sciences, Honolulu.

Fulk, J., Steinfield, C. W., Schmitz, J., & Power, J. G. (1987). A social information processing model of media use in organizations. *Communication Research, 14*(5), 529-552.

Galaskiewicz, J., & Wasserman, S. (1988). Mimetic and normative processes within an interorganizational field: An empirical test. *Administrative Science Quarterly, 34*, 454-479.

Gibson, W. (1989, June 15). Rocket Radio. *Rolling Stone Magazine, 554*, pp. 84-87.

Giddens, A. (1984). *The constitution of society: Outline of the theory of structuration.* Cambridge: Polity Press.

Granovetter, M. (1973). The strength of weak ties. *American Journal of Sociology, 78*, 1360-1380.

Granovetter, M. (1982). The strength of weak ties: A network theory revisited. In P. Marsden & N. Lin (Eds.), *Social structure and network analysis* (pp. 105-130). Newbury Park, CA: Sage.

Hiltz, S. R. (1981). *The impact of a computerized conferencing system on scientific research communities.* Newark, NJ: New Jersey Institute of Technology, Computerized Conferencing and Communications Center.

Huber, G. (1982). Organizational information systems: Determinants of their performance and behavior. *Management Science, 28*(2), 138-155.

Huber, G. (1984). The nature and design of post-industrial organizations. *Management Science, 30*(8), 928-951.

Jablin, F., & Krone, K. J. (1987). Organizational assimilation. In C. Berger & S. H. Chaffee (Eds.), *Handbook of communication science* (pp. 711-746). Newbury Park, CA: Sage.

Johansen, R. (1977). Social evaluations of teleconferencing. *Telecommunications Policy, December*, 395-419.

Johansen, R., & DeGrasse, R. (1979). Computer-based teleconferencing: Effects on working patterns. *Journal of Communication, 29*, 30-41.

Johnson, B., & Rice, R. E. (1987). *Managing organizational innovation: The evolution from word processing to office information systems.* New York: Columbia University Press.

Katz, D., & Kahn, R. (1978). *The social psychology of organizations* (2nd ed.). New York: John Wiley.

Kerr, E., & Hiltz, S. R. (1982). *Computer-mediated communication systems: Status and evaluations.* New York: Academic Press.

Kiesler, S. (1986). Thinking ahead: The hidden messages in computer networks. *Harvard Business Review, January-February*, 46-59.

Kling, R., & Scacchi, W. (1982). The web of computing: Computer technology as social organization. *Advances in Computers, 21*, 2-60.

Knoke, D., & Kuklinski, J. H. (1982). *Network analysis.* Newbury Park, CA: Sage.

Krackhardt, D., & Porter, L. (1986). The snowball effect: Turnover embedded in communication networks. *Journal of Applied Psychology, 71*, 50-55

Kraemer, K. L. (1982). Telecommunications/transportation substitution and energy conservation. *Telecommunications Policy, 6*, 39-59.

Leduc, N. (1979). Communicating through computers. *Telecommunications Policy, September*, 235-244.

Lievrouw, L. A., Rogers, E. M., Lowe, C., & Nadel, E. (1987). Triangulation as a research strategy for identifying invisible colleges among biomedical scientists. *Social Networks, 9*, 217-248.

Lincoln, J. R. (1982). Intra- (and inter-) organizational networks. In S. Bacharach (Ed.), *Research in the sociology of organizations* (pp. 1-38). Greenwich, CT: JAI Press.

March, J. G., & Simon, H. A. (1958). *Organizations.* New York: John Wiley.

Markus, L. (1987). Toward a critical mass theory of interactive media: Universal access, interdependence and diffusion. *Communication Research, 14*(5), 491-511.

Markus, M. L., & Robey, D. (1988). Information technology and organizational change: Causal structure in theory and research. *Management Science, 34*(5), 583-598.

Marsden, P. V. (1981). Introducing influence processes into a system of collective decisions. *American Journal of Sociology, 86,* 1203-1235.

Marwell, G., Oliver, P. E., & Prahl, R. (1988). Social networks and collective action: A theory of the critical mass. III. *American Journal of Sociology, 94*(3), 502-534.

McElroy, J. C., & Schrader, C. B. (1986). Attribution theories of leadership and network analysis. *Journal of Management, 12*(3), 351-362.

Mesthene, E. G. (1981). The role of technology in society. In A. H. Teich (Ed.), *Technology and man's future* (pp. 99-129). New York: St. Martin's Press.

Miller, K. I., & Monge, P. R. (1985). Social information and employee anxiety about organizational change. *Human Communication Research, 11*(3), 365-386.

Monge, P. R. (1987). The network level of analysis. In C. R. Berger & S. H. Chaffee (Ed.) *Handbook of communication science* (pp. 239-270). Newbury Park: Sage.

Monge, P. R., & Contractor, N. S. (1987). Communication networks: Measuring techniques. In C. Tardy (Ed.), *A handbook for the study of human communication* (pp. 107-138). Norwood, NJ: Ablex.

Monge, P. R., & Eisenberg, E. M. (1987). Emergent communication networks. In F. M. Jablin, L. L. Putnam, K. H. Roberts, & L. W. Porter (Eds.), *Handbook of organizational communication: An interdisciplinary perspective* (pp. 304-342). Newbury Park, CA: Sage.

Monge, P.R., & Miller, G. R. (1985). Communication networks. In A. Kuper & J. Kuper (Eds.), *The social science encyclopedia* (pp. 130-131). London: Routledge & Kegan Paul.

Ochs (1989). *Language, affect, and culture.* Cambridge: Cambridge University Press.

Olgren, C. H., & Parker, L. A. (1983). *Teleconferencing technology and applications.* Dedham, MA: Artech House.

Oliver, P. E., & Marwell, G. (1988). The paradox of group size in collective action: A theory of the critical mass. II. *American Sociological Review, 53,* 1-8.

Oliver, P. E., Marwell, G., & Teixeira, R. (1985). A theory of the critical mass. I. Interdependence, group heterogeneity, and the production of collective action. *American Journal of Sociology, 91,* 522-556.

Papa, M. J., & Tracy, K. (1988). Communicative indices of employee performance with new technology. *Communication Research, 15*(5), 524-544.

Parks, M. R. (1977). Anomie and close friendship communication networks. *Human Communication Research, 4*, 48-57.

Pelton, C. (1989, July 3). E-mail's message to corporate America. *Information WEEK, 227*, pp. 12-14.

Pennings, J. M. (1980). *Interlocking directorates.* San Francisco: Jossey-Bass.

Pfeffer, J. (1982). *Organizations and organization theory.* Marshfield, MA: Pitman.

Pfeffer, J., & Salancik, G. (1978). *The external control of organizations.* New York: Harper & Row.

Pool, I. S., Decker, C., Dizard, S., Israel, S., Rubin, P., & Weinstein, B. (1981). Foresight and hindsight: The case of the telephone. In I. S. Pool (Ed.), *Social impacts of the telephone* (pp. 127-157). Cambridge: MIT Press.

Poole, M. S., Seibold, D. R., & McPhee, R. D. (1986). A structurational approach to theory-building in group decision-making research. In R. Y. Hirokawa & M. S. Poole (Eds.), *Communication and group decision-making* (pp. 237-264). Newbury Park, CA: Sage.

Ranson, S., Hinings, B., & Greenwood, R. (1980). The structuring of organizational structures. *Administrative Science Quarterly, 25*, 1-17.

Rice, R. E. (1982). Communication networking in computer conferencing systems: A longitudinal study of group roles and system structure. In M. Burgoon (Ed.), *Communication yearbook 6* (pp. 925-944). Newbury Park, CA: Sage.

Rice, R. E. (1988). Collection and analysis of data from communication system networks. In R. Allen (Ed.), *Proceedings of the conference on office information systems* (pp. 134-141). Association for Computing Machinery.

Rice, R. E., & Borgman, C. (1983). The use of computer-monitored data in information science and communication research. *Journal of the American Society for Information Science, 34*, 247-256.

Rice, R. E., & Case, D. (1983). Electronic messaging systems in the university; A description of use and utility. *Journal of Communication, 33*(1), 131-152.

Rice, R. E., & Contractor, N. S. (in press). Conceptualizing effects of office information systems. *Decision Sciences.*

Rice, R. E., Grant, A., Schmitz, J., & Torobin, J. (1988). *Critical mass and social influence: A network approach to predicting the adoption use and outcomes of electronic messaging.* Unpublished manuscript, University of Southern California, Annenberg School of Communications, Los Angeles.

Riley, P. (1983). A structurationist account of political cultures. *Administrative Science Quarterly, 28*, 414-438.

Robertson, D. C. (1988). *Social determinants of information systems use.* Unpublished manuscript, Massachusetts Institute of Technology, Sloan School of Management, Cambridge, Massachusetts.

Rogers, E. M. (1983). *Diffusion of innovations.* New York: Free Press.

Rogers, E. M. (1987). Progress, problems and prospects for network research: Investigating relationships in the age of electronic communication technologies. *Social Networks, 9,* 285-310.

Rogers, E. M. (1988). Information technologies: How organizations are changing. In G. M. Goldhaber & G. Barnett (Eds.), *Handbook of organizational communication* (pp. 437-452). Norwood, NJ: Ablex.

Rogers, E. M., & Kincaid, D. L. (1981). *Communication networks: Toward a new paradigm for research.* New York: Free Press.

Salancik, G. R., & Pfeffer, J. (1978). A social information approach to job attitudes and task design. *Administrative Science Quarterly, 23,* 224-252.

Seghers, F., Rothfeder, J., & Hof, R. D. (1989, February 20). Electronic mail: Neither rain, nor sleet, nor software. *Business Week,* pp. 36-37.

Sherman, J. D., Smith, H., & Mansfield, E. R. (1986). The impact of emergent network structure on organizational socialization. *Journal of Applied Behavioral Science, 22,* 53-63.

Short, J., Williams, E., & Christie, B. (1976). *The social psychology of telecommunications.* London: Wiley.

Sproull, L., & Kiesler, S. (1986). Reducing social context cues: Electronic mail in organizational communication. *Management Science, 32*(11), 1492-1512.

Steinfield, C. W. (in press). Computer-mediated communications in the organization: Using electronic mail at Xerox. In B. Sypher (Ed.), *Case studies in organizational communication.* New York: Gilford Press.

Tichy, N. M (1981). Networks in organizations. In P. Nystrom & W. Starbuck (Eds.), *Handbook of organizational design* (pp. 225-249). New York: Oxford University Press.

Turkle, S. (1984). *The second self: Computers and the human spirit.* New York: Simon & Schuster.

Tushman, M. L., & Scanlan, T. J. (1981) Boundary spanning individuals: Their role in information transfer and their antecedents. *Academy of Management Journal, 24* 289-305.

Van de Ven, A., & Walker, G. (1981). *The dynamics of interorganizational coordination (Discussion paper 110).* Center for the study of Organizational Innovations, University of Pennsylania, the Wharton School.

Walker, G. (1985). Network position and cognition in a computer software firm. *Administrative Science Quarterly, 30,* 103-130.

Watson, R. W., DeSanctis, G. L., & Poole, M. S. (1988). Using a GDSS to facilitate group consensus: Some intended and unintended consequences. *MIS Quarterly, 12*(3), 463-478.

Weick, K. E. (1984). Theoretical assumptions and research methodology selection. In F. W. McFarlan (Ed.), *Proceedings of the The Information Systems Research Challenge* (pp. 111-132). Boston: Harvard Business School Press.

Wellman, B. (1983). Network analysis: Some basic principles. In R. Collins (Ed.), *Sociological theory 1983* (pp. 155-200). San Francisco: Jossey-Bass.

Wellman, B. (1988). Structural analysis: From method and metaphor to theory and substance. In B. Wellman & S. D. Berkowitz (Eds.), *Social structures: A network approach* (pp. 19-61). Cambridge: Cambridge University Press.

Wentworth, W. (1980). *Context and understanding: An inquiry into socialization theory.* New York: Elsevier.

Whetten, D. (1981). Interorganizational relations: A review of the field. *Journal of Higher Education, 52,* 1-28.

Williams, F., Rice, R. E., & Rogers, E. M. (1988). *Research methods and the new media.* New York: Free Press.

Zeitz, G. (1980). Interorganizational dialectics. *Administrative Science Quarterly, 25,* 72-88.

Zuboff, S. (1988). *In the age of the smart machine.* New York: Basic Books.

MARSHALL SCOTT POOLE
GERARDINE DeSANCTIS

8. Understanding the Use of Group Decision Support Systems: The Theory of Adaptive Structuration

Technologies for Groups

People spend an inordinate amount of time in meetings. One study estimated that there is a meeting every minute in the average large corporation. And this time is often badly spent—for many groups, meetings are dreaded and tiresome events. Bad jokes and bon mots chronicle this frustration: "A meeting is a cul de sac down which promising young ideas are lured and quietly strangled."

It is no surprise, then, that new computer-based technologies are being developed to aid meetings. A group decision support system (GDSS) combine communication, computer, and decision technologies to support the decision-making and related activities of work groups. Communication technologies available within a GDSS include electronic messaging, teleconferencing, and store and forward facilities. Computer technologies include multiuser operating systems, fourth generation languages, and graphics facilities. Decision support technologies include agenda setting, decision-modeling methods (such as decision trees or risk analysis), structured group methods (such as the Nominal Group and Delphi techniques), and rules for directing group discussion (such as parliamentary procedure) (DeSanctis & Gallupe, 1987).

The development of computer systems to support work groups represents an extension of systems such as personal computers, wordprocessors, and data management systems intended for the support of individual work. Traditional systems of this sort were designed around the notion of person-machine interaction, as opposed to person-to-person interaction. Unlike

Authors' Note: This work was supported by National Science Foundation grant SES-8715565 to the authors. The views expressed herein do not reflect the opinions of the research sponsors.

traditional systems, interpersonal communication is of central importance to the design and operation of social technologies such as GDSSs, both communication mediated by the technologies and the social interaction that forms the context for adoption and application of the technology. This introduces an added layer of complexity to research and explanation of GDSS effects, because we must figure social processes such as interpretation, restructuring, and negotiation into our theories. This chapter attempts to outline a theory of social technologies, with special attention to group decision support systems. The remainder of this section presents key variables describing GDSS configurations and considers the requirements for an adequate theory of GDSS impacts. The second section outlines a theory of social technologies, the theory of adaptive structuration, and its major constructs. The third section explicates some of the theory's predictions. Finally, the chapter covers some implications of the theory for research and practice.

Group Decision Support Systems

The fundamental goal of a GDSS is to support collaborative work activities such as idea creation, message exchange, project planning, document preparation, mutual product creation, and joint planning and decision making. Kraemer and King (1988) and Johansen (1988) present extensive reviews of available and potential GDSSs. Here we will mention just two examples. The SAMM[1] system (DeSanctis et al., 1987), developed at the University of Minnesota, is designed to promote participative, democratic decision making in 3- to-16-person groups. Designed to be operated by the group itself, SAMM provides public and private messaging and a number of decision tools such as Problem Definition, Idea or Solution Evaluation, Stakeholder Analysis, and Nominal Group Technique. SAMM has been used by a number of groups in government and business and is being adapted for use in computer conferences. The PLEXSYS system, developed at the University of Arizona (Nunamaker, Applegate, & Konsynski, 1987), can be used with large as well as smaller groups. It is operated by a facilitator and members interact largely through entering comments into the system's multifaceted text-processing system. PLEXSYS provides facilities for the analysis and discussion of ill-structured problems, as well as decision aids such as Nominal Group Technique and Stakeholder Analysis. PLEXSYS has been implemented in a number of large corporations and universities.

GDSSs can be described in terms of (a) the physical arrangement of the groups they support and (b) the degree of intervention into interpersonal communication that they provide (DeSanctis & Gallupe, 1985, 1987).

Physical Arrangement. There are GDSS implementations that support groups whose members are *dispersed*, working in their separate conference rooms, offices, homes, or other locations. And there are GDSSs that support *face-to-face* meetings that occur in one physical setting, such as a conference or board room. GDSSs may be further distinguished depending on whether they support *smaller* working groups or *larger* groups whose members may not know each other well. The Local Area Decision Network supports smaller groups, typically located in the same office building and working together on the same project or task. Systems such as Coordinator and others operating on local area networks (Alexander, 1988) are intended for project or office work groups who must structure their interactions to achieve specific work goals. The Computer-Mediated Conference supports a large number of people who are physically distant from one another but must work on common tasks. The Legislative Session supports larger groups whose members meet face-to-face; in these settings the GDSS may regulate member-to-member communication a good deal. The bulk of current GDSS research is centered on the Decision Room, which is the electronic equivalent of the traditional meeting. The meeting occurs in a conference room which is equipped with computer hardware and software for each meeting participant.

Level of Communication Intervention. Level 1 GDSSs provide technical features aimed at removing common communication barriers, such as large screens for instantaneous display of ideas, voting solicitation and compilation, anonymous input of ideas and preferences, and electronic message exchange between members. Level 1 features are found in some electronic-mail systems and in most computer-supported conference rooms. Level 2 GDSSs provide greater structure to the group through decision modeling and group decision techniques. Level 2 thus represents an enhanced GDSS, as opposed to Level 1, which is a communication medium only. Budget allocation models, utility and probability assessment models, and social judgment techniques are examples of Level 2 GDSS features. Level 3 GDSSs are characterized by machine-induced group communication patterns and can include expert advice in the selecting and arranging of rules to be applied during interpersonal communication. Hiltz and Turoff's (1985) description of computer-mediated communication systems that actively filter and structure information exchange are a type of Level 3 system.

An important implication of the notion of intervention levels is that a GDSS is not merely an additional communication channel for the group. A GDSS also provides communication patterns, decision methods, and alternative sequences for accomplishing group work. As such, these technologies not only create new and increased communication linkages among individuals

(Rice, 1984), but they also provide alternative ways of performing group work—different decision paths, new mechanisms for influence and conflict resolution, and systematic idea management.

Understanding GDSS Impacts

These possibilities stimulate several questions. How do the new group technologies change group interaction and outcomes? What other variables, individual and contextual, interact with or moderate technology effects? Are group technologies fundamentally different from individual technologies such as word processing or decision support systems? What can the study of group-technology use tell us about technology in general? Group use of technology may highlight features of the human-technology interaction that would go unnoticed in studies of individual use systems.

A striking feature of GDSS studies is the lack of consistency in their results. Two popular outcome variables, decision quality and level of member participation, illustrate this. Some studies have found that GDSSs encourage greater equality of member participation (e.g., Dubrovsky, 1985; Siegal, Dubrovsky, Kiesler, & McGuire, 1986), while others suggest they do not (e.g., Beauclair, 1987; Watson, DeSanctis, & Poole, 1988). Some studies have found performance improvements with groups using GDSSs (Gallupe, DeSanctis, & Dickson, 1988; Steeb & Johnston, 1981), while others find no meaningful differences in performance (Easton, Vogel, & Nunamaker, 1989; Zigurs, Poole, & DeSanctis, 1988). Similar inconsistencies have been found with other new technologies such as electronic mail systems (Kiesler, 1986; Rice, 1984).

These discrepancies can be explained in several ways. Differences in study design, tasks, or instrumentation is one possibility. Diversity in GDSS design across studies may also explain observed differences, although some replications with different GDSSs have yielded quite similar results (Watson et al., 1988; Easton et al., 1989). This essay will posit a different explanation: *Observed differences are attributable to the fact that various groups use the GDSSs differently.* On the surface, this seems obvious. Yet, if we probe more deeply, it becomes apparent that use of technologies, especially by groups, is a complicated issue that has not received adequate attention. The key to straightening out the tangle of findings concerning GDSSs and other technologies is to develop theories with adequate pictures of individual and social technology usage. To find our way to an adequate concept of use, we must reconsider our conceptions of technology.

Traditionally, technology has been thought of as something independent of the user, as an object or tool. But an important school of thought, represented by Heidegger (1977) and Ong (1982) claims otherwise. These thinkers regard technologies as inherently "social" in nature. Social processes create the conditions for the evolution of technology. Society is the matrix in which the technology and its application are embedded. There is a mutual determinism in that technologies also sustain and change society. As Heim (1987) notes, modern society and technology are so bound together that it is impossible to sort out which causes which.

There is also a complex interaction between technologies and users. While increasing user capabilities, technologies also channel and shape action. Writing on a word processor is very different from writing with pencil and pad. Heim (1987) and Ong (1982) have argued that new writing technologies change the process of thinking. It also seems likely that technologies such as GDSSs will change the nature of social thought and interaction. On the other hand, the user plays an important part in realizing technologies. No matter what features are designed into a system, users mediate technological effects, adapting systems to their needs, resisting them, or refusing to use them at all. The operative technology is determined by patterns of appropriation and use by human beings. Johnson and Rice (1985) indicate how word processing is "reinvented" by users, resulting in very different systems and different practices organized around those systems, with basically the same hardware and software. Human use makes a technology what it is. This implies what Giddens (1979) has termed a "dialectic of control"—the social technology shapes the user, but the user likewise shapes the technology, exerting some degree of control over its use and meaning in social action. User and technology are melded into an operating unit, and it is hard to tell where one leaves off and the other begins.

Notwithstanding this interplay of technologies, societies, and users, we tend to objectify technologies in our speech and writing (Finlay, 1987). We regard technologies as outside ourselves, objects to which we must somehow relate. Objectification is useful, in some respects. Taking this attitude helps us learn and master the technology, because we cast it up as an object to be manipulated and routinized. Objectification also helps us identify and understand the impact of the technology on our lives and on society; if we treat technology as an object, the contrast between "it" and "us" helps us understand its effects and implications.

Along with objectifying technologies, there is a tendency to decontextualize them, that is, to ignore the situation and circumstances surrounding their use. Finlay shows how writers tend to treat technologies such as word processing or GDSSs as general entities, with an identity all their own. So we read articles about "groupware" or "the word processing revolution" with no reference to specific adaptations. This ignores the fact that any technology is used in a specific context—for particular purposes, with particular users, at a particular place, subject to particular problems. Adaptation to these contexts often alters the nature of the technology, as Johnson and Rice (1985) suggest in their study of word processing.

Objectification and decontextualization conceal the social nature of technologies. Continually bombarded by such discourse, we forget that users constitute and give meaning to technologies. Until applied by a user in a specific context, a GDSS or any other technology is simply dead matter.

A theory of technological impacts must spell out the social aspects of technology and how context enters into use. But there are two ways in which we might take context into account. First, context can be regarded as a set of independent variables, themselves independent of the user and technology (McGrath, 1984). This approach runs into the same problems faced by attempts to separate user and technology. Contextual variables such as task and the larger organizational environment are mediated, reinterpreted, and reconstructed by users. The approach we will take attempts to show how context is "constructed" into the social process of technology use. The theoretical framework we will advance is called the *theory of adaptive structuration*. It draws on scholarship in social theory (Giddens, 1979; Bordieu, 1978; Garfinkel, 1968), literary studies (Barthes, 1974), and communication (Poole, Seibold, & McPhee, 1985), which explores how human beings actively structure the social world and how physical and social contexts enter into action.

Adaptive Structuration Theory

Groups are organized around common social practices: making decisions, accomplishing work, socializing, joking, teaching members skills and norms, fighting, establishing power and status relations, and meeting individual needs for sympathy, acceptance, self-development. Revolutionary though they promise to be, technologies such as GDSS will not suddenly change the nature of groups. The GDSS will be used to pursue these same practices, to make decisions, to support power moves, to show off, just as any other social resource would be.

The key to understanding group practices and how GDSSs might influence them is through analysis of structures and the role they play in group interaction. The term *structure* is used in a special sense here, which can best be understood in the distinction Giddens (1979) makes between system and structure. A *system* is a social entity such as a group, pursuing various practices that give rise to observable patterns of relations, such as the pecking order often seen in groups or organizations. *Structures* are the rules and resources that actors use to generate and sustain this system. For example, it might be the rule that older members with special experience are deferred to by others in a group. This rule enables them to talk more and to set up and sustain a pecking order with themselves at the top. Systems have patterns such as pecking orders, because of structuring processes. The observable system is of interest and can influence structures, but the structure is what does the real work.

The possible impact of GDSSs and other social technologies can be understood in these terms: they provide rules, such as voting routines, and resources, such as databases, which can be used by groups in the structuring process. What is important in determining GDSS effects is not the hardware or software per se, but the structures this technology promotes in the group. In our research (Poole & DeSanctis, 1989) we have distinguished two aspects of technological structures: their *spirit*, the general goals and attitudes the technology aims to promote (such as democratic decision making), and the specific *structural features* built into the system (such as anonymous input of ideas, or one vote per group member). A *structural feature* is a specific rule or resource that operates in a group, whereas the *spirit* is the principle of coherence that holds a set of rules and resources together. Obviously, the features of a GDSS are designed to promote its spirit. However, features are functionally independent of spirit and may be used in ways contrary to it by some groups.

But simply defining structures is not enough: we must show how structures enter into active use. The key to this is the concept of *structuration*, which refers to the process by which systems are produced and reproduced through members' use of rules and resources. This definition rests on several key assumptions and distinctions. First, not only is the system produced and reproduced through structuration, but the structures themselves are too. Structures have a dual nature: they are both the medium and the outcome of action. They are the medium of action because members draw on structures to interact. They are its outcome because rules and resources exist only through being applied and oriented to in interaction—they have no reality independent of the social practices they constitute. Hence, when a group uses a voting procedure built into a GDSS, it is employing these rules to act, but—more than this—it is reminding itself that these rules exist, working out a way of using the rules, perhaps creating a special version of them; in short, it is producing and reproducing the rules for its present and future use. So it is really somewhat misleading to focus on structures as though they were static entities. Structures exist only in a continuous process of structuration. A voting feature does not, for all practical purposes, exist for this group if the group never employs it nor makes it a regular part of its procedure.

One implication of this is that to study structuration we must focus directly on group interaction processes. Interaction is the locus of structuration. Through the various social processes that occur in interaction, each group produces and reproduces its own structures-in-use. Hence, the contextual features that influence group interaction play a direct and critical role in the structuring process.

Where do structures come from? In some cases, they are created by the group, but more often they are appropriated by the group from larger social institutions. In the case of GDSSs, structures such as voting, scratchpads, and idea generation are taken from general social knowledge of how decisions might be made and built into the system. This makes them available and possibly salient to members. Of course, members also bring in other structures when using a GDSS; a member familiar with parliamentary procedure, for example, might try to combine it with a GDSS. Each group forms its particular amalgam of structural features which it employs in its practices. Giddens (1979) calls these appropriations of general social structures into concrete situations *modalities of structuration*. Here we will simply call them *appropriations*.

The process of structuration accounts for stability of structural features as well as their change. Features are stable if the group appropriates them in a consistent way, reproducing them in similar form over time. This might happen, for example, if members emphasized learning the spirit behind the GDSS very thoroughly and dedicated themselves to using features in a way consistent with it. In the same vein, the group may intentionally or unintentionally change a structural feature; reproduction does not necessarily imply replication. Structures may change gradually, as in a group which, through a series of small, imperceptible stages, elevates one member to "system manager" of a GDSS originally designed to promote equal participation. They may also change when one structure is merged with another, for example, when a group accustomed to parliamentary procedure uses a multipurpose GDSS to put Roberts' Rules of Order into practice. Structures might also be eliminated through reproduction; overuse of voting facilities may lead groups to reject them ultimately. The rate at which these changes occur varies widely: they may come about in one fell swoop, or they may occur very gradually.

The fact that structuring occurs in interaction implies that users may plan and control this process. However, their control is limited in three respects. First, the context places limitations on how technologies may be used. The type of work a group must do, the amount of time it has, the group's power in the larger organization, membership composition, and other contextual features strongly influence how structures can by employed and, hence, how they are produced and reproduced. If a group has to make a complex decision quickly, for instance, it may be inspired to change GDSS procedures that it would follow faithfully, given enough time. Second, the social system and its interconnections are often so complex that users cannot fully grasp the implications of their actions. In such cases, the system may "get away" from members, reproducing structural features in unanticipated ways. For example, a democratically inclined leader may attempt to help followers learn how to use a GDSS in order to empower them. However, this could lead to the unintended consequence of even more dependence on the leader, whom members regard as an "expert" on the system. Finally, users' level of knowledge and self-awareness about the technology and group processes places limitations on what they can do and the degree to which they are able to control the structuring process.

Both technology and context, then, affect group outcomes through their influence on the structuring processes by which these outcomes are produced. A theory to explain technology effects should take the following factors into account: (1) The nature of the technology and the structures it supplies; (2) the context and the structures it supplies, and how contextual factors influence the use and reproduction of structures; and (3) the nature of the interactive structuring process itself, including how users appropriate and reproduce structures. Figure 8.1 summarizes these relationships. The next few pages will specify some of the dimensions of each of these three variable sets which our research suggests are important.

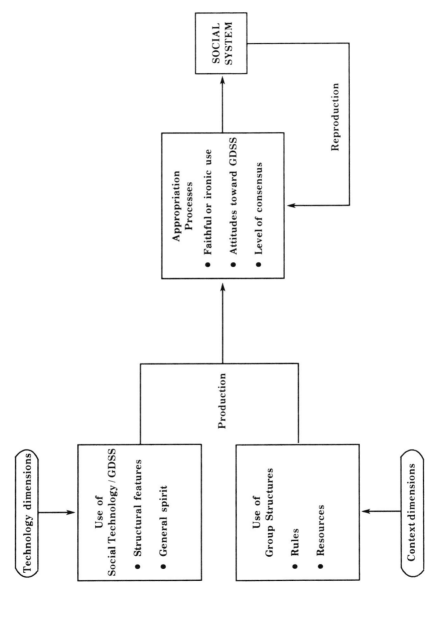

Figure 8.1 An Overview of the Adaptive Structuration Process

182

Dimensions of Technology

While design of GDSSs might vary along many dimensions, five factors that might influence group interaction are:

1. *Face-to-face versus dispersed meeting support.* This influences the quality of communication in the group. When the system is designed for dispersed meeting support, the GDSS is the only channel of communication available, reducing the richness of the information conveyed.
2. *Level of sophistication of the GDSS*: Level 1, Level 2, or Level 3.
3. *Degree of structure.* The extent to which the GDSS imposes its procedures on the group is an important determinant of group use.
4. *Degree of member control over the system.* Some systems are designed so that members directly control use of the system, whereas others require a facilitator or leader to manage use of the system.
5. *Asynchronous versus synchronous meeting support.* When members all meet at the same time, they directly regulate their own interaction. However, when members meet asynchronously, as in a computer conference, the system must regulate their interaction.

Dimensions of Context

McGrath (1984) provides an extensive analysis of contextual factors that influence group processes. Here we will focus on two dimensions that seem particularly important: nature of the group's task and degree of value agreement.

The *nature of a group's task* has been shown to exert powerful effects on group behavior and outcomes. There are many ways to classify tasks. Key task variables include: (1) *Degree of causal knowledge*, the degree to which decision makers have reliable knowledge about the effects of various possible actions, or can identify underlying cause-effect relationships with a high degree of certainty. This determines the degree of task difficulty. (2) The *operations* the task requires the group to perform. McGrath's (1984) task circumplex defines several operation types, including choosing, creating, and negotiating.

Degree of agreement on values is the extent to which members of the group agree on standards for judging an acceptable choice. It determines the conflict potential a decision has for a group. With high agreement on values chances of conflict are minimized, and the group (ideally) can focus on optimizing its performance. Low levels of agreement present a more fragile situation in which group members must manage conflict in addition to searching for a quality decision.

Other contextual factors might also be considered, including the group's power structure, leadership, group composition, and the degree of time pressure on the group.

The Nature of Structuring Interaction

Group interaction—how the group coordinates members' activities, manages conflict, and does its work—determines the nature of group products. The theory of adaptive structuration highlights an additional role for interaction in group practices: it is the locus for the group's appropriation and reproduction of both technology-based and nontechnology structures for its work.

Appropriation may be defined as the mode or fashion in which a group uses, adapts, and reproduces a structure. In a detailed analysis of appropriation, Poole and DeSanctis (1989) note that appropriation can be studied at several different levels of analysis: (1) as it occurs in the give-and-take of microlevel interaction, which determines the immediate system use; (2) in terms of global appropriation habits which groups develop after using a technology for some time; and (3) in terms of general social norms concerning use which hold throughout an organization or society. The concern of this essay is with microlevel and global appropriations by a single group.

At each level of analysis we can trace the mode in which groups appropriate GDSSs. There are at least three dimensions to modes of appropriation. Methods for measuring these dimensions are discussed in Poole and De Sanctis (1989), which offers a more detailed discussion of appropriation.

The first dimension of mode of appropriation involves whether the group is using the technology *faithfully* or *ironically*. As we noted above, the structure supplied by a GDSS can be described in terms of its spirit and its specific features. In appropriating and reproducing the GDSS structure, a group has four possibilities: (1) it may stick closely to both the spirit and the specific operations; for example, for a GDSS intended to promote member participation, the group might adhere to the letter of all procedures; (2) it may act in a way consistent with the spirit, but change and reinterpret operations; for the same GDSS, a group might use the scratchpad feature to gather opinions, but refuse to use voting features, on the grounds that votes reduce participation; (3) it may violate the spirit of the structure but retain its operations, using them in unintended ways (a group might use a majority vote to browbeat other members into agreement); or (4) it may alter both the spirit and operations of a structure; a group with the same GDSS might be taken over by a manager who uses voting to identify dissenters and pressure them into line. Options 1 and 2 are *faithful* appropriations, whereas options 3 and 4 represent *ironic* appropriations.

Related to this first dimension is a second, the *attitudes* the group has toward the GDSS. These set the tone for system usage and can reinforce productive or counterproductive trends in a group's experience with the GDSS. One critical attitude is the group's *level of comfort* with the technology, its confidence and ease in use of the system (Sambamurthy, 1988). *Degree of respect* for the technology is another important attitude. Some groups come to value the technology and presume it will be useful, while others conclude the GDSS has little value and distracts them from more important issues. Level of comfort and degree of respect determine the group's general approach to the GDSS and, in some measure, whether the group pursues its applications with sufficient vigor and confidence to carry them off.

The third dimension of appropriation mode is the *level of consensus* on the appropriation. Only when there is a fairly high level of consensus among a substantial proportion of group members does appropriation on the global or normative levels develop. If a group fails to converge on a common appropriation it may experience difficulty in coordinating member efforts.

Predictions

This theory allows us to derive predictions of how context and technology combine to affect structuration in user groups and how structural appropriation processes, in turn, affect group outcomes. Poole and DeSanctis (1987) present a lengthy list of hypotheses. For purposes of illustration, six predictions are presented here, along with relevant research results. They utilize only a few of the constructs defined in previous sections, but they illustrate the basic pattern of predictions the theory yields. All are based on the basic assumption of structurational theory: contextual and technology effects on group processes and outcomes are mediated by the interactive structuring process, as reflected in the group's mode of appropriation. There has been relatively little research on GDSS or other technological appropriation. Therefore, any results cited are not meant to prove the predictions, but merely to offer tentative support and justification. Future research by the Minnesota GDSS project and elsewhere will provide more definitive tests.

The first five predictions concern the effects of technology and context on structuring processes, and the final prediction concerns the effects of these appropriation processes on group outcomes. From the preceding discussion, it should be evident that appropriation processes are, of course, a function of the group's particular interaction dynamics. Consequently, we would not expect *all* groups to respond precisely as anticipated by these propositions. They do not depict determinations, but rather tendencies introduced into the structuring process.

Effects of Technology and Context on Structural Appropriation

In characterizing appropriation processes, it is useful to define a profile of a "stable" appropriation as a norm for comparison. A stable appropriation is one that is likely to promote the intended effects of a technology; it has a distinctive profile on three dimensions—the group makes a faithful appropriation, has high respect for and comfort with the technology, and has a high level of consensus on use. This is the way in which designers generally assume systems will be used. Other profiles of appropriation (e.g., when the group is not comfortable with the system or when it appropriates the system ironically) may lead to inconsistent or even harmful technological impacts.

Prediction 1: *Some GDSS designs are more conducive to stable appropriations than others.*

In particular, high structure and Level 2 GDSSs will tend to create faithful appropriations, and higher levels of respect, comfort, and consensus than will low structure or Level 1 GDSSs. High structure GDSSs constrain the group's use and leave fewer options for deviation than do low structure systems. DeSanctis, Donofrio, Sambamurthy, & Poole (1989) found lower variance in member perceptions of group process with high than with low structure GDSSs, supporting this prediction. A Level 2 system operates on data relevant to the group's work, thereby encouraging the group to use the system as it stands; with a Level 1 system, the group must decide how to reduce, integrate or otherwise manage data generated via Level 1 features, leaving members free to improvise and change the system. Sambamurthy (1988) found that groups using Level 2 GDSSs had higher levels of comfort than those with Level 1 GDSSs, providing partial support for this hypothesis.

Prediction 2: *The greater the knowledge members have of the GDSS's spirit, the more faithful their appropriation.*

Training in the use of GDSSs often emphasizes details of use rather than general philosophy. Learning to use features is important, but just as important is learning of the spirit behind the structures. Belief in this spirit can lead the group to enforce it and to improvise in line with the spirit. DeSanctis et al. (1989) manipulated the type of training groups were given prior to using a Level 1 system. Three treatment groups were given instructions in the mechanics of how to access and manipulate computer screen information. But one experimental condition was advised to follow a strict meeting agenda that included both a rational, democratic problem solving approach and consensus-oriented discussion rules which presented a "spirit" or philosophy of system use. A second condition was given the discussion rules and, separately, detailed instructions on systm use. The third was given no advice on the spirit of the system, but only instructions on system use. The three conditions presented different information to the group regarding the "spirit" of the technology. The first and second conditions, which taught the group the spirit of the system, obtained significantly higher consensus levels than the third.

Prediction 3:   *GDSSs will surface group conflicts, but a Level 2 GDSS will enable the group to handle conflict more effectively than will a Level 1 GDSS. Hence, consensus on appropriation will be more likely to be reproduced with a Level 2 GDSS.*

A Level 1 GDSS provides facilities for open expression of ideas and opinion and can result in member awareness of conflict (Gallupe et al., 1988; Watson et al., 1988). The decision models and techniques in a Level 2 GDSS should provide the group with tools for constructive management of conflict. In his study comparing a Level 1 and Level 2 GDSS, Sambamurthy (1988) attributed higher consensus in the Level 2 experimental condition to the ability of decision techniques to aid in conflict management. Poole, Holmes, & DeSanctis (1988), in a detailed interaction analysis of 40 group sessions, found that Level 1 GDSSs were less effective at managing conflict than "control" groups using a manual version of the structure built into the GDSS.

Prediction 4:   *Appropriation of the GDSS depends on the behavior of the group leader, particularly his or her willingness to act in a manner consistent with the spirit of the technology.*

In case studies of face-to-face meetings in the IDS Capture Lab, Mantei (1988) provided evidence that the actions of a group leader can strongly influence members' response to the GDSS and their behavior during meetings. Where the leader sits, his or her stance and movement with respect to the large viewing screen, and suggestions about how to use the technology can meaningfully affect group interaction. Dickson, Robinson, Heath, & Lee

(1989) noted the same pattern in student teams using a GDSS. Group members tended to resist, accept, or act neutral toward the technology depending on the comments and actions of the influence leader in the group.

Prediction 5:   *Task and agreement on values will interact with level and structure of the GDSS to influence how the group appropriates the GDSS.*

In general, favorable conditions (high causal knowledge; high agreement on values) would seem to favor explicit, direct appropriation of GDSS structures. On the other hand, low causal knowledge, low agreement situations are less organized and more ambiguous; members may tend to improvise and advocate different approaches to the problem, resulting in greater likelihood of less stable appropriation profiles. In addition, if members prefer a GDSS configuration, we would expect them to appropriate it more faithfully with greater comfort, respect, and consensus. Under favorable conditions, members will be more responsive to a Level 1, low-structure GDSSs that constrains them as little as possible and facilitates interaction. On the other hand, under unfavorable conditions, members will want a Level 2 GDSSs, because the structure reduces their uncertainty.

Effects of Structural Appropriation on Group Outcomes

Adaptive structuration theory implies that predictions about the effects of GDSSs, positive and negative, on group outcomes are not determinate. That is, predicted effects will emerge only if group interaction facilitates them, and this depends on the nature of the group's appropriation of the technology. Thus, there is a "double contingency": effects of GDSSs on group outcomes depend on (1) the nature of the GDSS design and contextual variables, and (2) whether group appropriation processes are well-suited to the technology and contextual demands placed on the group. This double contingency can be expressed as:

Given GDSS design and other contextual conditions, $n_1 \ldots n_k$, *and* stable group appropriation processes, *then* predicted outcomes of GDSS use will result.

This proposition emphasizes the mediating effects of appropriation on GDSS outcomes. Outcomes of interest include: quality of the group's judgment, plan, or decision; member consensus on the group's decision; and member satisfaction with the meeting process and the group's decision.

Prediction 6:   *The more stable the group's appropriation process, the more predictable outcomes of GDSS use will be.*

A GDSS has its best chance to channel a group's work in intended directions when group interaction provides no interference, that is, when there is a consensus on faithful use of a system members are comfortable with and respect. Conversely, if groups struggle with the technology and experience frustration in adapting it to their work needs, or if they have a conflict over how to apply the system, the GDSS is unlikely to produce the results for which it is designed. Efforts to channel the group's appropriation toward stable appropriation—a high structure agenda, level 2 structural features, effective training in the spirit and features of the GDSS, a perceptive leader—will improve the likelihood of predictable outcomes, that is, outcomes in line with deterministic propositions. In a study of conflict management in 13 groups using the SAMM GDSS, Poole et al. (1988) attempted to predict group effectiveness based on how groups appropriated the system. They observed that six groups appropriated the system in ways that were expected to promote positive outcomes, and seven adapted it in ways that should encourage negative outcomes or no net benefit. These predictions proved to be quite accurate, using increase in consensus level as an indicator of productive outcomes. The results of this study lend support to the notion that a GDSS does not have a direct, determinant effect on outcomes, but that individual patterns of appropriation mediates this effect. The importance of usage patterns in determining GDSS effects have also been noted by Mantei (1988), Sambamurthy (1988), and Nunamaker et al. (1987).

Conclusion

Adaptive structuration theory provides a model for understanding group use of technologies. Although there is much anecdotal evidence, there has been little direct research on appropriation. Our program of research is still in its early phases. The experimental results described in the previous section have been based on controlled experiments conducted in a decision room. In the future, we plan to study dispersed group meetings, compare synchronous with asynchronous conferences, and begin to examine in greater detail the effects of Level 2 GDSSs on group appropriation processes and outcomes.

Adaptive structuration theory emphasizes the importance of group interaction processes in determining group outcomes. It helps to explain why actual behavior in the context of technology frequently differs from the impacts intended by designers. For researchers, the theory implies that study of technology effects must take into account the unique ways in which people respond to the contextual demands surrounding the technology and that group interaction is a critical mediator in the ultimate effects of new technologies on organizations. Uneven and inconsistent results across studies may be the product of differential appropriations. The theory also implies a further complication, which this essay has not developed: The group's context influences outcomes not only by influencing the structuration process, but also by providing structures for the group's work. For example, groups form task representations that they use to plan and guide their work. But these structures too are produced and reproduced in interaction, and so they may change. Hence, context is structured and restructured in the same recursive process that shapes technology impacts. It is necessary to take this into account in order to predict outcomes.

For designers and users of technology, the theory calls for attention to the manner in which people *use* systems as critical to their success. Some technologies may work very well for some people, but not for others. When people struggle with a new technology, the solution may not always be to change the system but to explore ways in which to promote effective use of the technology, through training, advice giving, leadership, or the addition of structures that limit the possibility for misuse.

Training and explanation of the system offers one way to influence how groups structure it into their work. Results so far imply that training in the system's spirit or philosophy is more important than training in details about system features. To the extent that technology metaphors are provided in training and documentation (e.g., "the GDSS is an electronic chalkboard," "the GDSS is an electronic mediator"), designers should be sensitive to the spirit conveyed in these images and possible limitations put on user's interpretations of the system. Metaphors provide additional structures for users that may mediate or change GDSS appropriation. Of course, other structures that members bring in may alter the structuring process. Perhaps one goal of system designers might be to concoct systems that are resistant to misappropriation. This may be easier with Level 3 technology.

We have defined a stable appropriation as one likely to promote intended uses. This implies that stable appropriations are desirable. However, instability may also be beneficial. Struggles over the use of technologies may be part of larger struggles to alter or equalize the group's power structure.

Instability may also be part of learning to use technologies in creative ways. Even in cases where users "misuse" technology, perhaps designers should not be too concerned.

Note

1. The SAMM system copyright is held by the Regents of the University of Minnesota.

References

Alexander, M. (1988). Adapting tools to work groups. *Computerworld*, December 19, 31-37.

Barthes, R. (1974). *S/Z*. New York: Hill & Wang.

Beauclair, R. A. (1987). *An experimental study of the effects of GDSS process support applications on small group decision making*. Unpublished Ph.D. dissertation, Indiana University.

Bordieu, P. (1978). *Outline of a theory of practice*. Cambridge: Cambridge University Press.

DeSanctis, G., Donofrio, M. J., Sambamurthy, V., & Poole, M. S. (1989) *Comprehensiveness versus restriction in group decision heuristics: Effects of computer support on consensus decision-making*. Unpublished working paper, University of Minnesota.

DeSanctis, G., & Gallupe, R. B. (1985). GDSS: A new frontier. *Data Base*, *16*(2), 2-10.

DeSanctis, G., & Gallupe, R. B. (1987). A foundation for the study of group decision support systems. *Management Science*, *33*(5), 589-609.

DeSanctis, G., Sambamurthy, V., & Watson, R. (1987). Computer supported meetings: Building a research environment. *Large Scale Systems, 13*, 43-59.

DeSanctis, G., Sambamurthy, V., & Watson, R. (1988). Building a software environment for GDSS research. In E. Weber (Ed.) *DSS-88 Transactions*, Eighth International Conference on Decision Support Systems, 3-12.

Dickson, G. W., Robinson, L., Heath, R., & Lee, J. (1989). Observations on GDSS interaction: Chauffeured, facilitated, and user-driven systems. *Proceedings of the Twenty-Second Annual Hawaii International Conference on System Sciences*, Vol. III, 337-343.

Dubrovsky, V. (1985). Real-time computer-mediated conferencing versus electronic mail. *Proceedings of the Human Factors Society*, 29th Annual Meeting, 380-384.

Easton, A. C., Vogel, D. R., & Nunamaker, J. F., Jr. (1989). Stakeholder identification and assumption surfacing in small groups: An experimental study. *Proceedings of the Twenty-Second Annual Hawaii International Conference on System Sciences*, Vol. III, 344-352.

Finlay, M. (1987). *Powermatics*. London: Routledge & Kegan Paul.

Gallupe, R. B., DeSanctis, G., & Dickson, G. W. (1988). Computer-based support for group problem finding: An experimental investigation. *MIS Quarterly, 12*(2), 277-298.

Garfinkle, H. (1968). *Studies in ethnomethodology.* New York: Prentice-Hall.

Giddens, A. (1979). *Central problems in social theory.* Berkeley: University of California Press.

Heidegger, M. (1977). *The question concerning technology and other essays.* New Haven, CT: Yale University Press.

Heim, M. (1987). *Electric language: A philosophical study of word processing.* New Haven, CT: Yale University Press.

Hiltz, S. R., & Turoff, M. (1985). Structuring computer-mediated communication systems to avoid information overload. *Communications of the ACM, 28*(7), 680-689.

Johansen, R. (1988). *Groupware: Computer support for business teams.* New York: Free Press.

Johnson, B., & Rice, R. (1985). Reinvention in the innovation process: The case of word processing. In R. Rice (Ed.) *The new media: Communication, research, and technology.* Beverly Hills, CA: Sage.

Kiesler, S. (1986). The hidden messages in computer networks. *Harvard Business Review*, Jan-Feb, 46-59.

Kraemer, K. L., & King, J. L. (1988). Computer-based systems for cooperative work and group decision making. *ACM Computing Surveys, 20*(2), 115-146.

Mantei, M. (1988). Capturing the capture concepts: A case study in the design of computer-supported meeting environments. *Proceedings of the Conference on Computer-Supported Cooperative Work*, 257-270. Portland, OR, Sept. 26-28.

McGrath, J. E. (1984). *Groups: Interaction and performance.* Englewood Cliffs, NJ: Prentice-Hall.

Nunamaker, J. F., Applegate, L. M., & Konsynski, B. R. (1987). Facilitating group creativity: Experience with a group decision support system. *Proceedings of the Twentieth Annual Hawaii International Conference on System Sciences*, Vol. 1, 422-430.

Ong (1982). *Orality and literacy: The technology of the word.* London: Metheuen.

Poole, M. S., & DeSanctis, G. (1987). *Group decision making and group decision support systems.* MIS Research Center Working Paper No. 88-02, University of Minnesota.

Poole, M. S., & DeSanctis, G. (1989). Use of group decision support systems as an appropriation process. *Proceedings of the Twenty-Second Annual Hawaii International Conference on System Sciences*, Vol. IV, 149-157.

Poole, M. S., Holmes, M., & DeSanctis, G. (1988). Conflict management in a computer-supported meeting environment. Unpublished working paper, University of Minnesota.

Poole, M. S., Seibold, D. R., & McPhee, R. D. (1985). Group decision-making as a structurational process. *Quarterly Journal of Speech, 71*, 74-102.

Rice, R. (1984). Evaluating new media systems. In J. Johnston (Ed.) *Evaluating the new information technologies: New directions for program evaluation*, no. 23. San Francisco: Jossey-Bass.

Sambamurthy, V. (1988). *A comparison of two levels of computer-based support for communication and conflict management in equivocality reduction during stakeholder analysis.* Ph.D. dissertation proposal, Carlson School of Management, University of Minnesota.

Siegal, J., Dubrovsky, V., Kiesler, S., & McGuire, T. W. (1986). Group processes in computer-mediated communication. Working paper, Carnegie-Mellon University, 1984. *Organizational Behavior and Human Decision Processes, 37,* 157-187.

Steeb, R., & Johnston, S. C. (1981). A computer-based interactive system for group decision making. *IEEE Transactions on Systems, Man, & Cybernetics, 11* (8), 544-552.

Watson, R. T., DeSanctis, G., & Poole, M. S. (1988). Using a GDSS to facilitate group consensus: Some intended and unintended consequences. *MIS Quarterly, 12*(3), 463-480.

Zigurs, I., Poole, M. S., & DeSanctis, G. (1988). Computer support of group decision making: A communication-based investigation. *MIS Quarterly, 12*(4), 625-644.

M. LYNNE MARKUS

9. Toward a "Critical Mass" Theory of Interactive Media

One of the things that makes the telephone such a useful medium of communication in the United States today is that one can use it to reach almost anyone else. Long before telephone subscribers were able to realize this benefit, promoters had coined the phrase "universal service" to describe it (de Sola Pool, 1983). Years later, Federal Express learned the importance of universal service while introducing a new communication medium, overnight package delivery in the United States (Sigafoos, 1983).

The purpose of this chapter is to identify the key factors that determine whether or not an interactive medium introduced into a community will achieve *universal access*, that is, the ability of any member of the community to reach all other members through the medium. *Interactive media* are technologies that facilitate multidirectional communication. Older interactive media include the telephone and paper mail; newer ones include electronic mail, voice messaging, facsimile, computer-conferencing, video-conferencing, overnight mail, and many others.

A *community* is a group of individuals with some common interests and greater density of communication within than across its boundaries: Examples include an invisible college of academic researchers, a business organization, or a department within a firm. Some interactive media are used by the members of one community to communicate with outsiders as well as insiders, as when people in a business firm use U.S. mail to communicate with customers as well as with colleagues located in other cities. But some interactive media, such as interoffice mail and some electronic mail systems, are usable chiefly within communities and are introduced with the sole purpose of facilitating internal communication. This chapter focuses exclusively on use of interactive media within communities, while recognizing

Author's Note: The author gratefully acknowledges helpful comments from the editors and reviewers of the special issue of *Communication Research* and this volume and from J. D. Eveland, Mitchell Koza, Dan Robey, Jim Rule, Marvin Sirbu, Burt Swanson, Jon Turner, and, especially, Everett Rogers, on earlier versions of this chapter.

194

that the ability to use media with outsiders may promote internal use as well.

The Importance of Universal Access

Universal access is important to a community introducing an interactive medium for two reasons. First, only when all people in a community have access to an interactive medium does each member have the ability to realize full benefits from using it. Proponents argue that the newer interactive media, like electronic mail and voice messaging, are more efficient than traditional forms of communication, because they increase the speed and geographic scope of communication and reduce such nonproductive efforts as redialing busy telephone numbers (Rice & Bair, 1984). But individuals cannot achieve these benefits through their own independent efforts. In the extreme case, an isolated user of an interactive medium can obtain no benefits at all. (Imagine being the only person with a telephone.) At a minimum, two users are necessary for *either* to receive benefits. ("It takes two to tango," according to Katz, 1962.) In general, the benefits of using an interactive medium increase with the number of people who use it (Rohlfs, 1974; Steinfield, 1986) and will be greatest when universal access has been achieved.

Second, only when a new interactive medium has achieved universal access can communities afford to reduce their investments in older universal access media. Without a medium of universal access, communities risk disintegrating into noninteracting subgroups. While a newer interactive medium may be more efficient than an older one, an older one that is universally accessible may be indispensable until almost everyone uses the new one. For example, in a certain organization, members of a central processing unit do not have telephones, communicating with people through-out the organization via electronic mail (Markus, 1988). Clearly, this firm is able to dispense with telephones for the central processors only because all the people who need to reach them also have access to electronic mail. Other firms may find that they can reduce the number of interoffice mail deliveries when a new interactive medium achieves universal access, but not before.[1]

The Difficulty of Achieving Universal Access

But the same properties of interactive media that make universal access advantageous also make it difficult to achieve. The individuals who adopt an interactive medium before universal access has been achieved may experience less than full benefits from using the medium and high costs due to the need to maintain duplicate channels of communication. Consider the situation in which only half of a project team uses electronic mail. The communicator who wants to reach all team members and to use electronic messaging has to: (a) remember who is a regular user of messaging and who is not; (b) maintain different procedures for accessing different people (for example, lists of BITNET addresses, office addresses, and telephone numbers); and (c) prepare communications in two different media. This can be quite costly in time and effort.

Given the higher costs and lower benefits an individual can receive from an interactive medium that has not achieved universal access, one may well wonder how universal access could ever come about. The individual considering the adoption of an interactive medium is very likely to choose not to use it, unless a sizable number of communication partners are already using it. In the absence of a sizable number of initial users, not only may use of a medium fail to spread, but it may also be extinguished altogether (Hiltz, 1984, pp. 84-86; Uhlig, Farber, & Bair, 1979, pp. 251-252).

Economists have referred to situations of this sort as problems of "critical mass" (Rohlfs, 1974; Schelling, 1978), and the term has been widely used by people concerned with the implementation and diffusion of interactive media (Bair & Mancuso, 1985; Culnan & Bair, 1983; Hiltz, 1984; Hiltz & Turoff, 1978; Rogers, 1986; Uhlig, Farber & Bair, 1979). This chapter explores in detail one "critical mass" theory of interactive media use in communities, focusing on such questions as: Will it be possible to find enough people willing to "go first" with a newly introduced interactive medium? And, under what conditions will adoption spread from the earliest users to the rest of the people in the community? In this theory, the outcome of interest (universal access) is a property of the *community*, but the antecedents are properties of individuals. Thus, the theory relates micro (individual) inputs to macro (community) outcomes (Coleman, 1986; Granovetter, 1978; Granovetter & Soong, 1983), in contrast to research that explores the determinants of *individuals'* media choice behavior.

The plan of the chapter is as follows. The next section reviews diffusion of innovation theory and collective action theory and discusses their applicability to the interactive media. Next, one particular "critical mass" theory is applied to the interactive media and specific propositions for empirical testing are developed. The concluding secion of the chapter discusses the implications of this theory for future empirical research and for the practice of implementing interactive media.

Diffusion, Interdependence, and "Critical Mass"

In trying to explain when and how a newly introduced interactive medium spreads to all members of a community, diffusion of innovations theory (Rogers, 1983) is an obvious place to start. In diffusion theory, the first people to adopt do so because they can obtain benefits from performing the innovative activity. Either because they "need" the innovation more than others, or because the benefits derivable from an adoption are proportional to length and intensity of use, the "greatest profits go to the first to adopt" (Rogers, 1983, p. 252). Innovation spreads when others either observe the early adopters and imitate them to replicate their profits, or communicate with the early adopters and are persuaded or induced to adopt.[2]

In related work, Granovetter (1978) proposed threshold models to explain such collective phenomena as rioting and diffusion of innovation. In threshold models, someone throws the first brick because of the "utility" that activity provides. Whether or not others follow depends on the distribution of individual thresholds, defined as the number of other people who must be doing the activity before a given individual joins in. In threshold models, the intrinsic utility of the behavior to an individual may be more important in determining that individual's behavior than social influence, but even a small amount of social influence may have a strong effect on the collective outcome.

Interdependence

Both diffusion theory and threshold models allow for interdependence in individuals' decisions to adopt. However, the interdependence is generally assumed to be *sequential* (Thompson, 1967), in which later adopters are influenced by earlier ones, but not vice versa (Granovetter & Soong, 1983 [3]). An unsuccessful innovation or collective action is one in which few people follow early adopters; in a successful action, large numbers follow (Figure 9.1). While discontinuance ("a decision to reject an innovation after having previously adopted it" Rogers, 1983, p. 186) is higher in unsuccessful innovations than in successful ones, "later adopters are more likely to discontinue innovations than are earlier adopters," when success is held constant (Rogers, 1983, p. 188), because early adopters have higher benefits than later ones.

In attempting to apply these theories to the interactive media, however, it becomes clear that the assumption of sequential interdependence must be

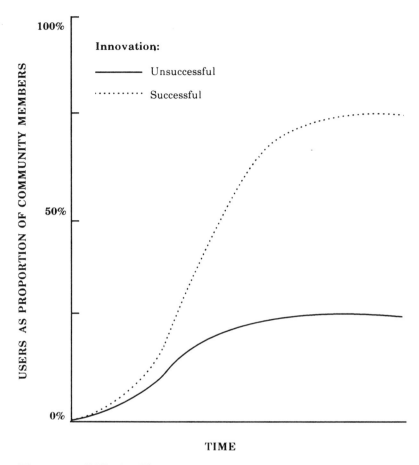

Figure 9.1 Diffusion Theory

replaced by one of *reciprocal* interdependence (Thompson, 1967), in which early adopters can be influenced by later adopters as well as the other way around. As previously explained, early adopters of an interactive medium may experience lower benefits and higher costs than those who adopt after many others have already done so. Thus, discontinuance can be a big problem among early adopters. In the unsuccessful case (see Figure 9.2), early adopters may defect if their communications through an electronic medium are not reciprocated (Rice, 1982) or if additional people do not follow the early adopters (Rohlfs, 1974; Schelling, 1978). If some defect, others may follow, leading to a complete extinction of use (Rohlfs, 1974; Schelling, 1978). On the other hand, if early users' communications are answered or new users

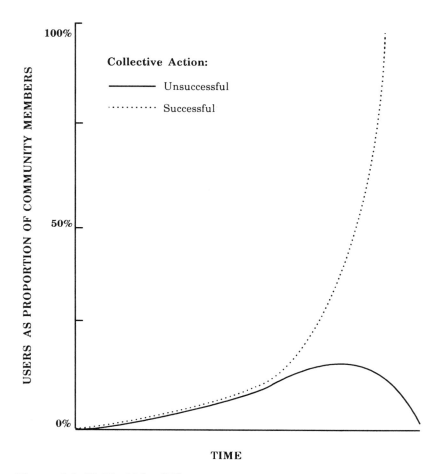

Figure 9.2 "Critical Mass" Theory

are attracted, the costs decrease and benefits increase, attracting still more users and creating a rapid acceleration of use (Figure 9.2).

This suggests that, in many situations, the diffusion of an interactive medium in a community may be an "all or nothing" affair. Either usage will spread to all members of the community (universal access is achieved) or no one will use the medium (for communication inside the community), because no one started using it or because early users defected.

Histories of some interactive media lend credence to this view. For example, Federal Express experienced a minor setback in its attempts to interconnect the 100 largest U.S. metropolitan areas with overnight package delivery service (Sigafoos, 1983). An operational test in an 11-city network yielded only 6 packages. It was declared a failure and discontinued. A second trial a month later—starting with 25 cities and adding 4 cities per 2-week period—was sufficient to launch the new medium of communication. Similarly, Hammer (1985) discusses the failure of a major bank's first attempt to implement electronic messaging; a subsequent attempt with different messaging technology was a huge success. And Eveland and Bikson (1987) note that a sizable number of people who tried a recently implemented electronic messaging system appear to have "dropped out" soon after.

However, the "all or nothing" phenomenon may be limited to situations in which an individual's adoption decision is influenced only by the *number* of other users, not by *who* they are (Rohlfs, 1974). Groups of people within a community may have sufficient common interest to adopt an interactive medium as a unit and to continue using it, even if use does not spread more widely in the community. And, if a large amount of individuals' communication takes place with a few principal contacts, a community may contain a large number of small, isolated sets of interactive medium users (Rohlfs, 1974).

For example, the first telephone subscribers bought telephones in pairs, along with a telephone line to connect, for example, an office to a factory, a home to an office, or a pharmacy to a physician's office (Aronson, 1977; de Sola Pool, 1983). Many of these early subscribers later failed to see the value of switched service that would allow them to reach all other subscribers: They were already communicating with their important contacts. Once enough people were recruited to the new switched service, however, use spread rapidly until universal access was achieved.

Thus, when one makes more realistic assumptions about the nature of the "demand" for an interactive medium (Rohlfs, 1974), the outcomes observed when an interactive medium is introduced into a community may not be so sharply different from those predicted by diffusion theory (Figure 9.1) as is suggested in Figure 9.2. Nevertheless, because interactive media entail reciprocal interdependence among their users, the process by which the media diffuse within communities should differ substantially from the diffusion processes of sequentially interdependent innovations.

In addition, rational decision makers contemplating early adoption of an interactive medium should use very different criteria from those that would be applied to innovations not entailing reciprocal interdependence. For example, a physician deciding whether or not to adopt a new antibiotic can consider the advantages to her patients and the costs to herself of failing to keep up with competing physicians (Burt, 1987). But the potential early adopter of electronic mail must worry about whether her communication partners will also follow suit. A theory that models such reciprocal decision processes and considers their consequences for the community is described below.

"Critical Mass" Theory

Sociologists Oliver, Marwell, and Teixeira (1985) developed their theory of "critical mass" to integrate and formalize theory about "collective action," defined as individuals' actions in service of "public goods." Public goods are benefits that individuals cannot be prevented from enjoying, whether or not they have helped to secure them (Olson, 1965; see also the chapter by Thorn & Connolly in this volume).

"Critical mass," in physics, is that amount of radioactive material necessary to produce a nuclear fission explosion. For Oliver et al., "critical mass" is defined as "a small segment of the population that chooses to make big contributions to the collective action while the majority do little or nothing" (Oliver et al., 1985, p. 524). Oliver et al.'s theory of "critical mass" seeks to predict the probability, extent and effectiveness of group action in pursuit of a public good. Their theory has two major sets of independent "variables": the shape of the *production function* and *heterogeneity* of resources and interests in the population.

The production function specifies the relationship between individuals' contributions of resources and achievement of the common good. Oliver et al. (1985) note that production functions may take many forms in addition to the general third-order curve (S-curve) usually assumed. In a *decelerating* production function, the first few units of resources contributed have the biggest effect on achieving the public good, and subsequent contributions progressively less (decreasing marginal returns—see Figure 9.3). In an *accelerating* production function, successive contributions generate progressively larger payoffs, thus making additional contributions more likely (increasing marginal returns—see Figure 9.3).

Interests are the values different individuals place on the public good; *resources* are what individuals must contribute to achieve it. ". . . [A] positive correlation between interests and resources is highly favorable for collective action, as it increases the probability of there being a few highly interested and highly resourceful people who are willing and able to provide the good for everyone" (Oliver et al., 1985, p. 530). In addition, heterogeneity (variation) in interests and resources is believed to affect the probability, extent and likelihood of collection action. If everyone could derive the same benefits from a public good, no one would have the incentive to contribute more than

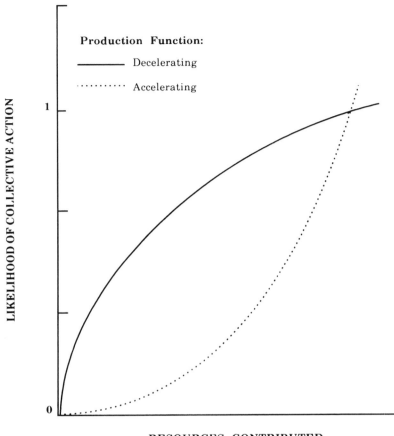

Figure 9.3 Production Functions

the others. Therefore, differential ability to derive benefit from the public good increases the likelihood that someone will value it enough to pay more for it than the others do. Variation in the resources available for contribution is believed to favor contributions in a similar way (Oliver et al., 1985).

Oliver et al. (1985) tested their theory using formal analysis and simulation and report that the probability, extent, and effectiveness of group action depend on the shape of the production function. Decelerating production functions favor the initiation of collective action but inhibit optimal levels of the collective good. On the other hand, when the production function is accelerating, individuals are unlikely to make the contributions necessary to provide the public good. However, once these contributions get started, they generally accelerate rapidly until the public good is completely provided. For accelerating production functions, both interest heterogeneity and resource heterogeneity were found to promote the achievement of the public good (Oliver et al., 1985).

Applying "Critical Mass" Theory to Interactive Media

The collective action relevant to a newly introduced interactive medium such as electronic mail, voice messaging, computer conferencing, facsimile, and the like, is the achievement of universal access. This public good enables any community member to reach any other member through the medium, whether or not that individual has helped to achieve it. The critical mass theory of Oliver et al. (1985) proposes conditions under which universal access is more or less likely to occur.

Resource Contributions

The theory formulated by Oliver et al. (1985) is very general, and "collective actions differ" (p. 523). An important step in applying it to interactive media is to determine the shape of the production function, which specifies the relationship between individuals' contributions of resources to the likelihood of the outcome.

Let us first consider the resources *required* for universal access. Other resources that may promote universal access, but are not required for it, are considered later. The required resources fall into two broad categories: equipment, comprising infrastructure and access devices, and effort, including knowledge and communication discipline.

Many interactive media require an *infrastructure*, such as the central computer, software, and telecommunications facilities used in electronic mail, or the private branch exchange, software, and wiring used in voice messaging. Second, each user of an interactive medium must have sole or shared use of one or more *access devices*, such as a computer terminal, a telephone handset, or a facsimile machine, and relevant ID numbers, accounts, and access codes.

Universal access requires expenditures of effort as well as investments in equipment. Each user must acquire the *knowledge and skills* to use the medium herself or employ an *intermediary* to use the medium for her.

Together with infrastructure and access devices, usage knowledge and skills provide *operational access* to a medium, that is, they enable a user to initiate communication through a medium.

But operational access is not sufficient for universal access. If people only used an interactive medium when they wanted to initiate communication, universal access could never come about. People must also ready themselves to reciprocate communication, that is, make themselves available to those who wish to reach them through the medium. The effort involved in this might be termed *communication discipline*. For example, the disciplined user of the telephone must answer the telephone when it rings, make provisions to have it answered in his/her absence, return telephone calls when requested to, and so forth. Holders of both voice and text mailboxes are urged to check for messages frequently, as many as three times every business day (Kneale, 1986; Turner, 1985), whether or not they have messages to send.

What is the relationship between the resources individuals contribute and the likelihood of universal access? In other words, what is the shape of the production function? An interesting property of the effort costs of usage knowledge and communication discipline is that no one individual can provide these for the entire community; each individual must supply her own. Each contribution of effort increases the ability of prospective users to benefit. And each additional contribution makes it more likely that others will contribute also. Thus, in general, the shape of the production function for interactive media is accelerating, and, according to Oliver et al. (1985), it may be difficult to create the critical mass of users necessary to assure the outcome of universal access.

Because universal access requires universal participation (or nearly so) among community members, it seems clear that the likelihood of the universal access will depend upon the magnitude of the resources members are required to contribute. The higher the costs, the less likely that a critical mass of users can be found. This suggests the following general proposition:

Proposition 1: Reducing the resources that early adopters of an interactive medium are required to contribute will increase the likelihood that universal access to the medium in the community will be achieved.

The resources required for universal access to an interactive medium are influenced by two major factors: the specific technological configuration of the interactive medium used in a particular community[4] and the mechanisms used within the community to fund the acquisition and operation of equipment.

First, interactive media vary considerably in their knowledge and skill requirements. For example, the instructions for using most voice messaging systems, which employ telephone handsets as terminals, can be printed on wallet-sized cards, whereas users of electronic messaging and computer-conferencing systems may need extensive training in typing skills and general computer literacy in addition to specific operational commands.

Another aspect of knowledge and skill requirements concerns the procedures for directing communications to a particular person. Some systems require message senders to memorize complicated, unmemorable new user-names for recipients, whereas other systems employ such easily remembered "addresses" as recipients' names or telephone numbers. Some systems provide directory services to identify members of the user group and their system-specific addresses; others do not.

This line of reasoning suggests:

Proposition 1A: The higher the skill and effort requirements of an interactive medium, the lower the likelihood that universal access will be achieved.

In particular, universal access should be more likely when interactive media are voice-based rather than text-based, when they employ simple or known addressing conventions, and when they provide good directory services.

Second, the interactive media vary considerably in the effort required of individuals to maintain communication discipline. Some media actively notify users that messages are waiting (e.g., secretaries hand managers their mail, terminals beep when new messages are delivered, red lights on telephones blink), while others require users to remember to check for messages by invoking a particular procedure (e.g., checking a mail slot or message board, dialing a special number and entering a sequence of codes). This suggests:

Proposition 1B: The higher the communication discipline requirements of an interactive medium, the lower the likelihood that universal access will be achieved.

In particular, universal access should be more likely when interactive media employ active rather than passive notification of new information or communication.

Third, different classes of interactive media vary widely in terms of their requirements for equipment. For example, in terms of equipment, electronic mail generally requires a central computer, telecommunications capability, software, and computer terminals. By contrast, much of the infrastructure needed for electronic mail via facsimile is generally already available (the public telephone network and telephone handsets); the only additional equipment needed are the facsimile machines themselves.

But it is not the costs of supplying infrastructure and access devices per se that affects the likelihood of achieving universal access, it is the extent to which these costs are borne by individual users. Communities differ in the extent to which they are willing and able to supply equipment and services for individual members. For example, business firms are much more likely than invisible colleges of academic researchers to subsidize the cost of equipment for an interactive medium. But some business firms require employees to purchase their own personal computers, which are the access devices for certain interactive media. And others will charge employees' budgets for equipment acquisition or media usage costs (Markus, 1987). This suggests:

Proposition 1C: The higher the equipment costs borne by early users of an interactive medium, the lower the likelihood that universal access will be achieved.

Heterogeneity

The preceding discussion has assumed that the members of a community are equivalent in their ability to benefit from and contribute to universal access. In other words, how many people adopt a medium early on is assumed to be more important than who those people are (Rohlfs, 1974). But, in many cases, there can be substantial variation within communities in the degree to which members can benefit from and contribute to universal access. Oliver et al. (1985) found that heterogeneity of interests (variation in the degree to which individuals can benefit) promotes collective action, whether the production function is accelerating or decelerating. And heterogeneity of resources (variation in the degree to which individuals can contribute) favors collective action especially when the production function is accelerating. This general proposition follows from our earlier argument that the production function for universal access is accelerating:

Proposition 2: Heterogeneity of interests and resources among the members of a community will increase the likelihood of universal access.

An earlier section of this paper discussed some of the resources that people can provide to the achievement of universal access. But what interests do individuals have in universal access? One important interest is the need for information from other people in the community. Communities differ in the degree to which members experience the need or desire to communicate widely with other members.

In task-oriented communities, the property of task interdependence influences members' needs and desires to communicate. Task interdependence often results from functional specialization and differentiation. Specialization creates sources of information that are not readily accessible to people outside the specialist group. At the same time, differentiation in the community increases the need for communication among specialist groups. Thus, task interdependence promotes heterogeneity of interests in and resources for universal access and, hence, should promote the achievement of universal access. By contrast, when tasks are highly independent, members are relatively homogeneous in their interests in and resources for universal access, and, in general, this condition should diminish the prospects for universal access.

In social communities, the concept of network density is a more meaningful indicator of important variations in communication patterns than task interdependence. In either case:

Proposition 2A: Task interdependence or network density increases the likelihood of universal access in a community.

We have already discussed the resources of equipment and effort that must be provided for all members of the community regardless of who they are. In addition, some individuals in the community may have resources that, while not necessary for universal access, can promote it. First, some individuals have *information* that they can exchange with others via the interactive medium. Second, some individuals have the personal characteristic of being *sought-after* by others as communication partners. In communities that are highly decentralized, these resources are widely distributed; in centralized communities, some people have much more of them than others (Marwell, Oliver, & Prahl, 1988). This suggests:

Proposition 2B: Centralization increases the likelihood of universal access.

Numerous studies have shown that *inaccessibility* of information sources or channels has a significant negative effect on information use (Allen, 1977; Allen & Gerstberger, 1967; Culnan, 1984; 1985; Steinfield, 1986). In communities which are highly centralized geographically, traditional universal access media such as face-to-face meetings, telephone, and physical mail deliveries generally work reasonably well to keep people accessible to each other. But as geographic dispersion increases, people become less accessible to each other through frequent travel, time zone differences, and language barriers. For people located far from the geographic or population centers of a community, newer interactive media become more attractive than traditional media (Goldstein, 1986; Hammer, 1985; Johansen, Vallee, & Spangler, 1979; Kerr & Hiltz, 1982; Steinfield, 1986; Steinfield & Fulk, 1986; Turner, 1985). Thus, geographic dispersion generally does not affect all members of the community equally, but increases heterogeneity of interest in universal access via an interactive medium. This suggests:

Proposition 2C: Geographic dispersion increases the likelihood of universal access.

Discussion

The previous section of this chapter derived a set of propositions about the likelihood that interactive media will diffuse widely in the communities into which they are introduced. This section discusses some of the implications of this theory of "critical mass" for future research on the interactive media and for the practice of implementing them.

Implications for Research

The *unit of analysis* in this "critical mass" theory is the community, not the individual. In other words, the theory attempts to predict the likelihood that interactive media will diffuse widely within communities rather than the likelihood that any particular individual will use an interactive medium. This means that the abundant research on individuals' media choice decisions does not provide direct evidence for or against the propositions stated in this chapter. For example, evidence that inaccessibility deters individuals' information use does not support or refute the proposition that geographic dispersion within a community promotes universal access. In order to support or refute the propositions stated in this chapter, new research must be done.

Perhaps the most difficult conceptual issue to be faced in research on the critical mass phenomenon is the appropriate definition of *the boundaries of "community."* Many communities, such as business organizations, consist of nested subunits, such as divisions, departments, and primary work groups. Each of these subunits might legitimately be considered communities in their own right by virtue of communication patterns, culture, or task interdependence. One way this issue might be resolved is with reference to the process of implementing the interactive medium: Has the medium been made available to people throughout the organization or only to the members of a particular subunit? In the former case, it might be better to take the entire organization as the unit of analysis, whereas, in the latter case, one might be justified in taking the subunit as the appropriate unit.

However this issue of boundaries is resolved, it suggests a promising avenue of future research: whether and how use of an interactive medium spreads from subgroup to subgroup within the community, not only from individual to individual (Olson, 1965, Chapter II passim; E. Rogers, personal communication, May 4, 1987). One plausible hypothesis suggests that, when use of the medium spreads from subunit to subunit, it does so through "weak ties" among individuals whose primary affiliation lies in different subgroups (Feldman, 1987; Granovetter, 1973).

A major practical difficulty in conducting "critical mass" research is determining whether sufficient *time* has passed for diffusion processes to have run their course. One might be reasonably confident of this if medium usage has fallen off to zero or achieved universality within the community. However, at the time of research, a medium may be used universally by a subgroup within the community, but not elsewhere, or by a number of relatively self-contained sets of individuals. In such a case, one might wonder whether these intermediate levels of usage are stable or whether, given sufficiently long time, they might change into something else. This suggests the usefulness of longitudinal research that tracks the diffusion of interactive media use over time.

The time issue complicates the question of *measurement*. The proportion of community members to adopt a medium in each time period seems a logical starting place for measuring "the likelihood of universal access" in research designed to test this "critical mass" theory. However, it follows from our earlier discussion of reciprocal interdependence that one must also consider the number who defect, or discontinue using the medium, in each time period. And one might wish to compare communities, not only in terms of the proportions of members who adopt and discontinue using the media, but also in terms of the speed with which universality of usage is achieved (when it is).

Another complicating factor in research on "critical mass" phenomenon is the *size of the community* into which interactive media are introduced. Oliver and Marwell (1988) have argued convincingly, contrary to Olson (1965), that large community size generally promotes the success of collective action. Small size only promotes collective action when a public good has zero *jointness of supply.*

For a good like a bridge, the jointness of supply is high, because if the good is supplied for one member, it is supplied for all. Jointness of supply is also high for the infrastructure (e.g., a central computer and software) required for some interactive media. This suggests that universal access to media with high infrastructure requirements will be more likely to occur in large communities rather than in small ones.

But, in general, the infrastructure comprises only part of the resource requirements for interactive media: Access devices, usage knowledge, and communication discipline are also required. The cost of supplying these resources is generally proportional to the number of users (zero jointness of supply). Consequently, the likelihood of universal access to media with low or no infrastructure requirements should be greater in small communities than in large ones.

This prediction, however, appears to run afoul of the special characteristics of interactive media. If the benefits of using these media increase with the number of users, very small communities should obtain very small benefits from using them, and, therefore, universal access should be unlikely to occur in very small communities. This is consistent with the frequently made assertion that the "critical mass" of users necessary for an interactive medium to succeed numbers about 30 individuals (Bair & Mancuso, 1985; Hiltz, 1984). Clearly, the effects of community size on the likelihood of universal access will not be decided by theory, but will require empirical research.

Although the "critical mass" theory developed in this chapter is primarily concerned with outcomes at the community, rather than the individual, level of analysis, it does have some implications for individual level research. Theories of media choice such as the theory of social presence (Short, Williams, & Christie, 1976) and the theory of information richness (Daft & Lengel, 1984; 1986; and Trevino, Lengel, & Daft, in this volume) predict that individuals will choose which medium to use on the basis of the appropriateness of a medium to a communication task. But a rational communicator is unlikely to choose on the basis of appropriateness if she knows or suspects that the intended recipient of the communication is not also a user of the appropriate medium. In other words, in settings where an interactive medium has not yet achieved universal access, individuals are likely to weigh the extent of a medium's diffusion (known or believed) more highly than appropriateness in deciding whether or not to use the medium.

Consequently, settings where some of the media of interest have not achieved universal access do not make particularly good settings for testing individual level media choice theories. Future media choice research should attempt to reduce threats to valid interpretation by reporting the extent of media diffusion (e.g., the percentage of subgroup and community members who use each medium), and by using extent of diffusion as a control variable in research involving multiple subgroups and communities, much as accessibility (e.g., the physical locations of terminals, medium use knowledge) is currently used.

Implications for Practice

A number of practical implementation tactics can be derived from the theory of "critical mass" and are outlined below. Before presenting these, however, two caveats are in order. First, it is important to note that the recommendations derived from theory are only as good as the theory itself. In the absence of rigorous empirical tests of the theory, caution should be taken in adopting implementation advice derived from it. Second, effective implementation strategies will vary depending on the relationship between the parties formulating the strategy and the community adopting the interactive medium. Many such relationships are possible. For example, the implementors might be a committee within a community that has no explicit "executive" subgroup, for example, an invisible college of researchers. Here, implementors may not be able to mandate compliance with their policy statements. In another case, the implementor might be a vendor of interactive media products and services. Here, again, coercion is not a viable strategy, and strategy will center on pricing policies.[5] In still a third possibility, implementors might occupy an executive role with coercive power in a hierarchically organized community such as a business firm or a government agency. This third situation is assumed in the advice derived below from the "critical mass" theory.

The implementation advice derived from "critical mass" theory centers on two major issues, the initial user group and the resources required for universal access. With respect to the first issue, the question is: How can one make sure that the initial group of users constitutes a critical mass, so that more people will be attracted than will defect, and the user group will grow?

The surest strategy, of course, is to have everyone in the community start to use the interactive medium at the same time. According to Oliver (1985), in cases where unanimity is required, negative incentives (punishments for those who do not comply) will be more efficient than positive incentives (rewards for complying). In other words, this strategy involves *mandating usage* and punishing those who fail to comply. Senior executives have employed such a strategy in a number of cases where universal access to an interactive medium was achieved (see Markus, 1988, for a case involving electronic mail[6]).

Sometimes, however, executives will be reluctant to coerce employees to use an interactive medium, even when the ability to impose negative sanctions lies within their power. The use of negative sanctions can evoke hostility and tension (Alter, 1980; Oliver, 1985), and may stimulate resistance directed toward the executive or the medium (Markus, 1981; 1984). In such a case, the best strategy is to *select the initial user set carefully* so that it contains people with high interests in universal access and high resources to contribute to universal access.

Individuals differ in their information processing behavior. Some are more active than others in using information, or *communication consumption*. Some are more active than others in information seeking, or *communication origination*. In general, active users and originators benefit more from interactive media than passive ones (Malone, Brobst, Grant, & Cohen, 1987; P. Strassmann, personal electronic communication, summer 1985) and so are good candidates for inclusion in an initial user group.

Individuals also differ in their ability to induce other members of a community to join them in media usage behavior. Some people are highly sought after as communication partners, because of high status, special expertise, coordination roles (e.g., secretaries), or frequent inaccessibility (e.g., travel, meetings). To the extent that these people make themselves more accessible through interactive media than through traditional media, they give others, who might otherwise choose not to use the systems, a powerful incentive to do so (Goldstein, 1986; Hammer, 1985; E. Rogers, personal communication, May 4, 1987[7]; Turner, 1985[8]). This incentive may be sufficient to initiate and sustain use of the medium. Thus, sought-after people are obvious candidates for inclusion in an initial group of users of an interactive medium. So are individuals who have discretionary resources for acquiring access devices, people with prior experience using such systems, and people with the ability to mandate use of an interactive medium within a subgroup of the community (e.g., product managers, unit heads).

A much weaker strategy is to *provide positive inducements*, reinforcements, or rewards to the early users of an interactive medium. Media support personnel might "remind" people who have not used the medium lately. Alternatively, implementors might attempt to capitalize on the "play value" of high technology (Dozier & Rice, 1984; Malone, 1984), for example, by tacitly permitting the medium to be used for nonwork purposes such as restaurant reviews and want ads (Feldman, 1987; Sproull & Kiesler, 1986).

It is little use to mandate that everyone in a community use an interactive medium if the individuals do not have the operational access resources required for use (e.g., infrastructure, access devices, and knowledge and skills about how to use the medium). Thus, the second part of an effective strategy for implementing an interactive medium concerns the resources of operational access. Consistent with our earlier arguments about mandating use, the surest way to ensure universal access is to *provide the resources* of operational access to all people in the community simultaneously. Obviously, however, this tactic may be prohibitively expensive, and it is certainly inefficient if a lower level of expenditure will suffice.

As explained earlier in this chapter, the costs that individuals must bear in order to use an interactive medium are affected by two factors: community policies concerning equipment acquisition and operation and the specific technological configuration of the interactive medium. Implementors unwilling or unable to bear all the costs of operational access might choose to *subsidize costs*, but only for an initial group of users, or to *modify organizational funding policies* that directly discourage media use (e.g., charging for electronic mail on a per access basis[9]).

Alternatively, implementors might *select a technological configuration* with relatively low costs to the individual (e.g., voice messaging instead of electronic mail, electronic mail with active notification instead of passive), or might *devise procedures* that compensate for lack of resources (e.g., printing out and delivering hard copies of messages for people who lack access to terminals, see Eveland & Bikson, 1987). For best results, implementors might manipulate technological configuration and organizational funding policies simultaneously.

Conclusion

Central to the "critical mass" theory outlined in this chapter is the explicit assumption that interactive media have two key properties not shared with all other technological innovations. The first of these is reciprocal interdependence, in which later adopters influence earlier adopters as well as the other way around. The failure of later adopters to reciprocate the communications of earlier adopters and to become regular users of the medium themselves can induce early adopters to stop using the medium. This may initiate a vicious cycle in which all medium usage is extinguished. Similarly, reciprocation and the attraction of new users may cause medium usage to spread to nearly everyone in the community. Because of reciprocal interdependence, the "critical mass" theory argues that the dynamics of diffusion of interactive media will differ from those of many other technological innovations.

The second important property of interactive media not shared with all other innovations is that universal access to interactive media comprises a public good, or collective benefit, that cannot be denied to people who have not worked to achieve it. When everyone in a community uses an interactive medium, users can generally derive greater benefits than if only some community members use it. But some people may provide more benefits to others by using the medium than they will personally receive from it. Because individuals may lack the incentive to contribute to this public good, the "critical mass" theory argues that interactive media will diffuse differently than many other technological innovations.

In short, the theory of "critical mass" directs attention away from the individual toward the community level of analysis. It highlights the tensions between an individual's ability to derive benefits from an interactive medium and the social or public benefits that can follow from the individual's use. Its central problematic is the situation in which the collective outcome differs from a simple aggregation of individuals' values, attitudes and behavioral predispositions. And the empirical research required to test this theory has only just begun.

Notes

1. A given community may choose not to reduce its investment in older media: Few organizations remove telephones when electronic mail has been introduced. But resources are required to maintain the availability of each medium of communication, and, under some conditions, communities may be motivated to reduce these costs.

2. An alternative theory hypothesizes that status equals compete to avoid being the last of their cohort to adopt a particular innovation (Burt, 1987).

3. Granovetter and Soong (1983) explore the negative effects of "dropouts" on those who have not yet tried the innovation, but appear not to expect widespread reversals among early adopters.

4. The technological configuration of a medium can also affect the interests individuals have in using it. For example, voice messaging can be used to record incoming messages from nonusers as well as to communicate asynchronously with other users. Thus, an early adopter of voice messaging is able to derive benefits from voice messaging even if no other members of her community adopt it. Clearly, this factor will improve the diffusion prospects of voice messaging relative to interactive media with little or no "independent" benefits. See Rohlfs, 1974.

5. See Rohlfs (1974) for a discussion of alternative pricing policies given different assumptions about the nature of demand for telephone service.

6. Another use of this implementation strategy occurred at AMOCO research center in Tulsa, Oklahoma (site visit in 1981).

7. "I remember that President Donald Kennedy at Stanford was enthusiastic about the new electronic messaging system introduced among the top 100 administrators at the university. A photo of Kennedy sitting at his computer monitor appeared in the student newspaper. He sent messages on the new system to the other 99, with the implication that they should reply on the system. His personal sponsorship of the interactive innovation helped reach a critical mass more quickly." (E. Rogers, personal communication, May 4, 1987)

8. Turner (1985) identified this instance of "top management support" as critical to the successful implementation of an integrated office system at Bankers' Trust: "As one middle level manager put it, 'when you called (the head of [one of the bank's major subunits]) his secretary would say, 'I'll have him call you back.'' But he was too busy. If you wanted to get a message to him, you had to send it over the system. At least I know he would read it by the end of the day.' " (Turner, 1985, p. 39)

9. A better scheme might be flat rate charging at least until a critical mass of users has been achieved, see Markus, 1987.

References

Allen, T. (1977). *Managing the flow of technology*. Cambridge: MIT Press.

Allen, T., & Gerstberger, S. (1967). Communication in the R&D lab. *Technology Review*, *70*,31-37.

Alter, S. L. (1980). *Decision support systems: Current practice and continuing challenges*. Reading, MA: Addison-Wesley.

Aronson, S. H. (1977). Bell's electrical toy: What's the use? The sociology of early telephone usage. In I. de Sola Pool (Ed.), *The social impact of the telephone* (pp. 15-39). Cambridge: MIT Press.

Bair, J. H., & Mancuso, L. (1985). *The office systems cycle: The process and technology of office automation*. Palo Alto, CA: Hewlett-Packard Company.

Burt, R. S. (1987). Social contagion and innovation: Cohesion versus structural equivalence. *American Journal of Sociology*, *92*(6), 1287-1335.

Coleman, J. S. (1986). Social theory, social research, and a theory of action. *American Journal of Sociology*, *91*(6), 1309-35.

Culnan, M. J. (1984). The dimensions of accessibility to online information: Implications for implementing office information systems. *ACM Transactions of Office Information Systems*, *2*(2), 141-150.

Culnan, M. J. (1985). The dimensions of perceived accessibility to information: Implications for the delivery of information systems and services. *Journal of the American Society for Information Science*, *36*(5), 302-308.

Culnan, M. J., & Bair, J. H. (1983). Human communication needs and organizational productivity: The potential impact of office automation. *Journal of the American Society for Information Science, 34*(3), 215-221.

Daft, R. L., & Lengel, R. H. (1984). Information richness: A new approach to managerial behavior and organizational design. In L. L. Cummings & B. M. Staw (Eds.), *Research in organizational behavior* (Vol. 6, pp. 191-233). Homewood, IL: JAI Press, 1984.

Daft, R. L., & Lengel, R. H. (1986). Organizational information requirements, media richness and structural design. *Management Science, 32*(5), 554-571.

de Sola Pool, I. (1983). *Forecasting the telephone: A retrospective technology assessment.* Norwood, NJ: Ablex.

Dozier, D. M., & Rice, R. E. (1984). Rival theories of electronic newsreading. In R. E. Rice & Associates. *The new media: Communication, research and technology* (pp. 103-127). Beverly Hills, CA: Sage.

Eveland, J. D., & Bikson, T. K. (1987). Evolving electronic communication networks: An empirical assessment. *Office: Technology and People, 3*(2), 103-128.

Feldman, M. S. (1987). Constraints on communication and electronic mail. *Office: Technology and People, 3*(2), 83-101.

Goldstein, D. K. (1986). *IBM Europe headquarters.* Harvard Business School, ICCH 0-187-025.

Granovetter, M. (1973). The strength of weak ties. *American Journal of Sociology, 78*(6), 1360-80.

Granovetter, M. (1978). Threshold models of collective behavior. *American Journal of Sociology, 83*(6), 1420-1443.

Granovetter, M., & Soong, R. (1983). Threshold models of diffusion and collective behavior. *Journal of Mathematical Sociology, 9,* 165-179.

Hammer, M. (1985). *Intra-company electronic mail: Its impacts on managers' working methods.* Technical Report, NYU Graduate School of Business Administration, New York. (Available from Prof. Jon A. Turner, NYU.)

Hiltz, S. R. (1984). *Online communities: A case study of the office of the future.* Norwood, NJ: Ablex.

Hiltz, S. R., & Turoff, M. (1978). *The network nation: Human communication via computer.* Reading, MA: Addison-Wesley.

Johansen, R., Vallee, J., & Spangler, K. (1979). *Electronic meetings: Technical alternatives and social choices.* Reading, MA: Addison-Wesley.

Katz, E. (1962). Notes on the unit of adoption in diffusion research. *Sociological Inquiry, 32*(1), 3-9.

Kerr, E. B., & Hiltz, S. R. (1982). *Computer-mediated communication systems: Status and evaluation.* New York, NY: Academic Press.

Kneale, D. (1986, February 24). The electronic in-basket. *The Wall Street Journal,* pp. 24D, 29D.

Malone, T. W. (1984). Heuristics for designing enjoyable user interfaces: Lessons from computer games. In J. C. Thomas & M. L. Schneider (Eds.), *Human factors in computer systems* (pp. 1-12). Norwood, NJ: Ablex.

Malone, T. W., Brobst, S. A., Grant, K. R., & Cohen, M. D. (1987). Intelligent message routing systems. *Communications of the ACM, 30*(5), 390-402.

Markus, M. L. (1981). Implementation politics: Top management support and user involvement. *Systems, Objectives, Solutions, 1*(4) 203-215.

Markus, M. L. (1984). *Systems in organizations: Bugs and features.* Cambridge, MA: Ballinger.

Markus, M. L. (1987). Chargeback as a tactic for implementing office communication systems. *Interfaces, 17*(3), 54-63.

Markus, M. L. (1988). *Information richness theory, managers and media choice.* Paper presented at the 1988 Annual Meeting of the Academy of Management, Anaheim, California.

Marwell, G., Oliver, P. E., & Prahl, R. (1988). Social networks and collective action: A theory of the critical mass. III. *American Journal of Sociology, 94*(3), 502-534.

Oliver, P. (1985). Rewards and punishments as selective incentives for collective action: Theoretical investigations. *American Journal of Sociology, 85* (6), 1356-1375.

Oliver, P. E., Marwell, G. (1988). The paradox of group size in collective action. *American Sociological Review, 53* (1), 1-8.

Oliver, P., Marwell, G., & Teixeira, R. (1985). A theory of critical mass I. Interdependence, group heterogeneity, and the production of collective action. *American Journal of Sociology, 91*(3), 522-56.

Olson, Jr., M. (1965). *The logic of collective action: Public goods and the theory of groups.* New York, NY: Schocken Books.

Rice, R. E. (1982). Communication networking in computer-conferencing systems: A longitudinal study of group roles and system structure. In M. Burgoon (Ed.), *Communication yearbook 6* (pp. 925-944). Beverly Hills, CA: Sage.

Rice, R. E., & Bair, J. H. (1984). New organizational media and productivity. In R. E. Rice & Associates. *The new media: Communication, research and technology* (pp. 198-215). Beverly Hills, CA: Sage.

Rogers, E. M. (1983). *Diffusion of innovations* (3rd ed.). New York, NY: Free Press.

Rogers, E. M. (1986). *Communication technology: The new media in society.* New York: Free Press.

Rohlfs, J. (1974). A theory of interdependent demand for a communication service. *The Bell Journal of Economics and Management Science, 5*(1), 16-37.

Schelling, T. C. (1978). *Micromotives and macrobehavior.* New York: W. W. Norton & Co.

Short, J., Williams, E., & Christie, B. (1976). *The social psychology of telecommunications.* London: John Wiley.

Sigafoos, R. A. (1983). *Absolutely positively overnight: Wall Street's darling inside and up close.* Memphis, TN: St. Luke's Press.

Sproull, L., & Kiesler, S. (1986). Reducing social context cues: The case of electronic mail. *Management Science, 32*(11), 1492-1512.

Steinfield, C. W. (1986). Computer mediated communication in an organizational setting: Explaining task-related and socioemotional uses. In M. L. McLaughlin (Ed.), *Communication yearbook 9* (pp. 777-804). Beverly Hills, CA: Sage.

Steinfield, C. W., & Fulk, J. (1986). *Information processing in organizations and media choice.* Paper presented at the International Communication Association Conference, Chicago, Illinois.

Thompson, J. D. (1967). *Organizations in action.* New York: McGraw-Hill.

Turner, J. A. (1985). *The organization of work with integrated office systems: A case study in commercial banking.* Unpublished manuscript, Center for Research on Information Systems, New York University, CRIS Working Paper 107.

Uhlig, R. P., Farber, D. J., & Bair, J. H. (1979). *The office of the future: Communication and computers.* Amsterdam: North-Holland.

TERRY CONNOLLY
BRIAN K. THORN

10. Discretionary Databases: Theory, Data, and Implications

Organizational members routinely have, or could readily acquire, information on a wide range of topics that would be of value to their colleagues: local expertise and experience, details of available technologies, assessments of specific markets, contact with individuals, evaluations of colleagues' abilities, and a vast array of other information. Some of this information is communicated to potential users by informal channels of various sorts, some (probably quite little) by formal channels. We label it *discretionary* to emphasize the fact that it is initially under the control of one organizational member, who can choose whether or not to make it available to others. Such technologies as computerized bulletin boards and the public distribution list capabilities of electronic mail systems are intended to facilitate distribution of this discretionary information.

The central contention of this paper is that discretionary information in organizations may have the properties of what are called *public goods* (Barry & Hardin, 1982). Related notions include the commons dilemma (Hardin, 1968); social traps (Platt, 1973); and the free rider problem (Sweeney, 1973)—all aspects of what are referred to as "social dilemmas" (see Dawes, 1980; Messick & Brewer, 1983, for reviews). The special kind of social dilemma involved in the provision of public goods is that, if provided, the good is available to everyone, regardless of whether or not they contributed to its provision; and one individual's consumption of it does not reduce what is available to anyone else. Public television, clean air, and lighthouses are often offered as exemplars (see Rapoport, 1987).

What makes public goods such a fascinating problem is that, if everyone acts in a perfectly sensible way, they won't get what they want. This is not

Authors' Note: Financial support for this work was provided in part under a contract from the Office of Naval Research # 14-83-K-0742 to the first author. Helpful comments on an earlier draft were received from Gary Wagner, Doug Vogel, the editors, and two anonymous reviewers. An earlier version appeared in *Communication Research, 14*, 1987, pp. 512-528.

the same problem as greed and altruism, where one person gives something up so that others can enjoy more. Your contribution to OXFAM or CARE costs you something, but you give because a lot of other people benefit more than you give up. With public goods problems, everyone would be better off if the "good" is provided, and everyone would be happy with their bargain (what they gained minus what they paid) in a quite self-interested way. The problem is that everyone would be happier still if they got the good without having to pay—that is, if they were able to enjoy a free ride. Unless there's a way to stop this free riding, everyone will try to take one and there will be no good for anyone.

Public radio is an excellent example. I enjoy the news and music on public radio and would be happy to spend, say, a dollar a week to keep it on the air. Suppose that, if all the potential listeners in town contributed at this rate, the service could continue. Because it is very unlikely that my contribution is the one that makes the difference between the station staying on the air and its folding, I can probably enjoy public radio *and* keep my $50 a year. But if everyone else makes the same calculation, the station will definitely fold, despite everyone's willingness to spend $50 to keep it alive.

As an organizational example, consider the local market information available to regional managers of a national organization. Each manager, we assume, will routinely monitor the economy of his or her region, tracking interest rates, employment trends, weather patterns, state and local tax bases, and a host of other factors. The manager could, with little effort, compile this information into a brief report on the local economy for distribution to other managers. But why should he or she do so? The cost, even if modest, is real; and the manager already knows that content of the report, and so gains nothing from its distribution. The manager might hope that distributing the report might induce other managers to contribute their own valuable information; or he or she might feel obliged by public spiritedness or company loyalty to absorb the cost at no gain. But to the extent that individual managers operate on a careful consideration of their own costs and benefits, the "public good" (a comprehensive, region-by-region database) will not come into existence, despite the desire of all concerned that it should. Both analytic and empirical study of public goods (see, for example, Marwell & Ames, 1979; Isaac, McCue, & Plott, 1985) suggest that such goods will generally be undersupplied.

The purpose of this chapter is to explore the idea that discretionary information in organizations is a public good, in the sense outlined above, and that this may be a serious problem in information sharing. Note that the analysis does not turn on any particular communication technology. It should be as relevant to traditional as to novel technologies. The key point is that, as in the regional economic assessment example, the cost of contributing the information falls narrowly on one person, while the benefits accrue more widely and indiscriminately. The analysis is thus relevant to organizational communication problems in general, as well as those raised by electronic communication media in particular.

In the first section, we outline the basic analysis that leads to the prediction of undersupply of discretionary information and explore some of the major variables that might affect the extent of such undersupply. In the second part of the chapter, we describe briefly a series of laboratory experiments we have conducted, testing some of the predictions of this theory. Some implications and suggestions for further development are noted in the Conclusion.

The Basic Model

We define a discretionary database as a shared pool of data to which several participants (individuals, departments) may, if they choose, separately contribute information. We will assume that a participant incurs some costs, if he or she contributes information, and enjoys some benefit from using the information that is available on the database. (Note that *costs* include effort, delay, reputational risk and loss of strategic opportunity, as well as money; *benefits* include time savings, decisional improvements, and career enhancement, as well as money savings.) For simplicity we shall also assume that the information has a limited lifetime, after which it disappears unless reentered, generating new cost for the enterer. (In some practical cases it might be more realistic to assume that outdated items remain in the system, imperiling the users. Such a case would require an extension of the present analysis).

These simple assumptions allow us to make some surprisingly strong predictions as to who will contribute to such a database, what information it will contain, and who will benefit from its use. Consider a system of $(N + 1)$ individuals such as those described above, each of whom may contribute, at cost c, one item of information. All users have free access to any information contributed by others, and each item generates, on the average, a benefit b to each user. A given user now faces each period a choice between two possible payoff functions, one for contributing, the other for withholding (see Figure 10.1). (Note that our assumptions imply a linear relationship between payoff and number of players contributing. More general, nonlinear payoff functions are discussed by Oliver, Marwell, & Teixeira, 1985).

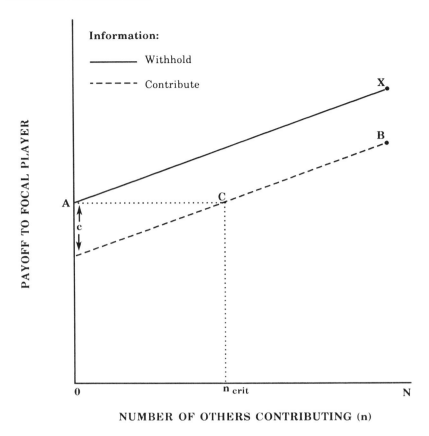

Figure 10.1 Payoffs to Focal Player as a Function of Number of Others Contributing

The focal user's ideal outcome, obviously, is point X, at which he enjoys the benefit of everyone else's contributions without having to incur the cost of contributing himself. Indeed, for any number, n, of other users contributing, the focal user is better off by the contribution cost, c, if he withholds his information. Withholding is, in game theoretic terms, a "dominant strategy," a strategy that leaves the focal player better off regardless of what the other players do. The temptation is to "free ride" on the contributions of others.

Unfortunately, the results of this dominant strategy may be undesirable. Recall that we assumed above that all users were in the same situation with regard to costs and benefits. (We will relax this assumption later). The logic that leads the focal user to withhold applies equally to all the users. No one contributes information, so each enjoys only payoff A, the payoff obtained

222

with no information on the database. If, as in Figure 10.1, there are enough players, and sufficient potential benefits from the contributions of each, a more satisfactory solution from everyone's point of view would be at point B, the payoff to each participant when everyone contributes. Withholding, the dominant strategy, leads to what is known as a *deficient equilibrium* (*equilibrium*, in the sense that no player has an incentive to move away from it on his own, *deficient* in the sense that a solution everyone likes better is available). By everyone acting in his self-interest, a solution is obtained that is no one's self-interest!

Another way to look at this result is to note that, given an equilibrium as A in Figure 10.1, trades are possible that would leave everyone better off. For example, in the deficient equilibrium just described, each user would benefit by an amount b from the focal user's information, so would presumably be prepared to pay up to b to get it. An outside agent could thus approach N such users, collect b from each of them, and offer the total, bN, to the focal user as an inducement to contribute his information. If bN is greater than c, the charge for contribution, the user would contribute, and everyone would be better off. This process would continue until all possible deals had been struck, and each user would then receive the resulting payoff, B. From this perspective the problem is seen as a failure of the system to bring together eager buyers and sellers of information. We shall return to this perspective later.

The practical implications of this analysis are straightforward and worrying: To the extent that the arrangements and incentives of a real information system are reflected in the model, we would expect to find discretionary information generally undersupplied. The arrangements and incentives we have postulated are, however, highly simplified. Do the conclusions change as we introduce elements of realism?

1. System-Wide Subsidies. One strategy for attacking the undersupply problem might be for the organization to subsidize contributions, reducing the effective cost, c. For example, the organization might provide data-entry personnel and equipment, provide training to contributors, eliminate computer charge-backs, or even make cash or budgetary awards based on amount of information provided. If this subsidy were made large enough, the cost, c, could even become negative (i.e., paying rather than charging for contributions), so that contributing became the dominant strategy. The obvious drawback to such subsidies is that they would apply equally to all classes of information, good, bad, and indifferent. If contribution is sufficiently subsidized, the problem flips from undersupply of valuable information to oversupply of useless or harmful information. (An incentive scheme of just this form may operate in scientific publishing, where the costs of publication are heavily subsidized by employers and substantial individual-level incentives exist for publishing, regardless of the merit of what is published. "Publish or perish" incentives thus endanger the value of the shared data base known as the "scientific literature.") Across-the-board subsidies, then, shift the problem from undersupply of good information to oversupply of bad.

2. Size and Information Quality. For the simple model we have considered so far, the equilibrium condition is always at A (total withholding), as long as c, the contribution charge, is positive. Whether or not this equilibrium is deficient, in the sense discussed above, depends on two things: the value of each player's information to each of the others, and the number of other players. If there are many other players or if the value of the information to each is large, then the noncontributing equilibrium is deficient. The point at which this happens is labeled C in Figure 10.1. It can be thought of as specifying the smallest number, n_{crit}, of system participants whose total gain from receiving an item of information, $b \times n_{crit}$, just offsets the contribution cost, c, incurred by the individual contributing the item to the system. Below this point, withholding information makes sense both for the individual and for the system as a whole; above this point, it makes sense for the individual, but not for the system. Alternatively, n_{crit} is the smallest viable coalition of contributors, in the sense that, if this many individuals contribute, they can do as well thereby as they would if they all withheld their information.

The condition that defines point C—that $n_{crit} \times b = c$—represents a range of very different situations. At one extreme there are only two participants, one of whom controls a single item of information whose value, b, to the other just balances the contribution cost, c. At the other extreme the focal player's information is of small value to a very large number of other players. In each case an omniscient system designer would like the contribution to occur, but it seems likely that the probability of this happening decreases as the size of the group increases. In the two-person case, for example, one individual's decision to contribute has a direct and obvious effect on the well-being of the other—and the other is in a position to know who is helping or harming him. If, as we assume, all players are in the same position, the recipient is able to reciprocate either cooperation or withholding, so the first player might contribute in hopes of inducing the other to cooperate. (The structure in this case reduces to that of a Prisoners' Dilemma, a game that has been very extensively studied; see, for example, Hardin, 1982.) In contrast, contribution or withholding in the many-player system is much less readily traced and punished, so one might expect contribution rates to be lower. Several studies of public goods provision (e.g., Sweeney, 1973; Marwell & Ames, 1979) have found lower contribution rates in larger groups.

3. *Asymmetries*. Perhaps the most obvious oversimplification of the basic model is the assumption that all participants hold information of equal value to others, benefit equally from the contributions of others, and pay the same cost to contribute. Clearly, in any real setting, none of these symmetries will necessarily hold. Some participants will have access to better information than others, some will stand to benefit more from information of a given quality than do others, some will be able to contribute more cheaply than others. We shall refer to these asymmetries as *sender*, *user*, and *cost* asymmetries respectively. We assume that the general case will contain asymmetries of both kinds.

Would asymmetries be expected to change the hypothesized pattern of contribution and withholding? Our prediction is that asymmetry will reduce contribution. Consider first a sender-asymmetric situation in which some participants control *good* information, others *bad* information. Exchanges amongst the good players will be governed by incentives as above, but a good player making his information available to a bad player can expect only bad information in return. The good player's overall incentive to contribute is thus reduced, if part of that incentive is taken to be the hope for reciprocity. Conversely, the bad player has little to offer to induce the good player to contribute.

Consider now the converse, user-asymmetric cases in which some users benefit greatly from getting a given item of information, while others benefit less. The high-benefit users might be expected to contribute heavily, in hopes of eliciting reciprocity; but the low-benefit users gain little from this largesse and have little incentive to reciprocate. Thus, assuming that the hope of reciprocity is part of the incentive to contribute, asymmetries should reduce overall contribution rates below those obtained in equivalent symmetrical conditions. (Note that the prediction here is directly opposed to that of conventional public goods theory, which predicts that the existence of a subset of actors having either large interest in the good or large resources to contribute to providing it increases the chances of achieving a "critical mass" and thus providing the good for everyone [see Oliver et al., 1985]. The contrast re-emphasizes the unusual nature of information as a public good: Each item of information contributed provides a separate benefit to everyone *except* the provider; his benefits arise only from the contributions of others, with no direct link to his own decisions.)

4. Potential Escape Strategies. One familiar proposal for the solution of public goods problems is the *privatization* of the good—that is, turning the public good into a private one that can be bought and sold (see, for example, Cross & Guyer, 1980). In the present context, this would involve providing each participant a proprietary interest in the information he controls and making users pay, so that income would balance contribution costs. In our earlier example each manager would simply offer for sale copies of the local market report and keep the proceeds. The difficulty with such a scheme is that establishing appropriate "markets" involves huge organizational overhead. We explore two primitive schemes of this type later in the chapter. Detailed analysis of either information markets linking individuals in pairwise transactions or shared data bases jointly funded by groups of individuals would add a great deal of complexity to our simple model.

A second approach is the incorporation of the participants into a single over-riding incentive structure, such as an organization-wide profit-sharing scheme. In such schemes, some fraction of the profits earned by the individuals separately is divided among them all. Each individual would then have a two-part incentive, one based strictly on his own performance, the other on the aggregate performance of his colleagues. Given appropriate numerical values, contribution charges incurred in providing information to one's colleagues might raise their performance enough to generate a net gain via the profit-sharing scheme. Careful experimentaion would be needed to get these systems to operate in the desired way.

Summary

We have outlined here a formal analysis of an abstract communication structure we call a *discretionary database*, which is intended to represent the key features of such real communication systems as simple bulletin boards, distribution lists and shared databases, conventional or electronic. The key features of these systems are: (a) that there is a cost for contributing information; (b) that participants can contribute or not, as they choose; and (c) that information on the system is freely available to all, and is of potential benefit to those who use it. These characteristics suggest that discretionary databases can be usefully considered as public goods. An immediate implication is that less information will be contributed to such systems than either the designers or the participants would want. If contribution costs are significant, participants will be deterred from contributing information that could be of significant value to colleagues, since there is no clear mechanism by which the recipients' gratitude can be converted into income for the contributor. If contribution costs are subsidized across the board to the point at which contribution becomes profitable, we would predict that information will, in fact, be contributed—but without regard to its value to potential recipients. Large systems will generally justify more contributions than small ones, as they involve more users. However, large systems weaken the possible linkage between contributor and beneficiary, diluting the hope for reciprocity. We therefore predict less contribution in large systems than in small. Finally, asymmetries caused by unequal information quality, unequal information benefit or unequal contribution cost will, we predict, further reduce contribution rates, as they also dilute the hope of reciprocity. Possible remedial strategies include market analogs with information bought and sold, and corporate incentive schemes with contribution rates raised by profit-sharing.

This highly simplified treatment of discretionary databases provides a useful starting point for studying real systems. The procedures and findings of some exploratory experiments are presented in the next section.

Some Experimental Results

In the series of experiments reported here, student subjects participated in a simple business game. They played the role of production manager in charge of agricultural output of an imaginary country, which produces a single agricultural product for world-wide distribution. Each period, the manager set the production level for his or her product for the subsequent period. Demand varied from period to period, and production above or below this level resulted in penalties. The task structure is discussed in detail in Connolly and Thorn (1986). The game was implemented on a network of up to eight microcomputers located in different rooms and connected to a central file-sharer.

Each manager was told that, being located in a different country, he or she was in an advantageous position to assess the local economy and thus the likely demand for the different products. Subjects were presented with this demand information at the start of each period and could, if they wished, contribute it to a database available to the other players, incurring a charge if they did so. They were then shown the content of the database, showing demand for each nation that had contributed market estimates, a *Not Available* (NA) code otherwise. They then set a production level for their own product for the subsequent period. Finally, they were shown actual demand for the period, penalties and charges were computed and displayed, and the game moved to another period.

Subjects were recruited from undergraduate business classes with offers of pay and credit towards a lab participation requirement. On arrival at the lab, they were briefed together on the experimental procedures and equipment, before being shown to separate rooms for the experiment proper. Direct communication between subjects, either by voice or computer, was not allowed. After 24 periods of play, the subjects completed a brief postexperimental questionnaire, were paid and debriefed, and released. Pay was based on performance, and typically ranged between $4 and $6 for a 1-hour experiment.

Experiment 1

Design: The initial experiment investigated the effect of c, the contribution charge, on contribution rates in 4-person groups. Subjects were given an initial money stake each trial and contribution charges and penalties were deducted from this. To equate possible earnings across conditions, the three experimental conditions were:

Low cost: Stake = 25 cents; Contribution charge = 1 cent;
Medium cost: Stake = 30 cents; Contribution charge = 6 cents;
High cost: Stake = 35 cents; Contribution charge = 11 cents.

Four groups were run in each condition, for a total of 48 subjects.

Results: As predicted, contribution rate declined as contribution charge increased. At $c = 1$, subjects contributed overall on 68% of the opportunities they had to do so; at $c = 6$, the rate dropped to 32%, and was 33% at $c = 11$. The effect of c is statistically significant ($F = 11.71$; $p<.0001$). There was evidence of a tendency to increase contribution rates from the first 12 trials to the second 12, ($F = 3.22$; $p<.08$), though the size of this effect was modest except for the $c = 1$ groups, where contribution rates rose from 63% to 73%.

Discussion: These findings indicate that the subjects do not behave as the narrow self-interest model predicts. Even with a very modest contribution charge of one cent, overall contribution rate is well below 100% (lowering actual earnings: net earnings in the $c = 1$ condition averaged $4.02 per subject, only 70% of the maximum $5.76 they would have earned by 100% contribution). Withholding is a heavy majority choice in both the $c = 6$ and $c = 11$ conditions, cutting average earnings to $3.51 and $4.32 respectively. The model predicts zero contribution in all 3 cases.

Experiment 2

Design: Two asymmetrical conditions were constructed. A source-asymmetric condition gave 2 group members information that was 9 times as valuable (in penalty avoidance) as that available to the other 2 members, with all 4 members facing identical contribution charges and error penalty schedules. A user-asymmetric condition gave 2 members error penalty schedules 9 times as steep as those for the other 2, with all 4 members controlling equally valuable information and equal contribution charges. Four groups were run in each asymmetry condition under low ($c = 1$) and medium ($c = 6$) contribution charges, for a total of 64 subjects.

Results: Mean contribution rates in the source asymmetric conditions were 55% ($c = 1$) and 29% ($c = 6$). In the user-asymmetric conditions, contribution rates were 49% ($c = 1$) and 22% ($c = 6$). Contribution rates in both asymmetrical conditions were thus lower than in the equivalent symmetrical cells: 68% ($c = 1$) and 32% ($c = 6$). Two-way analysis of variance showed a significant main effect for contribution charge ($F = 45.09$; $p<.0001$) and for symmetry condition ($F = 3.62$; $p<.03$).

Discussion: These results provide support for the hypothesis that asymmetries reduce contribution rates. They also suggest that user asymmetry is a stronger disincentive to contribution than is source asymmetry, an effect for which we have no immediate explanation.

Experiment 3

Design: We explored two alternative bidding arrangements by which users could compensate senders for their contribution charges. In the first, posted-price arrangement, each player established an asking price each period for his or her information, and users specified the amount they would be prepared to contribute to meet this price. If the total exceeded the posted price, that item was placed on the database, and the contributing player received the net of total bids and contribution charge. In the second, posted-bid arrangement, players first made offers of what they would be prepared to contribute to the purchase of each item of information. Each potential sender reviewed the total offers made for his or her information and decided whether or not to contribute at that price. If the sender did contribute, all transactions cleared as before.

Both posted-price and posted-bid procedures were run in symmetrical and both asymmetrical conditions under moderate contribution charge ($c = 6$ cents). With four groups in each of these six conditions, a total of 96 subjects participated.

Results: Recall that with $c = 6$ under nonbidding conditions, contribution rates averaged 32%, 29%, and 22% for the symmetric, source-asymmetric, and user-asymmetric conditions respectively. For the posted-price conditions, the corresponding rates were 50%, 40%, and 41%. For the posted-bid conditions, the rates were 64%, 58%, and 46%. Combining these observations into a 3 × 3 ANOVA shows significant main effects for bidding arrangement ($F = 21.11$; p<.0001) and symmetry ($F = 3.87$; p<.03).

Discussion: Even these crude bidding arrangements had a marked effect on the propensity of individuals to contribute their information to the database. Though it appears that the posted-bid arrangement is more effective than the posted-price arrangement in eliciting contribution, our primary interest is not in the differential effectiveness of alternative bidding arrangements. Rather we wish to emphasize the superior contribution rates achieved in either bidding system, as compared to the simple public good structure. "Privatization," if it could be implemented practically, could significantly improve information sharing in discretionary systems.

Experiment 4

Design: As a preliminary probe of the effects of group size, we selected the symmetrical, $c = 6$, 4-person groups as a baseline, and compared them to equivalent 8-person groups in nonbidding, posted-price, and posted-bid conditions. Using four groups in each condition required a further 96 subjects for these larger groups.

Results: With groups of size 4, contribution rates averaged 32%, 50%, and 64% for the nonbid, posted-price, and posted-bid conditions respectively. The corresponding rates for the 8-person groups were 34%, 47%, and 59%. A 3 × 2 ANOVA confirms the significant main effect for bidding condition ($F = 14.39$; p<.0001), but shows no effect for group size ($F = 0.21$; ns).

Discussion: The absence of an effect for group size is surprising, in light of the substantial body of evidence finding such an effect in other public goods studies. This is an obvious anomaly inviting further exploration. It should, perhaps, be noted that groups of size 8 are still much too small to allow anonymity to individuals; an explanation for the absence of a group size effect must come from elsewhere.

General Discussion

This chapter has outlined a formal theory of discretionary databases in organizations and shown how it can be tested and developed using normal laboratory methods. We are excited about the leads it opens up for further work. On the theory side, extension could address such issues as contribution costs that differ across participants; formation and stability of coalitions; information that persists or decays over time; and the effects of organizational boundaries (i.e., the contrast of intra- and inter-organizational databases). Empirical work both in the laboratory (extending to other tasks, populations, and settings) and in the field (adding the richness and realism of the organizational context) is clearly called for. Indeed, we sincerely hope that the incompleteness of the present sketch will attract others to contribute to the work. Our aim has been simply to suggest that the approach has serious promise. We are encouraged that Markus, in this volume, also demonstrates the power of public goods thinking for the analysis of organizational communication issues. Though her concerns and emphases differ from ours, the basic convergence in form of analysis suggests the beginnings of important new theorizing.

At root the theoretical proposal common to both Markus and ourselves is that we should take seriously the detailed incentive structure that operates on those who provide information to, and those who withdraw information from, discretionary data bases (see also Connolly & Porter, 1990). There is no reason to assume a priori that such incentive structures will stimulate communication behavior that is beneficial for either the organization or any of its members. It seems likely that public goods incentive structures operate commonly in organizations and lead to large undersupply of valuable information. The first part of the chapter developed a simple model of this process and derived hypotheses about how system-wide subsidies, size, information quality, and asymmetries among users and senders would affect information contribution. The general prediction is that discretionary information will be chronically undersupplied. Remedial mechanisms will thus be of interest. We sketched two such mechanisms, one based on bidding arrangements, the other on group-wide incentives.

Theoretical analysis is not enough, of course: we need evidence (Rapoport, 1987). The second part of the chapter described some experiments testing the theoretical propositions in the context of a simple organizational communication and decision-making task. The findings support the basic hypothesis that discretionary data is generally undersupplied, to the detriment of individuals and organization alike. At the same time the findings are rich enough to highlight the inadequacies of the theoretical model and to suggest directions for its extension and refinement.

The broad issue of discretionary information systems seems likely to be one of growing importance for organizations. The technology of storing and distributing information is advancing rapidly; but we see relatively little evidence of parallel growth in the understanding of how this technology can be best harnessed. Existing database thinking seems primarily concerned with data (e.g., financial, inventory) that is already entered to a corporate database for other purposes, so that "contribution charges" are effectively zero. At the other extreme are efforts in the spirit of "expert systems" work, where large, widespread, or long-term benefits justify large investment in information acquisition. This leaves a large intermediate region in which both information and need exist within the organization and for which mutually advantageous exchanges could be achieved if user(s) and supplier(s) were efficiently brought into contact. This is the domain of the "discretionary database." We are only beginning to get a handle on this domain, either theoretically or empirically.

Incomplete understanding or not, the area already has important practical implications. The most central, clearly, is that all of us, designers, users, and potential contributors, pay serious attention to the incentive systems that bear on our information exchanges. Getting information from A to B will often involve costs that fall on A and benefits that accrue to B. Is there any way by which B's gratitude, and B's needs, are regularly communicated to A? Can we arrange for this gratitude to be converted into assistance for A in gathering and contributing the relevant information? How can we organize groups of As and Bs so that their information can be packaged and transmitted as it is needed? Are the costs justified by the payoffs? And how can the two be brought together in one place, so that benefits and costs can be realistically balanced? These are not familiar questions to the information system designer and user. The analysis of discretionary databases suggests that they should be.

References

Barry, B., & Hardin, R. (Eds.). (1982). *Rational man and irrational society?* Beverly Hills, CA: Sage.

Connolly, T., & Thorn, B. K. (1986). Predecisional information acquisition: Effects of task variables on suboptimal search strategies. *Organizational Behavior and Human Decision Performance, 39*, 397-416.

Connolly, T., & Porter, A. L. (1990). Discretionary databases in forecasting. *Journal of Forecasting, 9,* 1-12.

Cross, J. G., & Guyer, M. J. (1980). *Social traps.* Ann Arbor: University of Michigan Press.

Dawes, R. M. (1980). Social dilemmas. *Annual Review of Psychology, 31,* 169-193.

Hardin, G. (1968). The tragedy of the commons. *Science, 162,* 1243-1248.

Hardin, R. (1982). *Collective action.* Baltimore, MD: John Hopkins University Press.

Isaac, R. M., McCue, K. F., & Plott, C. R. (1985). Public goods provision in an experimental environment. *Journal of Public Economics, 26,* 51-74.

Marwell, G., & Ames, R. (1979). Experiments in the provision of public goods. I. Resources, interest, group size, and the free-rider problem. *American Journal of Sociology, 84,* 1335-1360.

Messick, D. M., & Brewer, M. B. (1983). Solving social dilemmas: A review. In L. Wheeler & P. Shaver (Eds.), *Review of personality and social psychology* (Vol. 4, pp. 11-44). Beverly Hills, CA: Sage.

Oliver, P, Marwell, G., & Teixeira, R. (1985). A theory of the critical mass. I. Interdependence, group heterogeneity, and the production of collective action. *American Journal of Sociology, 91,* 522-556.

Platt, J. (1973). Social traps. *American Psychologist, 28,* 641-651.

Rapoport, A. (1987). Research paradigms and expected utility models for public goods. *Psychological Review, 94,* 74-83.

Sweeney, J. W. (1973). An experimental investigation of the free-rider problem. *Social Science Research, 2,* 277-292.

PART V

Information Technology and Organizational Design

We conclude our series of theoretical essays with three chapters that examine the interface between information technology and organizational design. The authors of these three chapters work from the premise that the availability of new information and communication technologies has important implications for the way we design and structure organizations. They invite a re-examination of classic theories of design, prompted by the possibility that new technological capabilities obviate many of the core assumptions upon which design principles are based. Each chapter then suggests how theories of organization can be modified to incorporate new challenges from advanced, computer-based information and telecommunications technologies.

George Huber integrates findings from studies of information technology with organizational theory to arrive at a theory of the effects of advanced information technologies on organizational design, intelligence, and decision making. He focuses attention on two classes of information technologies—computer assisted communications and decision aiding technologies. He proposes that use of these technologies affects two key organizational parameters: (1) characteristics of organizational intelligence and decision making, such as timeliness and quality of decisions, and (2) aspects of organizational design related to intelligence and decision making, such as the size and composition of decision units. Huber's chapter presents a set of integrated propositions and concepts which form the core of his theory.

Thomas Allen and Oscar Hauptman also invoke principles of organizational design, although they limit their focus to research and development organizations. Allen and Hauptman propose that at the core of any R&D endeavor is a tension between two communication-related goals: (1) the coordination of activities across specialties on multidisciplinary tasks, and (2) the acquisition of state-of-the-art information in a functional area. The former goal is best met by a structure that groups researchers from diverse fields into project teams. Staying abreast of current developments in a particular field, however, is best supported by grouping people of like specialties together in a functional design. The choice of either design constrains an organization's ability to effectively meet the goals served by the other design. Allen and Hauptman analyze project needs for coordination and information acquisition by deriving a three-dimensional model of R&D design in relation to structural forms: task interdependence, task duration, and the rate of change in knowledge. They define an area in the three-dimensional space in which use of new information technologies can shift beneficially the boundaries of effectiveness of each form. The net effect is to increase the structural options available to R&D organizations for pursuing *both* project and functional goals.

The final chapter by Keen reminds us that organizations exist within an ongoing competitive environment. He is concerned that organizations have responded to complexity in their environment by themselves becoming more complex. This creates a number of organizational design pathologies that reduce effectiveness. Keen also proposes that technologies can enable new organizational designs, but his focus in less on specific media than on the broader telecommunications infrastructure. Keen recognizes the often massive investment required to establish the infrastructure, but suggests that telecommunications can be a means to achieving less complex and more effective organizational designs. In a less formal fashion than preceding chapters, Keen illustrates how the implementation of a telecommunications infrastructure can enable such simplifying strategies as the reduction in management levels and in associated bureaucratic procedures.

GEORGE P. HUBER

11. A Theory of the Effects of Advanced Information Technologies on Organizational Design, Intelligence, and Decision Making

This article draws on the work of organizational researchers, communication researchers, and information systems researchers to set forth, in the form of a set of propositions, a theory concerning the effects that *advanced information technologies* have on organizational design, intelligence, and decision making. The motivations for such an article are four.

One motivation concerns the need to reinvestigate and possibly revise certain components of organization theory. A large part of what is known about the factors affecting organizational processes, structures, and performance was developed when the nature and mix of communication technologies were relatively constant, both across time and across organizations of the same general type. In contrast, the capabilities and forms of communication technologies have begun to vary, and they are likely to vary a great deal in the future. For example, communication technology (or communication medium) is now a variable whose traditionally relatively constant range (from face-to-face at one extreme to unaddressed broadcast documents at the other, Daft & Lengel, 1984, 1986) is being expanded by organizations to include *computer-assisted communication technologies* (e.g., electronic mail, image transmission devices, computer-conferencing, and videoconferencing) that facilitate access to people inside and outside the organization with an ease that previously was not possible. Also, more sophisticated and more

Author's Note: This research was largely supported by the U.S. Army Research Institute for the Behavioral and Social Sciences. I am indebted to Janice Beyer, Richard Daft, John Huber, Reuben McDaniel, Chet Miller, Ronald Rice, and Robert Zmud for their helpful suggestions on earlier versions of this paper and to Reuben McDaniel for his earlier contributions to my thinking on this subject. This chapter draws upon and expands upon Huber (1988) and is reprinted, by permission, from Huber (1989).

user-friendly forms of *computer-assisted decision-aiding technologies* (e.g., expert systems, decision-support systems, on-line management information systems, and external information retrieval systems) are in the late stages of development or early stages of implementation. Consequently, as the uses, capabilities, and forms of communication and decision-aiding technologies increase in their range, researchers must reassess what is known about the effects of these technologies because what is known may change. "That is, new media impacts may condition or falsify hypothesized relationships developed by past research" (Williams & Rice, 1983, p. 208). Thus, one motivation for setting forth propositions concerning the impact of advanced information technologies is to encourage investigation and debate on what the nature of organizational design, intelligence, and decision making might be when these technologies become more sophisticated and more widely used.

The second motivation is to take a step toward creating a theory of the effects that advanced information technologies have on organizations. *Advanced information technologies* are devices (a) that transmit, manipulate, analyze, or exploit information; (b) in which a digital computer processes information integral to the user's communication or decision task; and (c) that have either made their appearance since 1970 or exist in a form that aids in communication or decision tasks to a significantly greater degree than did pre-1971 forms. (For expanded discussion of the term *advanced information technologies*, see Culnan & Markus, 1987; Gibson & Jackson, 1987; Johansen, 1988; Rice & Associates, 1984; and Strassman, 1985a.) The need for such a theory has been exemplified in a review by Culnan and Markus (1987) and in a special issue of *Communication Research* (Steinfield & Fulk, 1987). In that special issue, the guest editors noted that, although there are many empirical findings concerning the effects of advanced information technologies on organizations, "there has been little synthesis, integration, and development of theoretical explanations [and] that it is time for theory development and theory-guided research" (Steinfield & Fulk, 1987, p. 479).

Together, the propositions in this article comprise a theory such as that called for by Steinfield and Fulk, but like any theory, it is limited. It includes as dependent variables only (a) characteristics of organizational intelligence and decision making, such as timeliness, and (b) aspects of organization design associated with intelligence and decision making, such as the size of decision units. Further, within this still rather large set of dependent variables, the theory includes only those (a) that seem to be significantly affected by advanced information technology, (b) that are of interest to organization

Table 11.1

Dependent Variables Included in the Theory (and the numbers of the propositions related to them)

Design Variables (Subunit Level)	Design Variables (Organizational Level)	Design Variables (Organizational Memory)	Performance Variables
Participation in decision making (1)	Centralization of decision making (4,5)	Development and use of computer-resident data bases (8)	Effectiveness of environmental scanning (10)
Size and heterogeneity of decision units (2)	Number of organizational levels involved in authorization (6)	Development and use of computer-resident in-house expert systems (9)	Quality and timeliness of organizational intelligence (11)
Frequency and duration of meetings (3)	Number of nodes in the information-processing network (7)		Quality of decisions (12)
			Speed of decision making (13, 14)

scientists or administrators, or (c) whose variance seems to have increased with the advent of advanced information technologies. The dependent variables included in the theory are shown in Table 11.1. Variables that are not included in the theory, but whose omission is briefly discussed, include horizontal integration, specialization, standardization, formalization, and the distribution of influence on organizational decisions.

As independent variables the theory includes only (a) the use of computer-assisted communication technologies and (b) the use of computer-assisted decision-aiding technologies. The theory does not encompass the use of computer-assisted production technologies or the use of transaction-enacting technologies such as computerized billing systems. (For ideas concerning the effects of advanced information technologies, broadly defined to include computer-assisted automation, on a broader set of organizational attributes, see Child, 1984, 1988; Gibson & Jackson, 1987; Strassman 1985a; Zuboff, 1984.) Finally, the theory does not explicitly address use of advanced information technologies for impression-management purposes such as those described by Sabatier (1978) and Feldman and March (1981).

The third motivation for integrating the work of organizational researchers, communication researchers, and information systems researchers is to help researchers in each of these fields become more aware of the existence, content, and relevance of the work done by researchers in other fields. Without such awareness, the efficiency of the research establishment is less, opportunities for synergy are lost, and progress in theory development is inhibited.

The fourth and last motivation is of practical, administrative importance. Advanced information technologies are becoming a pervasive aspect of organizations, but their relatively recent appearance and rapidly changing nature virtually guarantee that administrators and their advisors will not have experience as a guide in anticipating and planning for the impacts they may have. In the absence of experience, the value of theory is considerable.

It is important to note that the theory described here is not based on a great deal of directly applicable empirical research. There are two reasons for this. The first is that the components of organization theory that were drawn upon in developing the propositions were not validated under conditions in which decision and communication systems were computer assisted; consequently, they may not be valid for organizations that presently use a good deal of advanced information technology. The second reason is that many of the empirical studies that were drawn upon inductively in developing the propositions pertain to forms of technology that are not necessarily representative of the more sophisticated forms now in use or expected to be in use in the more distant future. (See Hofer, 1970; Pfeffer, 1978; Rice, 1980; Robey, 1977; Whistler, 1970, for brief reviews of some of these early studies, and Olson and Lucas, 1982, for some thoughtful speculations concerning the effects of advanced information technologies on a variety of organizational attributes and behaviors.) Thus most propositions about the organization-level effects of advanced information technology must be viewed with some caution, whether derived from mature, but possibly outdated, organization theory or from recent, but perhaps soon-to-be outdated, empirical findings.

The above cautions notwithstanding, the propositions set forth are supportable to the degree necessary to be responsive to the motivations just noted, especially if the qualifications attendant to each proposition are seriously considered by users. In any case, these propositions can serve as a basis for the development of specific hypotheses.

Nature of Advanced Information Technologies

What are the critical characteristics of advanced information technologies that might cause these technologies to have effects on organizational design, intelligence, and decision making different from the effects of more traditional technologies?

For purposes of discussion, characteristics of information technologies will be divided into two groups. *Basic characteristics* are related to data storage capacity, transmission capacity, and processing capacity. Advanced information technologies, largely as a result of their digital computer component, usually provide higher levels of these basic characteristics (Culnan & Markus, 1987, p. 420; Rice & Associates, 1984, p. 34). [No distinction is made in this definition or in this chapter between data (stimuli and symbols) and information (data conveying meaning as a result of reducing uncertainty).]

Characteristics of the second group I will call *properties*. Although the above basic dimensions are relevant to users, often it is the multi-dimensional configuration of the levels characterizing a particular technology that is most relevant for a particular task. Some authorities have considered these configurations when comparing advanced information technologies with traditional information technologies, and have made generalizations about the resultant properties of advanced information systems. Because these properties cause the use of advanced information systems to have effects such as those noted in this paper, some of these generalizations are reviewed here. (See Culnan & Markus, 1987; Rice & Associates, 1984, especially Chapter 2, for discussions of how these properties follow from the levels that the technologies attain on the basic dimensions.)

In the context of *communication*, these properties include those that facilitate the ability of the individual or organization (a) to communicate more easily and less expensively across time and geographic location (Rice & Bair, 1984); (b) to communicate more rapidly and with greater precision to targeted groups (e.g., Culnan & Markus, 1987; Sproull & Keisler, 1986); (c) to record and index more reliably and inexpensively the content and nature of communication events; and (d) to more selectively control access and participation in a communication event or network (Culnan & Markus, 1987; Rice, 1984).

In the context of *decision aiding*, the properties include those that facilitate the ability of the individual or organization (a) to store and retrieve large amounts of information more quickly and inexpensively; (b) to more rapidly and selectively access information created outside the organization; (c) to more rapidly and accurately combine and reconfigure information so as to create new information (as in the development of forecasting models or financial analyses); (d) to more compactly store and quickly use the judgment and decision models developed in the minds of experts, or in the mind of the decision maker, and stored as expert systems or decision models; and (e) to more reliably and inexpensively record and retrieve information about the content and nature of organizational transactions. (Discussions of these properties of computer-assisted decision-aiding technologies, richer in detail than space allows here, are contained in Sprague & McNurlin, 1986; Sprague & Watson, 1986; Zmud, 1983.)

Mistaken Impressions

It may be helpful to draw upon the above discussion of the basic characteristics and properties of information technologies to dispel some occasionally held, but mistaken, impressions. One such mistaken impression is that advanced information technologies are universally inferior or superior to traditional technologies. This impression is erroneous because the properties just delineated may be less important than other properties possessed by a more traditional technology. In addition, particular uses of the advanced technologies may have undesirable side effects (Culnan & Markus, 1987; Markus, 1984; Zuboff, 1984). Further, traditional technologies often score higher with respect to acceptability, ease of use, and richness (Culnan & Markus, 1987; Fulk, Steinfield, Schmitz, & Power, 1987; Trevino, Lengel, & Daft, 1987), or have scores that overlap on these properties with the scores of advanced information technologies. For these reasons, use of advanced information technologies will not eliminate use of traditional technologies. However, when the properties of advanced information technologies are useful for enhancing individual or organizational effectiveness, and when retarding forces such as those just noted are not potent, it is reasonable to believe that organizations will use the advanced technologies.

The availability of the advanced information technologies increases the communicating or decision-aiding options for the potential user, and thus in the long run, unless the selected technology is inappropriately employed, the effect is to increase the quality (broadly defined) of the user's communication or decision-making processes. Presumably, through experience or observation, organizational members learn which communication or decision-aiding technology is most likely to achieve their purpose, and then adopt it. Field studies, which will be cited later, verify this belief.

In a related vein, it is a mistake to view advanced information technologies solely as substitutes for traditional technologies. To the contrary, advanced information technologies are frequently used more as supplements and complements to traditional technologies, rather than as substitutes. For example, electronic mail is often used to confirm with text what was said in a phone conversation or to set up face-to-face appointments, and image transmission devices are often used to make available drawings that will be discussed after all the parties have had a chance to study them. Of course, people do substitute computer-assisted media for traditional media when it seems efficacious to do so. Overall, the effect of availability of user-friendly computer-assisted communication technology is to increase the range of options for the communicator. Presumably, through experience or observation, organizational members learn to choose communication technologies wisely. Evidence, which will be cited, indicates that this presumption is correct. An analogous discussion applies to computer-assisted decision-aiding technologies, but limits of space force its omission.

A final mistaken impression is that, although advanced information technologies may lead to rational outcomes (such as information that is more accurate and comprehensive or decisions that are more timely) in organizations characterized by strong adherence to a norm of economic rationality, these outcomes are unlikely in more highly politicized or power-driven organizations. In the absence of scientific evidence with which to develop the required contingency theory, three observations are offered. The first is that the external environments of many organizations are sufficiently competitive that, in order to survive, the organizations must adopt and properly use rationality-enhancing communication and decision-aiding technologies. If organizational politics interferes with such adoption or use, the marketplace or parent organization intervenes until universal conformance is achieved. Thus, in their time, the telegraph became a pervasive technology in railroads, the calculator in brokerage houses, and the radio in armies. In the organizations that survived, those managers whose proprietary inclinations caused them not to use the technologies to further organizational goals (such as timely delivery of freight, accurate and comprehensive information for investors, or effective coordination in battle) were evidently converted or purged. In essence, superordinates or organizations require subordinates or subunits to help them compete effectively or otherwise satisfy environmental demands, and if rational use of technology is necessary, it occurs in the long run, whatever the proprietary inclinations of the subordinates or subunits.

The second observation is that highly politicized or power-driven organizations also have highly competitive internal environments, and in such environments it is necessary for managers to maximize their own competitive effectiveness by appearing to satisfy the goals of resource controllers on an issue-by-issue basis. In these environments, technical or financial analyses are widely used to persuade the resource controllers that the manager's proposals best satisfy the resource controller's goals (Burgelman, 1982; Kelley, 1976; Shukla, 1982). Thus, even in organizations where power plays a significant role in resource allocation, so also do "the numbers" (Gerwin, 1979; Pfeffer & Moore, 1980; Sabatier, 1978; Shukla, 1982). Managers who do not employ the most appropriate technologies in developing and selling analyses are at a competitive disadvantage; they must adapt or lose out.

The third observation is that, in almost all organizations, effective fulfillment of organizational responsibilities contributes to the development and maintenance of a manager's reputation. Thus, aside from whatever a manager might do to negatively or positively affect the quality or timeliness of the design, intelligence, or decision making of superordinate units, he or she is likely to employ any communication or decision-aiding technologies that can contribute to his or her personal effectiveness or the effectiveness of his or her own unit (Daft, Lengel, & Trevino, 1987).

Together, these observations suggest that even though power and politics influence organizational design, intelligence, and decision making, so too do information technologies; *for advancement of their own interests, organizational participants will use advanced information technologies in ways that increase their effectiveness in fulfilling organizational goals.* This fundamental assumption underlies many of the propositions included in the theory and seems to be validated in the studies referenced.

The Propositions

The propositions are grouped for expositional purposes into four sections. The propositions in the first three sections portray the effects of advanced information technologies on organizational design, that is, the effects on (a) subunit structure and process, (b) organizational structure and process, and (c) organizational memory. Although these effects will most often result from evolved practices rather than from prior managerial intentions, I expect that in the future, as administrators and their advisors learn about whatever functional effects of advanced information technologies on organizational design and performance may accrue, more and more of the effects will be the outcomes of intentions. In the short run, however, many managers will probably continue to introduce advanced information systems in order to reduce the number of personnel, to increase managerial efficiency, or to imitate other managers. After the systems are implemented for these purposes, these managers or other organizational participants will sometimes see that the systems can accomplish other purposes and will adjust the organization's design to facilitate accomplishment of these purposes (e.g., by extending the scope of responsibility of an organizational unit that now has easier access to a broader range of information).

The propositions of the fourth section set forth the effects of advanced information technology on organizational intelligence and decision making. Some of these effects are direct and some occur indirectly through changes in design. (Organizational intelligence is the output or product of an organization's efforts to acquire, process, and interpret information external to the organization [Porter, 1980; Sammon, Kurland, & Spitalnic, 1984; Wilensky, 1967]. It is an input to the organization's decision makers.)

Each of these four sections contains specific suggestions concerning research that would seem to be useful for examining the validity and domains of particular propositions. The last section of the paper contains more general recommendations for researchers in the areas of organization science and information systems.

Effects at the Subunit Level

The focus in this section is on those aspects of organizational design that ultimately affect organizational intelligence and decision making. For example, aspects of structure that affect the accuracy of communications or the timeliness of decisions are considered. The first three propositions of the section deal with variables generally thought of in the context of organizational subunits. The remaining six propositions deal with variables more associated with the design of the organization as a whole. (This distinction is made solely for expository purposes—the categorizations are not intended to have theoretical merit.)

Participation in Decision Making

In many organizational decisions, technical and political considerations suggest that the development, evaluation, or selection of alternatives would benefit from exchanges of information among a moderate to large number of experts or partisans. But communicating takes time and effort, and so the variety and number of participants is often narrower than post hoc analyses determine to be appropriate. Assuming that the time and effort involved in communicating are critical determinants of the number of individuals who become involved, *what is the effect of computer-assisted communication technology on the breadth of participation in decision making?*

Because computer-assisted communication technologies can greatly reduce the effort required for those individuals who are separated in time or physical proximity to exchange information (Hiltz & Turoff, 1978; Culnan & Markus, 1987; "Special Report," 1988), it is probable that more people would serve as sources of information. Thus, we have the story where

a product developer sent a message to distribution lists that reach thousands of people asking for suggestions about how to add a particular new product feature. Within two weeks, he had received over 150 messages in reply, cutting across geographical, departmental, divisional, and hierarchical boundaries, almost all from people the product developer did not know. (Sproull & Keisler, 1986, p. 1510)

And, of course, teleconferencing and other similar computer-assisted communication systems are useful for sharing information (Johansen, 1984, 1988; Rice, 1984).

In contrast, authorities have argued that computer-assisted communication technologies do not enable decision makers to obtain "soft" information (Mintzberg, 1975), "rich" information (Daft et al., 1987), the "meaning" of information (Weick, 1985), or information about sensitive matters. To the extent that this argument is correct, it would preclude the use of computer-assisted communication technologies where the need for such information is paramount. However, the circumstances where the arguments of these authorities are salient may be fewer than first thought. For example, the argument that computer-assisted technologies provide fewer cues than does face-to-face communication is valid, but it misses the fact that managers and other professionals usually choose the communication medium that fits the communication task (Daft et al., 1987; Rice & Case, 1983; Trevino et al., 1987). Thus, computer-assisted communication technology might still be used to exchange factual or technical information, whereas other media are used to elaborate on this information or to exchange other types of information.

The issue is not one of the technologies driving out the use of richer media, but rather of the technologies enabling communications that otherwise would be unlikely to occur. For example, Foster and Flynn (1984), Sproull and Keisler (1986), and others (Palme, 1981; Rice & Case, 1983) reported that the availability of electronic mail caused organizational participants to increase the overall amount of their communication; there was not a one-for-one trade-off between media. Overall, the preponderance of arguments and the available empirical evidence suggest that:

Proposition 1: Use of computer-assisted communication technologies leads to a larger number and variety of people participating as information sources in the making of a decision.

There will be exceptions to the relationship explicated in this and all propositions. A proposition states that across a large number of cases, *ceteris paribus*, there will be a tendency for the stated relationship to be observed.

Extensive testing of hypotheses derived from the proposition will, eventually, identify any *systematic* exceptions to the relationship.

Further research is needed, of course, to determine (a) if the increase in participation is of practical significance; (b) if the increase in participation leads to higher quality decisions or better acceptance of decisions; (c) if the information includes "hard" information, soft information, or both; and (d) if the decision process becomes more effective. (For reviews of the effects that computer-assisted communication technologies have on group behaviors, see Johansen, 1984, 1988; Rice, 1984. For a review of the behavioral effects of teleconferencing in particular, see Svenning and Ruchinskas, 1984.)

It is important to note that although organizational members tend to use the technologies that communicate their messages with timeliness and veracity (Trevino et al., 1987), they also consider the social acceptance of the technology (Fulk et al., 1987), the ease of use (Huber, 1982), and other attributes (Culnan & Markus, 1987).

Size and Heterogeneity of Decision Units

In many situations, organizational subunits are responsible for developing, recommending, or selecting a proposal for action. Thus, aside from the many individuals who might participate in this process, there is usually one individual or one group of individuals who is formally accountable for the decision. Such an individual or group is referred to as a *decision unit* (Duncan, 1974).

What is the effect of computer-assisted communication technology on the size and heterogeneity of decision units? To answer this question, note that small groups provide more satisfying experiences for their members (Jewell & Reitz, 1981; Kowitz & Knitson, 1980), and that small groups are less costly in terms of human resources. Also note that homogeneous groups provide more satisfying experiences and, if they have the necessary expertise, accomplish decision-related tasks more quickly (Jewell & Reitz, 1981; Kowitz & Knutson, 1980). Finally, note that the discussion associated with Proposition 1 suggests that computer-assisted communication technologies can help decision units to become relatively smaller and more homogeneous by obtaining information beyond that obtainable using traditional communication media; both experts and constituency representatives can often make their knowledge and concerns available through electronic mail, teleconferencing, or videoconferencing. Cost considerations suggest that organizations will seek such efficiencies in their use of human capital. For example:

You cannot afford to have an expert in very rare kidney disease on your team, just in case you might need him or her someday. . . . The technology allows you to have experts available electronically. (Strassman, 1985b, pp. 22, 27)

What is the effect of computer-assisted decision-support technology, as contrasted with communication technology, on the size and heterogeneity of decision units? Sometimes experts can be replaced by expert systems and information keepers can be replaced by management information systems. To the extent that a decision unit can properly use the expert system for resolving some uncertainties, the expert need not be a member of the decision unit; therefore the unit's size and heterogeneity will be decreased.

Research is needed, of course, to determine if these changes occur. They may not. For example, it may be that organizational aspirations will rise and information technologies will be used to acquire additional diverse information, information whose acquisition and interpretation will require approximately the same size face-to-face decision-group membership as is presently found. If the group's task involves less the acquisition of information than it does the routine processing of information, then the increase in the unit manager's span of control that is facilitated by increased internal communication capability may lead to an overall increase in unit size. It will be interesting to see if future studies can ascertain the net effect of the conflicting forces under various conditions. However, it seems that there are many situations where the increasing efficacy of the technologies and the need for efficient use of human resources will make valid the following:

Proposition 2: Use of computer-assisted communication and decision-support technologies leads to decreases in the number and variety of members comprising the traditional face-to-face decision unit.

Thus, although Proposition 1 suggests that the total number and variety of *participants serving as information sources* is likely to increase with use of computer-assisted communication technologies, Proposition 2 suggests that the number and variety of *members within the traditional face-to-face decision unit* will decrease with use of either computer-assisted communication or decision-support technologies.

It was noted earlier that people consider multiple criteria when selecting communication media. Similarly, it is important to recognize that even though organizational members tend to choose decision aids and decision procedures that facilitate the making of timely and technically satisfactory decisions (Lee, McCosh, & Migliarese, 1988; Sabatier, 1978), they also consider other criteria when making this choice (Feldman & March, 1981; Sabatier, 1978).

Meetings

Research confirms the everyday observation that completing an organizational decision process often takes months or years (Mintzberg, Raisinghani, & Theoret, 1976; Witte, 1972). Meetings are often used to speed up decision processes by creating situations where the rate of decision-related information exchange among the key participants is generally higher than that which occurs outside of meetings. Meetings, whether ad hoc processes or co-joined with more permanent structures, such as standing committees, are an important component of organizational decision processes and occupy a good deal of the time of managers and other professionals.

What is or what will be the effect of computer-assisted communication and decision-support technologies on the time absorbed by meetings? Some arguments and evidence suggest these technologies will result in fewer meetings with no loss of progress in the overall organizational decision-making effort. For example, many times discussion is halted and another meeting scheduled because needed information is missing. On-line management information systems or other query-answering technologies, including expert systems, may be able to provide the information, avoiding the need to schedule a subsequent meeting. Also, electronic mail and other computer-assisted communication media sometimes can be used to access soft information that can be obtained only be querying people. Further, decision-support systems can sometimes be used within meetings to conduct analyses that provide new information with which to resolve disagreements about the significance of effects of different assumptions, and thereby allow progress to continue rather than forcing adjournment until subsequent staff work can clarify the effects and another meeting can be scheduled.

Reflection suggests that each of the technologies just mentioned as facilitating the completion of meetings can sometimes lead to the cancellation of meetings. That is, with the added communication and computing capabilities, organizational members can occasionally accomplish the task of the meeting before the meeting takes place. Finally, it seems that because group-decision support systems enhance information exchange, they contribute to the effectiveness of the meeting and, thus, may enable groups to complete their tasks with fewer meetings (Benbasat & Konsynski, 1988; Johansen, 1988).

In contrast, if managers and others involved in making organizational decisions believe that use of the technologies will result in more effective meetings, the availability of the technologies may encourage them to have *more* decision-related meetings than they would otherwise. In addition, electronic mail, decision support systems, and other information sharing and generating technologies may facilitate mini-meetings. This might preempt the need for the larger, formal meetings, but the result may be more meetings in total. The outcome of the increase in technologically supported mini-meetings versus the decrease in traditional meetings is a matter for future empirical investigation. However, because such mini-meetings are likely to be shorter, and in view of the several preceding arguments, it seems reasonable to believe that on balance and across time:

Proposition 3: Use of computer-assisted communication and decision support technologies results in less of the organization's time being absorbed by decision-related meetings.

It is important to note that, because computer-assisted communication technologies facilitate participation in meetings by persons remote in time or geography, more people may ultimately participate in a meeting (see Kerr & Hiltz, 1982, and the discussion surrounding Proposition 1). In contrast, the mini-meetings that sometimes preempt the larger, formal meetings will typically involve fewer people. Because the net effects of these two phenomena are likely to be highly variable, no proposition is offered with *person-hours* as the dependent variable.

Validation of Proposition 3 would be a significant step in documenting the effect that computer-assisted technology has on organizational processes. It would be desirable to test this proposition for each technology separately. This may not always be possible, however, because many technologically progressive organizations will have a variety of technologies in place. (For a review of the effects of advanced information technologies on the overhead costs and benefits of technologically supported meetings, such as document preparation and meeting summaries, see Rice and Bair, 1984.)

Effects at the Organizational Level

Centralization of Decision Making

By enabling top managers to obtain local information quickly and accurately, management information systems reduce ignorance and help the managers to make decisions that they, otherwise, may have been unwilling to make (Blau, Falbe, McKinley, & Tracey, 1976; Child & Partridge, 1982; Dawson & McLoughlin, 1986). Motivations for top managers to make decisions that address local, lower level problems might include lack of confidence in subordinates (Vroom & Yetton, 1973), desire to reduce stress (Bourgeois, McAllister, & Mitchell, 1978), need for achievement (Miller & Droge, 1986), or concern that information about the organization's overall situation or about its policies be appropriately utilized (Huber & McDaniel, 1986). Thus, it seems likely that, on occasion, management information systems would cause decisions to be made at hierarchically higher organizational levels than if these systems were not available (Carter, 1984). The opportunity to obtain contextual clarification with electronic mail and other computer-assisted communication technologies would amplify this tendency.

Conversely, electronic bulletin boards enable lower- and middle-level managers to stay better informed about the organization's overall situation and about the nature of the organization's current problems, policies, and priorities (Fulk & Dutton, 1984) and, consequently, permit decisions made by these managers to be more globally optimal, rather than more parochial and suboptimal, as observed by Dawson and McLoughlin (1986). Further, computer-assisted communication technologies allow lower level units to clarify information in a more timely manner. Thus, on some occasions it seems that computer-assisted communication technologies would cause decisions to be made at organizational levels lower than if such technologies were not available. Motivations that lead top managers to permit this practice include the desire to decrease the time for organizational units to respond to problems or the desire to provide autonomy for subordinates. Some evidence suggests that this downward shift in decision making occurs: After observing the implementation of networked personal computers in the General Motors' Environmental Activities Staff, Foster and Flynn (1984, pp. 231-232) concluded that "from the former hierarchy of position power there is developing instead a hierarchy of competency. . . .Power and resources now flow increasingly to the obvious centers of competence instead of to the traditional hierarchical loci."

Therefore, *is the net effect of the use of computer-assisted communication and decision-support technologies to increase centralization or to decrease it?* Perhaps this is the wrong question. Together, the arguments in the previous two paragraphs suggest that computer-assisted and decision-support communication technologies, when used to provide most organizational levels with information that was formerly known to only one or a few levels, enable organizations to allow decision making to occur across a greater range of hierarchical levels without suffering as much of a loss in decision quality or timeliness as would be the case if the technologies were not available. Which hierarchical level would actually make a particular decision would depend on the inclination and availability of the relevant decision makers at the various levels (Cohen, March, & Olsen, 1972) or other idiosyncratic factors, as noted by Fayol (1949/1916) and Duncan (1973). Thus, given that the technologies can reduce the one-to-one correspondence between certain organizational levels and certain types of information, it is likely that:

Proposition 4: For a given organization, use of computer-assisted communication and decision-support technologies leads to a more uniform distribution, across organizational levels, of the probability that a particular organizational level will make a particular decision.

Corollaries to Proposition 4 are:

Proposition 4a: For a highly centralized organization, use of computer-assisted communication and decision-support technologies leads to more decentralization.

and

Proposition 4b: For a highly decentralized organization, use of computer-assisted communication and decision-support technologies leads to more centralization.

Propositions 4, 4a, and 4b follow from the arguments presented, but are not directly based on empirical studies. It may be that the forces implied in the arguments are weak relative to those that influence traditional practices. For example, advanced information technologies enable centralized organizations to become even more centralized without incurring quite the loss in responsiveness that would occur without their presence. Similarly, they enable decentralized organizations to operate in an even more decentralized manner. I believe that, on balance, the arguments preceding Propositions 4, 4a, and 4b will be the more predictive, but empirical studies may prove this judgment to be incorrect. Certainly, the propositions require empirical study.

It is important to emphasize that by increasing the hierarchical range across which a particular type of decision may be made without a corresponding loss in decision quality or timeliness, computer-assisted communication and decision-support technologies allow other decision-location considerations to be applied without prohibitive costs. Such considerations include political matters; adherence to organizational traditions, norms, or culture; and the preferred style of top managers. Because the relative influence of these considerations will vary from organization to organization it seems that:

Proposition 5: For a population of organizations, broadened use of computer-assisted communication and decision-support technologies leads to a greater variation across organizations in the levels at which a particular type of decision is made.

Number of Organizational Levels Involved in Authorization

Consider the common situation where at least some conclusions of lower-level units about what actions should be taken must be authorized by higher level units before being acted upon, and these are forwarded upward as proposals. In their study of the approval process for a research and development budget, Shumway and his associates (1975) found that the organizational design caused seven hierarchical levels to be involved in the proposal authorization process. Because each hierarchical level requires time to process a proposal in addition to the time required to render its judgments, the more levels involved, the longer the process takes. Each corresponding increment in the duration of the approval process can, in turn, adversely affect both the timeliness of the authorized action and the enthusiasm with which the proposers carry out the action once it is authorized.

Why then do organizations commonly involve several levels in authorizations? Frequently, the answer is that each level in the hierarchy has knowledge or decision-specific information that qualifies it to apply criteria or decision rules that less well-informed lower level units cannot apply (Meyer & Goes, 1988). For example, each higher level in an organization tends to know more about organizationwide issues, needs, and resources, and more about the nature of currently competing demands for resources, than does its subordinate units. The greater the amount of such information needed, the greater the number of hierarchical levels that will be involved in the authorization process. (In some respects this is the basis for vertical differentiation.)

What is the likely effect of communication and decision-support technologies on the number of hierarchical levels involved in authorizing a particular decision? It seems that the technologies will cause a decrease in the number of hierarchical levels involved in authorizing a proposal because technologies such as management information systems, expert systems, electronic mail, and electronic bulletin boards make information more widely available. In some cases organizational levels can obtain information that was previously unavailable and, thus, they can apply criteria or decision rules that they previously were not qualified to apply. Consequently, because the technologies facilitate the vertical distribution of information and knowledge (understanding about how to use information), there is more commonality (less extreme differentiation) of information and knowledge across organizational levels. Therefore, except when information technologies are allowed to create a problem of information overload, a given organizational level is more likely to be qualified to apply more criteria and decision rules than it could without the technologies. Assuming that use of the technologies does not somehow cause the number of decision rules to increase greatly, it follows that:

Proposition 6: Use of computer-assisted communication or decision-support technologies reduces the number of organizational levels involved in authorizing proposed organizational actions.

Possible support for Proposition 6 is found in the observations of managers that use of information technology is associated with a decrease in the number of organizational levels ("Special Report," 1983a, 1983b; "Special Report," 1984). The link between these observations and Proposition 6 is questionable, however, since the observed decreases could follow from decreases in the number of employees. Apparently few systematic studies have examined the relationship between the use of information technology and the number of organizational levels involved in decision authorization. This is unfortunate, because more sophisticated studies may find that the two variables (i.e., the increases in the use of advanced information technology and the reductions in the number of levels) are less causally related to each other than they are related to other variables (e.g., attempts to reduce direct labor costs). Thus, such studies may find that observed correlations between the use of advanced information technology and reduction in the number of middle-level managers or organizational levels have much less to do with the seeking of improved decision processes than they have to do with general reductions in the size of organizations when robots replace blue-collar workers and when computers replace clerical workers (Child, 1984).

Number of Nodes in the Information Processing Network

Decision-making individuals and units obtain much of the information used to identify and deal with decision situations through an information processing network. The outer boundaries of the network are the sensor units that identify relevant information from either inside or outside the organization. (Examples of sensing units include market analysts, quality control personnel, radar operators, and accountants.) These units serve as information sources, and in many situations they pass on their observations in the form of messages to intermediate units closer to the ultimate user, the decision-making unit. Quite often these intermediate units are at hierarchical levels between the sensor unit and the decision-making unit.

The recipients of the sensor unit's message process the message and pass it on to a unit that is closer still to the decision-making unit. The information processing performed by such intermediate units ranges from straightforward relaying to elaborate interpreting. For a variety of reasons the number of such units—the number of nodes on the network path connecting the sensor unit to the decision unit—may be greater than warranted. "Most managerial levels don't do anything. They are only relays" (Drucker, 1987, p. 61).

Besides the unnecessary costs implied in Drucker's observation, each information-handling unit in the network path tends to contribute distortions and delays, as detailed by Huber (1982). For these reasons, top managers sometimes attempt to reduce the role and number of such units and to use computer-assisted technologies as alternative means for obtaining the information ("Special Report," 1983a, 1983b; "Special Report," 1984). This reduces the workload used to justify the existence of these intermediate units and levels. Computers sometimes can be used to merge, summarize, filter, and even interpret information, thus eliminating clerical workers, managers, and the organizational units of which they are a part. These observations suggest that use of computer-assisted information processing and communication technologies would lead to the elimination of human nodes in the information processing network.

There is, however, a contrary argument. Elimination of intermediate nodes in the network results in an information overload on the decision unit. When the processing functions performed by intermediate information-processing units cannot be as efficiently or effectively performed with technology or changed practices, such as those suggested by Huber (1984) and Hiltz and Turoff (1985), the units will be retained. *So, do the aforementioned technologies actually decrease the number of nodes in the organization's information-processing network?*

Informal surveys ("Special Report," 1983a, 1983b; "Special Report," 1984) have found correlations between the use of computer-assisted communication technology and decreases in the number of managers. However, as mentioned previously, these surveys did not determine the cause of the correlation, and it may be the result of concomitant reductions in the over-all number of employees. Certainly, there is a need for more sophisticated, in-depth studies to determine the nature of the cause-effect links between the use of computer-assisted technology and the number of nodes in the information-processing network. On balance, however, it seems that in some instances reductions would take place. Thus,

Proposition 7: Use of computer-assisted information processing and communication technologies leads to fewer intermediate human nodes within the organizational information-processing network.

(Note that Proposition 7 deals with the number of intermediate nodes, Proposition 1 deals with the number of information sources, and Proposition 2 deals with the number of members in the traditional face-to-face unit.) If the network processes information across hierarchical levels, then a corollary of Proposition 7 is:

Proposition 7a: Use of computer-assisted information processing and communication technologies reduces the number of organizational levels involved in processing messages.

The last two propositions of this section deal with the design of the organization's memory. Designing the organization's memory is a novel idea to organizational scientists, but will become more familiar as organizational learning becomes a more mature area of study and as top management increases its emphasis on intellectual capital.

Effects on Organizational Memory

In their discussion of information search routines in organizational decision making, Mintzberg and his colleagues (1976) distinguished between an organization's memory search and the active or passive search of its environment. *Memory search* refers to "the scanning of the organization's existing memory, human or paper" (or, today, computer-resident) (Mintzberg, Raisinghani, & Theoret, 1976, p. 255).

Everyday experience and some research suggest that the human components of organizational memories are less than satisfactory. For example, research shows that forecasts about the time necessary to complete organizational tasks are quite erroneous, even when such tasks have been carried out in the organization on many occasions. Kidd (1970), Abernathy (1971), and Souder (1972) studied the judgments of project completion times made by managers, and found them to be woefully inaccurate, even though the managers had a good deal of experience with similar projects. Given what is known about the many factors contributing to inaccurate learning and incomplete recall (Nisbett & Ross, 1980; Kahneman, Slovic, & Tversky, 1982) and to motivational distortions in sharing information (Huber, 1982), it is not at all surprising that the human components of organization memories are less than satisfactory.

The problem of poor memory is, however, much more complex than simple considerations of the deficiencies of humans as repositories of organizational information and knowledge might suggest. Everyday observations make clear (a) that personnel turnover creates great losses of the human components of an organization's memory; (b) that nonanticipation of future needs for certain information results in great amounts of information not being stored or if stored not being easily retrieved; and (c) that information is often not shared by organizational members. For at least these reasons, organizational information and knowledge frequently are less available to decision makers than they would wish.

What are the effects of computer-assisted communication and decision-support technologies on the nature and quality of organizational memory? One answer to this question follows from the fact that more and more organizational activities are conducted or monitored using computer-assisted technology. For instance, it is possible to obtain and maintain information about the times necessary to carry out many organizational activities just as readily as it is to obtain and maintain information about the financial expenditures necessary to carry out the activities (e.g., times necessary to fabricate certain products, to receive shipments, to recruit or train employees, or to deliver services). With sufficient foresight such information can be readily indexed and retrieved through computer technology (Johansen, 1988). Although much organizational knowledge is computer-resident at some point, its users often do not recognize its potential usefulness for future decision making.

Another type of useful computer-resident information is information that is exchanged across the organizational boundaries. In the future, smart indexing (Johansen, 1988) or artificial intelligence will facilitate retrieval of this transaction information and will result in computer-resident organizational memories with certain properties, such as completeness, that are superior to the human components of organizational memories. Ongoing increases in the friendliness and capability of computer-based information retrieval systems suggest that today and even more so in the future:

Proposition 8: Availability of computer-based activity and transaction-monitoring technologies leads to more frequent development and use of computer-resident data bases as components of organizational memories.

Research is needed to understand what incentives are necessary for those organizational members whose actions produce the data to share it or to maintain its quality.

Since much of what an organization learns through experience is stored in the minds of its members, many organizations nurture members who are expert with respect to an intellectual task such as (a) diagnosing quality problems or equipment malfunctions; (b) learning the identities of extra-organizational experts, influence peddlers, resource providers, or other useful nonmembers; and (c) locating information or resources that cannot be located using official, standard sources. As the processes for eliciting knowledge, building expert systems (Welbank, 1983), and validating information (O'Leary, 1988) become standardized, organizations are creating computer-based expert systems using the knowledge of their own experts (Rauch-Hindin, 1988; Waterman, 1986). These expert systems have properties such as accessibility, reliability, and "own-ability," that are both superior to humans and useful as components of organizational memories. Thus, even though expert systems have properties that are inferior to human experts, it seems reasonable to believe that:

Proposition 9: Availability of more robust and user-friendly procedures for constructing expert systems leads to more frequent development and use of in-house expert systems as components of organizational memories.

How do experts react when asked to articulate knowledge and, perhaps, their secrets, so that these can be incorporated into software that might diminish their importance? How do local managers react in such a situation when their influence and status, which are derived from this information or knowledge, is lessened by giving others the ready access to expert systems possessing much of this local information or knowledge? What incentives are appropriate and effective for motivating experts to explicate their knowledge so that it can be used without their future involvement? These are questions in need of investigation.

Propositions 8 and 9 suggest that certain advanced information technologies increase the range of memory components for an organization, just as other advanced information technologies increase the range of media with which the organization can communicate its information and knowledge.

Effects on Other Design Variables

Before leaving this discussion of organizational design variables, it seems useful to comment on the effects of advanced information technologies on some design variables that have not yet been explicitly mentioned: (a) horizontal integration, (b) formalization, (c) standardization, and (d) specialization. *Horizontal integration*, important as it is, requires little additional comment. Since it refers to the use of communication structures and processes for facilitating joint decision making among multiple units or individuals, the effects are the same as those discussed in Propositions 1, 2, and 3, and, as will be seen, in Proposition 14.

Formalization is used to ensure adherence to standards, especially when behavioral norms cannot be counted on to provide the desired behavior. Thus, early in the adoption of any new technology, because the required norms have not had time to develop and to take hold, the level of formalization is often high. (Of course, very early in adoption, standards might not exist, so control might not be exercised through either norms or formalization.) As the new technology becomes familiar and "ages," it seems reasonable to believe that the degree of formalization associated with it approaches the degree of formalization associated with the technology being replaced. Consequently, the long-term effect of new technology on formalization might be nil. Although advanced information technology greatly facilitates the recording and retrieval of information about organizational events and activities and, thus, makes control of behaviors and processes through formalization more viable, the use of advanced information technology for closely controlling intelligence development and decision making has not been reported in the literature, to my knowledge. This may be due to the frequent need for initiative and non-routine activities by those engaged in these processes (Wilensky, 1967). (For a discussion of the use of advanced information technology for controlling other behaviors and processes in organizations, see Zuboff, 1984.)

Standardization is the reduction of variability in organizational processes. As noted earlier, advanced information technologies have greatly increased the range of communication and decision procedures. If organizational members can use discretion when choosing which information technology to use (and such discretion seems commonplace), the variation of technologies will increase, and standardization will decrease: This is so apparent that no proposition is needed.

With the regard to *specialization*, advanced information technology can either lead to the addition of job categories (e.g., computer programmer) or the deletion of job categories (e.g., bookkeeper), and, therefore, will affect the degree of specialization within the organization. However, such specialities support, make operational, or become part of technologies. The increase or decrease in the variety of support personnel has little or no impact on intelligence or decision making, independent of the technologies. For this reason, *specialization* was not discussed as a design variable that affects organizational intelligence and decision making.

Propositions 1 through 9 describe the effects that advanced information technologies have on those aspects of organizational design that, ultimately, influence organizational intelligence and decision making. The next section deals with more direct effects of the technologies on organizational intelligence and decision making and, ultimately, on organizational performance in these areas. Of course, the development of organizational intelligence and the making of decisions are organizational processes inextricably intertwined with an organization's design. The present conceptual separation of these processes from design is primarily for expository purposes.

Effects on Organizational Intelligence and Decision Making

This section sets forth two propositions dealing with information acquisition and then three propositions concerned with decision making and decision authorization.

Environmental Scanning and Organizational Intelligence

To some degree, all organizations scan their external and internal environments for information about problems or opportunities. Yet sometimes managers do not learn about problems or opportunities in time to act with maximum effectiveness. In many cases the alerting message is delayed as it moves through the sequential nodes in the communication network. In other instances incumbents of adjacent nodes in the communication network have difficulty connecting across time, as in "telephone tag." *What is the effect of advanced information technologies on these impediments? What is the effect on information acquisition overall?* With regard to these questions, recall that the reasoning surrounding Proposition 7 suggested that the use of computer-assisted information processing and communications technologies leads to rifle-shooting of messages and ultimately to fewer intermediary nodes in the information-processing network. This idea, in combination with the fact that the probability and duration of message delay and the probability and extent of message distortion are both positively related to the number of sequential links in the communication chain connecting the receiver to the information source, suggests that use of computer-assisted information processing and communication technologies would facilitate rapid and accurate identification of problems and opportunities.

A contrary line of reasoning exists, however. Since an important role of many information network nodes is to screen, package, and interpret messages, the use of advanced information technologies and the consequent elimination of nodes can result in an overload of irrelevant, poorly packaged, or uninterpretable messages. One study indicated that this danger may not be as serious as it appears. Hiltz and Turoff (1985) found that social norms and management practices tend to develop to reduce the problem to a level below what might be imagined. It is likely that computer-assisted technologies will be used to enhance information retrieval, especially from lower organizational levels and outside sources. Thus, on balance:

Proposition 10: Use of computer-assisted information processing and communication technologies leads to more rapid and more accurate identification of problems and opportunities.

Use of these technologies can aid not only in the identification of problems and opportunities, but also in a wide variety of more focused probes and data acquisitions for the purpose of analysis. Recalling Mintzberg et al.'s (1976) *active search*, and Mintzberg's (1975) notion that managers require timely information, consider that computer-assisted information systems can bring facts to the organization's decision makers almost immediately after the facts occur (e.g., check-out scanners and commodities market data).

Together, technologically advanced systems for the acquisition of external information and the development of computer-enhanced organizational memories enable organizations to increase the range of information sources that the producers and users of organizational intelligence can draw upon. Thus, in summary:

Proposition 11: Use of computer-assisted information storage and acquisition technologies leads to organizational intelligence that is more accurate, comprehensive, timely, and available.

This proposition is based on the assumption that the external information sources are accurate, comprehensive, timely, and available. Otherwise, "garbage in, garbage out."

A matter of some interest is how inclined information users are to employ accessible sources, rather than those with the highest quality information (Culnan, 1983; O'Reilly, 1982). How computer-assisted communications and information acquisition systems affect the trade-off between perceived accessibility and perceived quality, and the resultant information-seeking behavior, is an issue much in need of investigation.

Decision Making and Decision Authorization

It is reasonable to believe that the quality of an organizational decision is largely a consequence of both the quality of the organizational intelligence (as implied in Proposition 11) and the quality of the decision-making processes. Further, the discussion associated with Propositions 1 and 3 (and perhaps other of the propositions related to organizational design) strongly suggests that, by facilitating the sharing of information, computer-assisted communication technologies increase the quality of decision making, and that by aiding in the analysis of information within decision units, computer-assisted decision-aiding technologies increase the quality of decision making. Thus, in helping with Propositions 1, 3, and 11:

Proposition 12: Use of computer-assisted communication and decision-support technologies leads to higher quality decisions.

Because reducing the number of levels involved in authorizing an action will reduce the number of times the proposal must be handled (activities of a logistical, rather than a judgmental nature), it seems likely that:

Proposition 13: Use of computer-assisted communication and decision-support technologies reduces the time required to authorize proposed organizational actions.

Authorization as a particular step in the decision-making process has received little attention from organizational scientists (for exceptions, see Carter, 1971; Gerwin, 1979), and the time required for organizations to authorize action also has received little attention (for exceptions, see Mintzberg et al., 1976; Shumway et al., 1975). These topics are worthy candidates for study in general, and the potential effects of information technology seem to be especially in need of examination, given their probable importance and the total absence of systematic research on their effect on decision authorization.

Once a problem or opportunity has been identified, several types of activities are undertaken that might be more effective if undertaken using advanced information technology. For example, management information systems and electronic mail might enable decision makers to immediately obtain the information they seek when deciding what to do about problems and opportunities (see Proposition 11). Decision support systems might enable decision makers or their assistants to analyze this information quickly (at least for some types of problems). Electronic mail and video- or teleconferencing might help decision makers obtain clarification and consensus without the delays imposed by the temporary nonavailability, in terms of physical presence, of key participants (see Proposition 1). Finally, forms of advanced information technology might reduce the time required to authorize proposed organizational actions (see Proposition 13). These facts suggest that:

Proposition 14: Use of computer-assisted communication and decision-support technologies reduces the time required to make decisions.

Available evidence supports this proposition:

For instance, managers in the Digital Equipment Corporation reported that electronic mail increased the speed of their decision making and saved them about seven hours a week (Crawford, 1982). Managers at Manufacturers Hanover Trust reported that electronic mail saved them about three hours a week, mostly by eliminating unreturned phone calls and internal correspondence (Nyce & Groppa, 1983). (Sproull & Keisler, 1986, p. 1492)

However, studies employing casual self-report data need to be supplemented with more systematic studies, such as some of those noted by Rice and Bair (1984). Sophisticated studies may find that the actual reduction in time is marginal, and that the net benefit may be offset to some extent by the losses in decision quality that may follow from a reduction in the time spent cogitating, as noted by Weick (1985).

Toward a Conceptual Theory

Extensive organizational use of advanced information technologies is too new, and systematic investigation of their use is too limited, for a theory of their effects to have evolved and received general acceptance. As a result, the propositions set forth here were not derived from a generally accepted theory. Instead, they were pieced together from organizational communication and information systems research, extrapolating only when it seemed reasonable.

A *theory* may be defined as a set of related propositions that specify relationships among variables (cf. Blalock, 1969, p. 2; Kerlinger, 1986, p. 9). The set of propositions set forth in this article, related to one another (at the very least) through their possessing a common independent variable, advanced information technology, passes this definitional test of a theory. Yet, more is expected from a theory, such as a framework that integrates the propositions.

If other connecting relationships can be found to link them, perhaps the propositions of this paper can serve as building blocks for the development of a less atomistic, more conceptual theory. The result would, of course, be quite tentative, in that the propositions require additional substantiation and in that any one author's connective framework must be subjected to review, critique, and discussion across an extended period before gaining general acceptance. As a step in the development of a conceptual theory of the effects of advanced information technologies, the following concepts and constructs are offered. The constructs summarize and the concepts connect ideas that were mentioned previously but served a different purpose at the time.

Concept 1: Advanced information technologies have properties different from more traditional information technologies. *Availability of advanced information technologies* (Construct A) extends the range of communication and decision making options from which potential users can choose. On occasion a technology will be chosen for use, and when chosen wisely—such that the chosen technology's properties better fit the user's task—use of the technology leads to improved task performance. This reinforcement in turn leads to more frequent use of advanced information technology (Construct B).

Concept 2: Use of advanced information technologies (Construct B) leads to more available and more quickly retrieved information, including external information, internal information, and previously encountered information, and thus leads to increased information accessibility (Construct C). Concept 2 follows from Propositions 1, 4, and 7 through 11.

Concept 3: Increased information accessibility (Construct C) leads to the *changes in organizational design* (Construct D). Concept 3 follows from Propositions 1 through 7.

Concept 4: Increased information accessibility (Construct C), and those changes in organizational design (Construct D) that increase the speed and effectiveness with which information can be converted into intelligence or intelligence into decisions, lead to organizational intelligence being more accurate, comprehensive, timely, and available and to decisions being of higher quality and more timely, decisions that lead to *improvements in effectiveness of intelligence development and decision making* (Construct E). Concept 4 follows from Propositions 11 through 14.

These constructs and concepts are summarized in Figure 11.1.

Summary and Recommendations

In the form of propositions and their corollaries, this article sets forth a theory concerning the effects that computer-assisted communication and decision-aiding technologies have on organizational design, intelligence, and decision making. Subsequently, the propositions were connected with constructs and concepts, and from these a more conceptual theory was developed.

Some boundaries on the original theory (here called *the theory*) were delineated early in the paper. The theory is, nevertheless, a candidate for elaboration and expansion. For example, it was not possible, within the space available, to extend the scope of the theory to include propositions having to do with the effects of advanced information technologies on the distribution of influence in organizational decision making (see Zmud, in press). Examination of some relevant literature makes clear that numerous propositions would be necessary because (a) the technologies may vary in their usefulness for generating the particular types of information used by decision participants having different sources of influence, (b) the technologies may vary in their usefulness for enhancing the image or status of

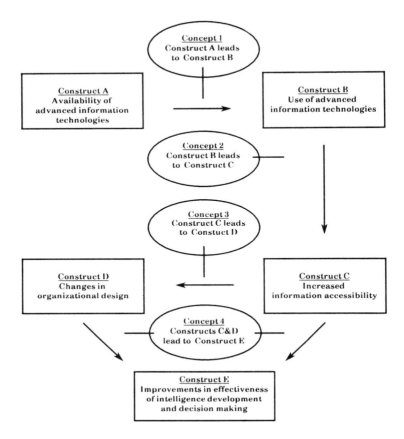

Figure 11.1 Conceptual Theory of the Effects of Advanced Information Technologies on Organizational Design, Intelligence, and Decision Making

participants having different organizational roles, and (c) the technologies may vary in their usefulness to different types of participants as aids in the building of decision-determining coalitions. Certainly, the theory is a candidate for elaboration and expansion, just as it is a candidate for empirical testing and consequent revision.

The process used to generate the propositions comprising the theory included drawing on components of established organization theory and on findings from communication and information systems research. Specific suggestions were made, with respect to many of the propositions about matters in need of empirical investigations. In addition to these specific suggestions, three somewhat more global recommendations are in order. The first is directed to any researchers exploring the effects of advanced information technologies. In this article, different forms of advanced information technology were discussed by name (e.g., electronic mail) yet the propositions were stated in general terms. This latter fact should not obscure the need to specify more precisely the particular technology of interest when developing hypotheses to be tested empirically. As more is learned about the effects of computer-assisted communication and decision-support technologies, it may be found that even subtle differences count (cf. the discussion by Markus & Robey, 1988). Even if this is not so, as researchers communicate about these matters among themselves and with administrators, it behooves them to be clear and precise about what it is that they are discussing.

The second suggestion, directed to organizational researchers, is to believe (a) that information technology fits within the domain of organization theory and (b) that it will have a significant effect on organizational design, intelligence, and decision making. Organization researchers, in general (there are always welcome exceptions), may not believe that these technologies fit within the domain of organization theory. This would be an erroneous belief. Organization theory has always been concerned with the processes of communication, coordination, and control and, as is apparent from the research of communication and information systems researchers (Culnan & Markus, 1987; Rice & Associates, 1984), the nature and effectiveness of these processes are changed when advanced information technologies are employed. Organizational researchers also may not have recognized that organizational designs are, at any point in time, constrained by the capability of the available communication technologies. Two of the infrequent exceptions to this important observation are cited by Culnan and Markus (1987):

> Chandler (1977) for example, argues that the ability of the telegraph to facilitate coordination enabled the emergence of the large, centralized railroad firms that became the prototype of the modern industrial organization. Pool (1983) credits the telephone with the now traditional physical separation of management headquarters from field operations, and in particular with the development of the modern office skyscraper as the locus of administrative business activity. (p. 421)

Also, Huber and McDaniel (1986) state that:

> Without telephones corporations could not have become as large as they have; without radios military units would be constrained to structures and tactics different from those they now use; without

computers the processes for managing airline travel would be different from what they are. Any significant advance in information technology seems to lead eventually to recognition and implementation of new organizational design options, options that were not previously feasible, perhaps not even envisioned. (p. 221)

Since information technologies affect processes that are central to organization theory, and since they also affect the potential nature of organizations design (a principal application of organization theory), a corollary of this second global recommendation is added: Organizational researchers should study advanced information technology as (a) an intervention or jolt in the life of an organization that may have unanticipated consequences with respect to evolved organizational design, (b) a variable that can be used to enhance the quality (broadly defined) and timeliness of organizational intelligence and decision making, and (c) a variable that enables organizations to be designed differently than has heretofore been possible. (A review of recent discussions of emerging organizational and interorganizational forms [Borys & Jemison, 1989; Luke, Begun, & Pointer, 1989; Miles & Snow, 1986; Nadler & Tushman, 1987] suggests that use of computer-assisted communication technologies can enhance the usefulness of such designs, requiring, as many will, communication among dispersed parties.)

The third global research recommendation is directed toward information systems researchers. It is straightforward. As is easily inferred by observing organizational practices, much information technology is intended to increase directly the efficiency with which goods and services are produced, for example, by replacing workers with computers or robots. But organizational effectiveness and efficiency are greatly determined by the quality and timeliness of organizational intelligence and decision making, and these, in turn, are directly affected by computer-assisted communication and decision-aiding technologies and are also indirectly affected through the impact of the technologies on organizational design. Therefore, it is likely that administrators will ask information systems researchers to help anticipate the effects of the technologies. In addition, builders and users of computer-assisted communication and decision-aiding technologies generally do not explicitly consider the effects that the technologies might have an organizational design, intelligence, or decision making. Thus, information systems researchers should arm themselves with the appropriate knowledge by increasing the amount of their research directed toward studying the effects that advanced information technologies have an organizational design, intelligence, and decision processes and outcomes.

References

Abernathy, W. M. (1971). Subjective estimates and scheduling decisions. *Management Science, 18,* 80-88.

Benbasat, I., & Konsynski, B. (1988). Introduction to special section on GDSS. *Management Information Systems Quarterly, 12,* 588-590.

Blau, P. M., Falbe, C. M., Mckinley, W., & Tracey, P. K. (1976). Technology and organization in manufacturing. *Administrative Science Quarterly, 21,* 20-40.

Blalock, H. M., Jr. (1969). *Theory construction: From verbal to mathematical formulations.* Englewood Cliffs, NJ: Prentice-Hall.

Borys, B., & Jemison, D. (1989). Hybrid arrangements as strategic alliances: Theoretical issues in organizational combinations. *Academy of Management Review, 14,* 234-249.

Bourgeois, L. J. III, McAllister, D. W., & Mitchell, T. R. (1978). The effects of different organizational environments upon decision and organizational structure. *Academy of Management Journal, 21,* 508-514.

Burgelman, R. A. (1982). A process model of internal corporate venturing in the diversified major firm. *Administrative Science Quarterly, 28,* 223-244.

Carter, E. E. (1971). The behavioral theory of the firm and top-level corporate decisions. *Administrative Science Quarterly, 16,* 413-428.

Carter, N. M. (1984). Computerization as a predominate technology: Its influence on the structure of newspaper organizations. *Academy of Management Journal, 27,* 247-270.

Chandler, Jr., A. D., (1977). *The visible hand: The managerial revolution in American business.* Cambridge, MA: Harvard University Press.

Child, J. (1984). New technology and developments in management organization. *OMEGA, 12,* 211-223.

Child, J. (1988). Information technology, organization, and response to strategic challenges. *California Management Review, 30*(1), 33-50.

Child, J., & Partridge, B. (1982). *Lost managers: Supervisors in industry and society.* Cambridge, England: Cambridge University Press.

Cohen, M. D., March, J. G., & Olsen, J. P. (1972). A garbage can model of organizational choice. *Administrative Science Quarterly, 17,* 1-25.

Crawford, A. B., Jr. (1982). Corporate electronic mail—A communication-intensive application of information technology. *Management Information Systems Quarterly, 6,* 1-14.

Culnan M. J. (1983). Environmental scanning: The effects of task complexity and source accessibility on information gathering behavior. *Decision Sciences, 14,* 194-206.

Culnan, M. J., & Markus, L. (1987). Information technologies: Electronic media and intraorganizational communication. In F. M. Jablin, L. L. Putnam, K. H. Roberts, & L. W. Porter (Eds.), *Handbook of organizational communication* (pp. 420-444). Newbury Park, CA: Sage.

Daft, R. L., & Lengel, R. H. (1984). Information richness: A new approach to managerial information processing and organizational design. In B. M.

Staw & L. L. Cummings (Eds.), *Research in organizational behavior* (pp. 191-233). Greenwich, CT: JAI Press.

Daft, R. L., & Lengel, R. H. (1986). Organizational information requirements, media richness, and structural design. *Management Science, 32,* 554-571.

Daft, R. L., Lengel, R. H., & Trevino, L. K. (1987). Message equivocality, media selection and manager performance: Implications for information systems. *Management Information Systems Quarterly, 11,* 355-368.

Dawson, P., & McLoughlin, I. (1986). Computer technology and the redefinition of supervision. *Journal of Management Studies, 23,* 116-132.

Drucker, P. (1987, September 28). Advice from the Dr. Spock of business. *Business Week,* pp. 61-65.

Duncan, R. B. (1973). Multiple decision-making structures in adapting to environmental uncertainty. *Human Relations, 26,* 273-291.

Duncan, R. B. (1974). Modifications in decision structure in adapting to the environment: Some implications for organizational learning. *Decision Sciences, 5,* 705-725.

Fayol, H. (1949/1916). *General and industrial management* [Constance Storrs, trans.] London: Pitman.

Feldman, M., & March, J. (1981). Information in organizations as signal and symbol. *Administrative Science Quarterly, 26,* 171-186.

Foster, L. W., & Flynn, D. M. (1984). Management Information technology: Its effects on organizational form and function. *Management Information Systems Quarterly, 8,* 229-236.

Fulk, J., & Dutton, W. (1984). Videoconferencing as an organizational information system: Assessing the role of electronic meetings. *Systems, Objectives, and Solutions, 4,* 105-118.

Fulk, J., Steinfield, C. W., Schmitz, J., & Power, J. G. (1987). A social information processing model of media use in organizations. *Communication Research, 14,* 529-552.

Gerwin, D. (1979). Towards a theory of public budgetary decision making. *Administrative Science Quarterly, 14,* 33-46.

Gibson, C. F., & Jackson, B. B. (1987). *The information imperative.* Lexington, MA: Heath.

Hiltz, S. R., & Turoff, M. (1978). *The network nation: Human communication via computer.* Reading, MA: Addison-Wesley.

Hiltz, S. R., & Turoff, M. (1985). Structuring computer-mediated communication systems to avoid information overload. *Communications of the ACM, 28,* 680-689.

Hofer, C. W. (1970). Emerging EDP patterns. *Harvard Business Review, 48*(2), 16-31, 168-171.

Huber, G. (1982). Organizational information systems: Determinants of their performance and behavior. *Management Science, 28,* 135-155.

Huber, G. (1984). The nature and design of post-industrial organizations. *Management Science, 30,* 928-951.

Huber, G. (1988). Effects of decision and communication technologies on organizational decision processes and structures. In R. M. Lee,

A. McCosh, & P. Migliarese (Eds.), *Organizational decision support systems* (pp. 317-333). Amsterdam: North-Holland.

Huber, G. P. (1989). A theory of the effects of advanced information technologies on organizational design, intelligence, and decision making. *Academy of Management Review, 15*(1), 47-71.

Huber, G., & McDaniel, R. (1986). Exploiting information technology to design more effective organizations. In M. Jarke (Ed.), *Managers, micros, and mainframes* (pp. 221-236). New York: John Wiley.

Jewell, L. N. & Reitz, H. J. (1981). *Group effectiveness in organizations.* Glenview, IL: Scott, Foresman.

Johansen, R. (1984). *Teleconferencing and beyond.* New York: McGraw-Hill.

Johansen, R. (1988). *Groupware: Computer support for business teams.* New York: Free Press.

Kahneman, D., Slovic, P., & Tversky A. (Eds.) (1982). *Judgment under uncertainty: Heuristics and biases.* Cambridge, England: Cambridge University Press.

Kelley, G. (1976). Seducing the elites: The politics of decision making and innovation in organizational networks. *Academy of Management Review, 1*, 66-74.

Kerlinger, F. N. (1986). *Foundations of behavioral research.* New York: Holt, Rinehart & Winston.

Kerr, E. B., & Hiltz, S. R. (1982). *Computer-mediated communication systems: Status and evaluation.* New York: Academic Press.

Kidd, J. S. (1970). The utilization of subjective probabilities in production planning. *Acta Psychologica, 34*, 338-347.

Kowitz, A. C., & Knutson, T. J. (1980). *Decision making in small groups: The search for alternatives.* Boston, MA: Allyn & Bacon.

Lee, R. M., McCosh, A., & Migliarese, P. (1988). *Organizational decision support systems.* Amsterdam: North-Holland.

Luke, R. D., Begun, J. W., & Pointer, D. D. (1989). Quasi firms: Strategic interorganizational forms in the health care industry. *Academy of Management Review, 14*, 9-19.

Markus, M. L. (1984). *Systems in organizations: Bugs and features.* Marshfield, MA: Pitman.

Markus, M. L., & Robey, D. (1988). Information technology and organizational change: Conceptions of causality in theory and research. *Management Science, 34*, 583-598.

Meyer, A. D., & Goes, J. B. (1988). Organizational assimilation of innovations: A multilevel contextual analysis. *Academy of Management Journal, 31*, 897-923.

Miles, R., & Snow, C. (1986). Organizations: New concepts for new forms. *California Management Review, 28*(3), 62-73.

Miller, D., & Droge, C. (1986). Psychological and traditional determinants of structure. *Administrative Science Quarterly, 31*, 539-560.

Mintzberg, H. (1975). The manager's job: Folklore and fact. *Harvard Business Review, 53*(4), 49-61.

Mintzberg, H., Raisinghani, D., & Theoret, A. (1976). The structure of 'unstructured' decision processes. *Administrative Science Quarterly*, *21*, 246-275.

Nadler, D., & Tushman, M. L. (1987). Strategic organization design. Glenview, IL: Scott, Foresman.

Nisbett, R., & Ross, L. (1980). *Human inference: Strategies and shortcomings of social judgment.* Englewood Cliffs, NJ: Prentice-Hall.

Nyce, H. E., & Groppa, R. (1983). Electronic mail at MHT. *Management Technology*, *1*, 65-72.

O'Leary, D. E. (1988). Methods of validating expert systems. *Interfaces*, *18*(6), 72-79.

Olson, M., & Lucas, H. C. (1982). The impact of office automation on the organization: Some implications for research and practice. *Communications of the ACM*, *25*, 838-847.

O'Reilly, C. A. (1982). Variations in decision makers' use of information sources: The impact of quality and accessibility of information. *Academy of Management Journal*, *25*, 756-771.

Palme, J. (1981). *Experience with the use of the COM computerized conferencing system.* Stockholm, Sweden: Forsvarets Forskningsanstalt.

Pfeffer, J. (1978). *Organizational design.* Arlington Heights, IL: AHM.

Pfeffer, J., & Moore, W. L. (1980). Power in university budgeting: A replication and extension. *Administrative Science Quarterly*, *19*, 135-151.

Pool, I. de Sola. (1983). *Forecasting the telephone: A retrospective assessment.* Norwood, NJ: Ablex.

Porter, M. E. (1980). *Competitive strategies: Techniques for analyzing industries and competitors.* New York: Free Press.

Rao, H. R., & Lingaraj, B. P. (1988). Expert systems in production and operations management: Classification and prospects. *Interfaces*, *18*(6), 80-91.

Rauch-Hindin, W. B. (1988). *A guide to commercial artificial intelligence.* New York: Prentice-Hall.

Rice, R. E. (1980). The impacts of computer-mediated organizational and interpersonnel communication. In M. Williams (Ed.), *Annual review of information science and technology* (Vol. 15, pp. 221-249). White Plains, NY: Knowledge Industry Publications.

Rice, R. E. (1984). Mediated group communication. In R. E. Rice & Associates (Eds.), *The new media* (pp. 129-154). Beverly Hills, CA: Sage.

Rice, R. E., & Associates. (1984). *The new media.* Beverly Hills, CA: Sage.

Rice, R. E., & Bair, J. H. (1984). New organizational media and productivity. In R. E. Rice & Associates (Eds.), *The new media* (pp. 185-216). Beverly Hills, CA: Sage.

Rice, R. E., & Case, D. (1983). Electronic message systems in the university: A description of use and utility. *Journal of Communication*, *33*, 131-152.

Robey, D. (1977). Computers and management structure. *Human Relations*, *30*, 963-976.

Sabatier, P. (1978). The acquisition and utilization of technical information by administrative agencies. *Administrative Science Quarterly, 23*, 396-417.

Sammon, W. L., Kurland, M. A., & Spitalnic, R. (1984). Business competitor intelligence: Methods for collecting, organizing, and using information. New York: Wiley.

Shukla, R. K. (1982). Influence of power bases in organizational decision making: A contingency model. *Decision Sciences, 13*, 450-470.

Shumway, C. R., Maher, P. M., Baker, M. R., Souder, W. E., Rubenstein, A. H., & Gallant, A. R. (1975). Diffuse decision-making in hierarchical organizations: An empirical examination. *Management Science, 21*, 697-707.

Souder, W. E. (1972). A scoring methodology for assessing the suitability of management science models. *Management Science, 18*, B526-B543.

Special Report: A new era for management. (1983a, April 25). *Business Week*, pp. 50-64.

Special Report: How computers remake the manager's job. (1983b, April 25). *Business Week*, pp. 68-76.

Special Report: Office automation. (1984, October 8). *Business Week*, pp. 118-142.

Special report: The portable executive. (1988, October 10). Business Week, pp. 102-112.

Sprague, R. H., & McNurlin, B. C. (1986). *Information systems management in practice*. Englewood Cliffs, NJ: Prentice-Hall.

Sprague, R. H., & Watson, H. J. (1986). *Decision support systems: Putting theory into practice*. Englewood Cliffs, NJ: Prentice-Hall.

Sproull, L., & Keisler, S. (1986). Reducing social context cues: Electronic mail in organizational communication. *Management Science, 32*, 1492-1512.

Steinfield, C. W., & Fulk, J. (1987). On the role of theory in research on information technologies in organizations: An introduction to the special issue. *Communication Research, 14*, 479-490.

Strassman, P. (1985a). *Information payoff: The transformation of work in the electronic age*. New York: Free Press.

Strassman, P. (1985b). Conversation with Paul Strassman. *Organizational Dynamics, 14*(2), 19-34.

Svenning, L., & Ruchinskas, J. (1984). Organizational teleconferencing. In R. E. Rice & Associates (Eds.), *The new media* (pp. 217-248). Beverly Hills, CA: Sage.

Trevino, L. K., Lengel, R., & Daft, R. L. (1987). Media symbolism, media richness, and media choice in organization: A symbolic interactionist perspective. *Communication Research, 14*, 553-574.

Vroom, V. H., & Yetton, P. W. (1973). *Leadership and decision-making*. Pittsburgh: University of Pittsburgh.

Waterman, D. A. (1986). *A guide to expert systems*. Reading, MA: Addison-Wesley.

Weick, K. E. (1985). Cosmos vs. chaos: Sense and nonsense in electronic contexts. *Organizational Dynamics, 14*(2), 50-64.

Welbank, M. (1983). *A review of knowledge acquisition techniques for expert systems.* Ipswich, England: Martlesham Consultancy Services.

Whisler, T. (1970). *Impact of computers on organizations.* New York: Praeger.

Wilensky, H. L. (1967). *Organizational intelligence.* New York: Basic Books.

Williams, F., & Rice, R. E. (1983). Communication research and the new media technologies. In R. N. Bostrom (Ed.) *Communication yearbook 7* (pp. 200-225). Beverly Hills, CA: Sage.

Witte, E. (1972). Field research on complex decision-making processes—The phase theorem. *International Studies of Management & Organization, 2,* 156-182.

Zmud, R. W. (1983). *Information systems in organizations.* Glenview, IL: Scott, Foresman.

Zmud, R. W. (1990). Opportunities for manipulating information through new technology. In J. Fulk & C. Steinfield (Eds.), *Organizations and communication technology.* Newbury Park, CA: Sage.

Zuboff, S. (1984). *In the age of the smart machine.* New York: Basic Books.

THOMAS J. ALLEN
OSCAR HAUPTMAN

12. The Substitution of Communication Technologies for Organizational Structure in Research and Development

Introduction: Communication and Performance in R&D

The determinants of technical communication patterns in R&D organizations have been the subject of a considerable amount of study in recent years (e.g. Allen, 1984; Allen, Tushman, & Lee, 1979; Allen, Lee, & Tushman, 1980; Katz & Allen, 1982).

A very large body of research (Allen, 1984; Pelz & Andrews, 1976) shows communication among technical professionals in R&D laboratories to be a significant determinant of the technical performance and productivity of R&D project teams. A recent study carried out in a major computer firm by Hauptman (1986a, 1986b) corroborated these findings for software development and production, as well.

A major question today is what impact the explosive development in communication-related information technologies will have on communication in R&D. To what extent do these technologies have the potential to show results at the bottom line and in what ways? Clearly some organizational tasks are more amenable to productivity increase through information technologies than others, which might appear quite similar. It is clear that the exploitation of these technologies has to be administered with considerable awareness concerning both communication-related and organizational issues.

In contrast to the general notion that these technologies will have a significant impact, the critical question of what are the specific capabilities of communication-related information technologies is still unanswered. Because the new technological options are not omnipotent panacea for all communication problems, their limits need to be explored. The extent to which the existing technological options such as electronic mail, computer-conferencing, bulletin boards, and document search and retrieval systems

275

differ from each other in accomplishing organizational objectives is still unclear. Probably an equally important question revolves around the task types for which they provide comparative advantages. For both theoretical and practical reasons, this situation prevents the matching of specific organizational tasks with their optimal communication-related information technologies.

The development of models that can test those limits is an important first step addressing these issues. In this chapter we present an initial formulation of a model for how new information technologies might be employed to increase the range of options available for structuring organizational tasks. Although it is clear that communication technologies cannot substitute for other structural arrangements, they may be able to extend the reach of current organizational options. We begin by a general review of the promise of new information technologies, followed by a description of key communication needs in R&D and the typical structural arrangements that are employed to meet these needs. Then, we suggest how several communication technologies might be employed to extend the capabilities of different organizational structures.

New Information Technologies and Communication

One cannot discuss organizational communication at the present without at least speculating about the impact the explosive development in communication-related technologies will have on them. The following rational-economic assessment of digital communication is probably typical of the enthusiastic perception of their benefits:

> The phone also shares a problem with all speech communication: the information density of speech is very low. Generally, the electronic transmission of speech requires about 60,000 bits per second. These 60,000 bits of speech carry about the same information as 15 characters of written text. . . . But you can transmit 15 characters directly as text by transmitting only 120 bits of information, rather than 60,000 bits of speech. . . . In a very fundamental sense, speech is not an economic medium of communication (Marill, 1980, p. 185).

It might seem that the new technologies, such as electronic mail or computer-mediated conferencing, would offer many advantages in comparison with oral communication. Hiltz and Turoff (1978, pp. 8-9) in their detailed study of a computer-conferencing system suggest that:

1. Time and distance barriers are removed. Participants can send and receive communications whenever it is convenient for them. . . .
2. Group size can be expanded without decreasing actual participation by either member. No one can be interrupted or "shouted down."
3. A person participates at a time and rate of his or her choice.

This positive outlook is shared by some practitioners. For instance, Roger Smith, Chairman of General Motors, refers to information technologies as the vehicle for what he calls the *21st Century Corporation*. It entails:

an integrated, coordinated, decision-making way of functioning which comprehends business plans, budgets, product programs, corporate volumes, and everything else that helps run the business. It must create an integrated worldwide data base that brings all parts of the business together. (Smith, 1985, p. 5)

The natural questions of effectiveness and efficiency have also been addressed. For instance Hiltz and Turoff (1978) and Siegel, Dubrovsky, Kiesler, and McGuire (1984) found that participation in discussions is more equally distributed among participants than what could be expected in a similar face-to-face meeting. In addition, Sproull and Kiesler (1986) found that much of the information conveyed through this medium would not have been conveyed without it. On the other hand, computer-mediated groups took longer to reach a solution (Siegel et al., 1984). These findings are indicative of the potential benefits and limitations imposed by the medium. Obviously, the efficiency of transmitting digital data, described by Marill (1980), narrows the "band" in the same ratio, in this case by 500 (60,000 to 120). The 60,000 bits of speech are transmitting not only 15 characters of verbal data but also vocalization. In addition, even the traditional voice medium, the telephone, is incomparably more narrow-banded than face-to-face interaction, totally lacking in visual attributes of the persons.

Because our focus is on the relatively complex tasks of research and development, the issue of task-technology compatibility is very relevant. This important issue was addressed by Steinfield (1984, 1985), who found that at least 50% of his respondents had never carried out such tasks as "carry on negotiations/bargaining" and "resolve conflicts/disagreements" by computer. His results support Picot, Klingenberg, and Kranzle (1982), who warn against overestimating the impact of these technologies on complex tasks. In this context, studies by McKenney and collaborators (McKenney, 1986; McKenney, Doherty, & Sviokla, 1986) suggest that electronic mail systems could be effective for complex managerial communication only when supplemented by face-to-face contact (McKenney et al., 1986, p. 22).

The Influence of Structure of Communication in R&D

Communication plays a central role in achieving two goals that are critical to performance in an R&D organization.[1] First, tasks must be provided with state-of-the-art information from their technological knowledge base. This need is critical: R&D project teams that were provided with this information significantly outperformed those that lacked it (Katz & Allen, 1982; Allen, 1984). This knowledge input is organized around disciplines, subdisciplines, technologies and technical specialties, or some combination of one of these with a broad area of application. To effectively manage the coupling to this source of knowledge, many research and development organizations are designed in a manner that emulates this structure. This is nothing new, as universities have been organized in this way for centuries. Because engineers keep abreast of developments in their specialties far more through discussion with colleagues than by any other means (Allen, 1984), this input-focused, or *functional* form of organization, will most effectively accomplish this goal of keeping project members up-to-date in what are often rapidly changing technical areas. By grouping together people who share a common base of knowledge, functional structures enable them to keep one another informed on new developments in that area of knowledge. Of course, by focusing so strongly on inputs, this form of organization almost invariably creates difficulties on the output side.

The output of an R&D organization, on the other hand, does not normally take the form of disciplines or technical specialties. It is generally in the form of designs for new products (or processes). Such designs usually require complementary and simultaneous application of different technical specialties. Thus, there is a strong need to coordinate these activities across the various disciplines and specialties in order to accomplish the work of multidisciplinary tasks. The project organization successfully solves this problem by insuring that all the individuals working on the common task share the project relevant information about technical progress, schedule and resources. When R&D professionals are grouped into project teams working toward a common output goal, *coordination of activities will be accomplished more effectively*. Obviously, by satisfying the informational requirements for output, the project structure creates a problem on the input side discussed above.

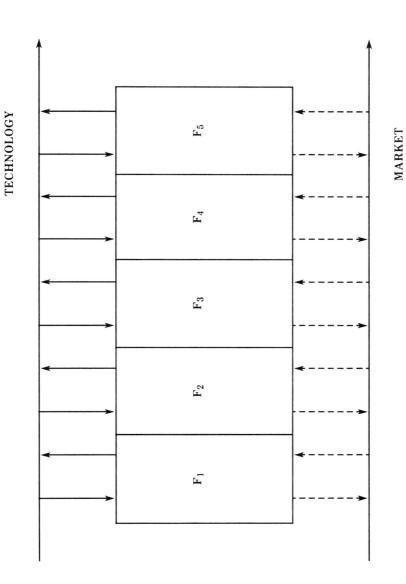

Figure 12.1 The Functional Organization and the Innovation Process

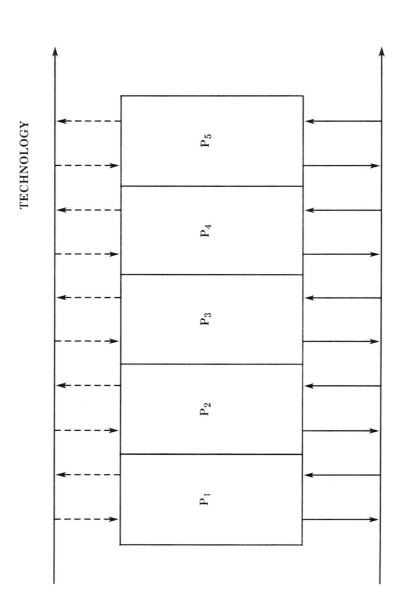

Figure 12.2 The Project Organization and the Innovation Process

To summarize, there is a clear trade-off between these two goals. Functional organizations promote *communication to facilitate technological currency* within specific disciplines or specialties, but *at the cost of coordination* across disciplines. Project organizations achieve this coordination by *facilitating communication across disciplines*, but at the *cost of not maintaining state-of-the-art knowledge within specialties*.

The conceptual model in the next section is based on the communication needs of typical R&D tasks and shows how functional and project structures help accomplish them. The model is closely linked with organizational information processing theory (Daft & Macintosh, 1981; Tushman & Nadler, 1978) and its more recent articulation in studies of advanced information technologies (see Steinfield, 1985, for a review). The model addresses information processing on the task level, with implications for organizational design.

Organizational Structure Space: A Conceptual Model

Our model defines a three-dimensional "Organizational Structure Space" based on three parameters that Allen (1984) has shown determine which of the two organizational forms will be preferred in any instance (Figure 12.3). The first dimension recognizes that technologies vary in their rate of development and in the rate at which new knowledge is generated. Some technologies, such as metal processing or oil refining, are presently mature and stable. Others, such as bioengineering or the development of superconducting materials, are more dynamic. The *rate of change of technological knowledge*, defined as the first derivative of knowledge with respect to time, dK/dt, serves as the first coordinate of the organizational structure space. The higher the value of dK/dt, the stronger is the need for effective transfer of state-of-the-art technology. Consequently, there is a greater need for the specialty oriented functional structure to accomplish this. Although there is some similarity between the dK/dt dimension and Perrow's (1967) typology of technological *nonroutineness* (see also Whithey, Daft, & Cooper, 1983), or to Tushman and Nadler's (1978) environmental uncertainty, their constructs lack the specific meaning of this dimension for technical activities on the task level. Thus the model prescribes that: *If the technology is advancing rapidly,* ceteris paribus, *functional structures are more effective for task performance than are project teams.* The second dimension of the organizational structure space is also related to the need for acquisition of technical information—the duration of the task. If the task duration (T) is comparatively short, a person working in even a rapidly advancing technology is unlikely to lose touch with current knowledge. On the other hand, in a long assignment of several years, being isolated from peers in the specialty or discipline will carry the dangers of professional obsolescence. This notion is reinforced on the group level by the effects of the "Not Invented Here Syndrome," investigated by Katz and Allen (1982). All this suggests that: *If the scale of the task is such that the assigned personnel will be expected to spend a long period of time on the task*, ceteris paribus, *the functional structure will be more effective than project teams*.

The third dimension of the decision space is related to the requirement for organizational coordination, of bringing together the expertise of different professionals toward a single output goal. It is the *interdependence among subsystems and components* that the task comprises. The higher this interdependence (I_{ss}) of these subtasks in the joint effort, the stronger is the demand upon the task team for coordination of its activities. This dimension cuts across Tushman and Nadler's (1978) intra- and inter-unit task interdependence by looking at it as a task attribute, rather than a structural relationship. On the other hand, it is based to some extent on Thompson's (1967) typology of task interdependence and its articulation by Van de Ven and Delbecq (1974) and Van de Ven, Delbecq, and Koenig (1976). Consequently, the following is proposed: *If the subtasks of the joint effort seem to be highly interdependent*, ceteris paribus, *project structure will result in better task performance by accomplishing effective coordination of these subtasks*.

A key question is: How will information technologies, such as electronic mail, computer bulletin boards, computer conferencing, and scientific information retrieval technologies influence this model? In other words, how might new information technologies affect the prescribed division of the organizational structure space into *functional* or *project* areas? Although there are still insufficient data for a meaningful answer as to whether or not communication-related information technologies are powerful enough to change individual and organizational behavior and performance, we can put forth some tentative hypotheses for future investigation.

Alternatives for Meeting Communication Needs

The first hypothesis is that improvements in information technologies will make it easier for technical professionals to communicate and thereby maintain up-to-date technological knowledge. Document search and retrieval systems are available to provide direct access to 3,800 documentation data bases (Cuadra Associates, 1984). Although they have proven at best moder-

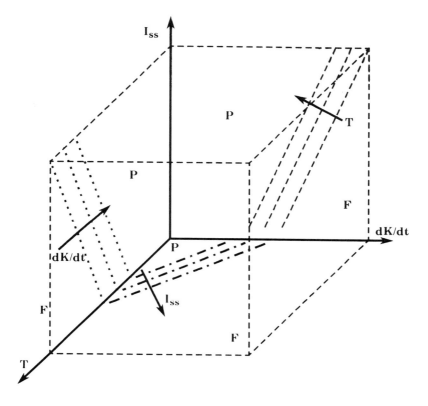

Legend:

dK/dt - Rate of change of
        knowledge
T   - Task duration
I_{ss} - Task interdependence
F   - Functional structure
        recommended
P   - Project structure
        recommended

Figure 12.3 Organizational Structure Space

ately successful for some disciplines or specialties, some can now be augmented by selective dissemination services based on artificial intelligence. These can learn a user's need and determine which journal articles or documents will be of interest. All of these systems unfortunately suffer from the same fatal flaw. They can provide information, but it still must be read. And there is a substantial body of research to show that for the average engineer that is a very high barrier (Allen, 1984).

Knowledge is best transferred to engineers through personal contact. The connection to literature and documentation is best accomplished with the aid of intermediaries known as *technological gatekeepers* (Allen, 1984; Allen & Cohen, 1969). More recent developments in information technology may very well aid in the process of connecting an engineer to an appropriate gate-keeper. Some companies, for example, have encouraged the development of computer-based bulletin boards or "forums" that are organized around technical subjects. Anyone can "post" on these bulletin boards questions, answers, or simple declarations of fact or discovery. Recent research (George, 1987) shows that there are key individuals associated with these forums who maintain them and enable those interested in a particular subject to communicate about that subject. Thus, the average member of the technical staff of an organization is provided with a communication channel that provides more ready access to the gatekeepers in a specialty. In other words, the forum serves as a mechanism to connect people to the appropriate gatekeeper. This should certainly assist in the process of disseminating knowledge among the technical staff, thereby assuming one of the principal functions of functional or departmental organization.

The second hypothesis is that the use of information technologies will also contribute to coordination within a project team. The type of information system employed for this purpose would accomplish a goal presently served by project structure. For example, there are sophisticated forms of electronic mail in which computer bulletin boards are organized by topic. These bulletin boards can be further organized hierarchically into subtopics or sub-sub-topics. Each of these topical subdivisions can be a subsystem, element, or component of a project (Stevens, 1981). Different access levels can be assigned to different individuals. Some people have *read* access only; others have both *read* and *write* access. Status reports can be maintained and regularly updated through this medium. The bulletin board can also be used for queries and for managing interfaces among subsystems. With the use of this form of communication medium, the problems of coordinating project work across several functional departments should be lessened considerably. This technology should even make the matrix form of organization easier to manage. The potential contributions of these information technologies are summarized in Table 12.1.

Table 12.1
Communication Need, Organizational Solution, and Technological Contributions

Organizational Need	Solution	Information Technology Contribution
Coordination of subsystem or sub-element work on a project	Project organization	Hierarchically organized bulletin boards for project status reporting and configuration control
Knowledge transfer	Functional or departmental organization	Document search and retrieval systems
		Expert system-based selective dissemination of information
		Bulletinboards for forums for information search

Combining Structure with Technology

The development of the new technologies affords an opportunity to use them to augment organizational structure. Despite attempts to link them through the matrix, the project and functional structures remain essentially separate. In choosing one, the organization forgoes or at least makes it more difficult to obtain the benefits of the other. What can now potentially be done is to use either the project or functional structure and augment that with the appropriate information technology to achieve some of the advantages of the alternative form. The potential effects of this are shown in Figure 12.4.

When using functional departments, coordination of work can be facilitated by using hierarchically organized computer bulletin boards for configuration control and subsystem status reporting. This allows team members to be dispersed among functional departments, thereby maintaining contact with their specialties and coordinating their joint effort electronically. In effect, this may shift the boundary for using functional structures to encompass a broader territory of high interdependence (I_{ss}) situations.

When using project organization, individuals can be connected to their knowledge bases by means of computer-based topical bulletin boards organized around their technical specialties. They thereby gain not just the advantage of coordinating their work, through the organizational structure; they are also, despite organizational and physical separation from colleagues in their own specialties, provided some assistance in keeping abreast of the state of the art electronically. Thus, the use of topical bulletin boards may shift the boundary to accommodate a greater use of project organizations when demand for technical updating remains high (i.e., higher rates of technological change, dK/dt, and longer duration tasks, T).

Note that in the dK/dt-T plane, there are two opposing forces. The greater the capability of the knowledge-enhancing systems (i.e., topical bulletin boards and retrieval systems), the larger will be the region in which project organization can be used. Conversely, the more capable are the coordinating systems (e.g., hierarchical bulletin boards), the larger will be the area in which functional organization can be employed. On the other hand, because the two variables dealing with knowledge transfer (change in knowledge and task duration) are not, as far we know, differentially affected by advances in information technology, we don't expect significant changes in the slope of the function-project separating line in this plane.

In the dK/dt-I_{ss} plane, there are also two forces that will operate in opposite directions. In this case, because one has more effect in dealing with subsystem interdependence, and the other with changes in knowledge, they will result in a rotation of the project-function boundary. Because the coordination requirements of the task may be more amenable to technological treatment, the dividing line will probably shift more toward the dK/dt coordinate, increasing the set of tasks for which the functional structure is recommended. The impact of document search and retrieval systems and of topical bulletin boards organized around specialties is expected to be somewhat less discernible for the reasons cited earlier. Even though documents can be located and retrieved, they still must be read. Topical bulletin boards, at this point, have been shown to be effective for software developers,[2] but it remains to be seen how well they will work in other specialties. As a result, the location of the dividing line in this plane will shift only slightly from the I_{ss} coordinate, somewhat increasing the set of tasks for which the project structure is recommended. Consequently, the more significant shift, increasing the functional area, will occur for tasks of low interdependence and slow advancement of knowledge. On the other hand, the increase in the project area will be smaller and mostly for tasks of rapidly changing technologies and high interdependence. The net change in the set of tasks in the two structure areas will be a function of the power, effectiveness, and usability of the two information technologies.

This can be seen diagrammatically in Figure 12.5, in which the trade-off between coordination and knowledge transfer is illustrated. Moving along one of the curves, better coordination requires the sacrifice of some knowledge-transfer, and vice versa. Improvements in the technology of communication may encourage a shift to a new curve. The new curve does not have to

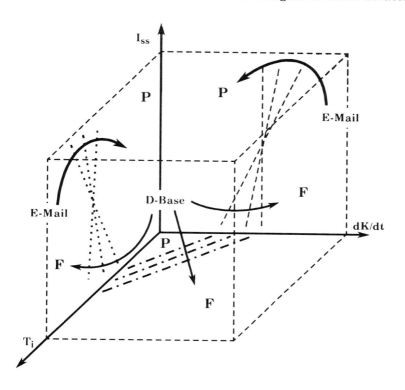

Legend:

dK/dt	-	Rate of change of knowledge	E-Mail	-	Electronic mail
T_i	-	Task duration	D-Base	-	Database for access of scientific and technological literature
I_{ss}	-	Task interdependence			
F	-	Functional structure recommended			
P	-	Project structure recommended			

Figure 12.4 Influence of Communication Related Information Technologies on the Organizational Structure Space

assume the same shape as its predecessor. Depending on whether the improvement is principally in the area of coordination or of knowledge, transfer will cause a tilt of the curve in one direction or the other. In the figure, an assumption is made that the advances in technology will affect coordination more than knowledge transfer.

The added flexibility in organizational design achieved through information technologies can be seen as similar to the impact of Flexible Manufacturing Systems (FMS) on the traditional matching between product and process attributes (Hayes & Wheelwright, 1984, pp. 209, 216). As they suggest, through this information-based technology the effective achievement of customer needs on the basis of product variety does not necessarily have to be traded off against efficient mass production.

Theoretical Implications and Future Research

Theoretically, the proposed conceptual model is one of many that are useful in studying organizational behavior. It will mainly apply at the task and departmental level, the operational and not the strategic organizational domain. The unit of analysis for a hypothetical study utilizing this model should be a group of professionals performing an organizational task.

In addition, we would suggest that the concepts described here, while developed in the context of research and development tasks are applicable to other organizational tasks if they are based on dynamic knowledge or expertise. This expertise does not have to be technical in nature; marketing or financial tasks, based on consumption psychology or simply dynamic market needs and economic theory, often face similar trade-offs between coordination and better knowledge of the underlying phenomena, in which case communication-related information technologies will hold the same potential for them that they do for research and development.

Thus, defining the general domain of the proposed model, the next question will be how to operationalize it for empirical research. Although the suggested model does not preclude qualitative, and case investigation, the final objective should be quantification of the model's dimensions. This will not be easy, but there are certainly possibilities.

Measurement of the Parameters

Of the three parameters, the easiest to measure is, of course, project duration. Measurement of the other two is a bit more difficult, but estimates can be made or values can at least be influenced by managerial action.

The rate of change of knowledge can be estimated on an ordinal basis by those familiar with the technologies. In addition, for those technologies or subdisciplines which have a central set of journals in which work is reported, there is a more objective measurement. *Science Citation Index* annually reports on the "half life" of citations for all journals within its coverage. This

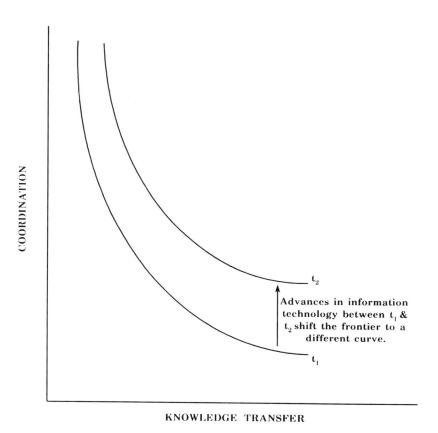

Figure 12.5 The Trade-Off Between Coordination and Knowledge
Transfer in Project Management

measure of citation half-life can certainly be regarded as an indicator of the
rate at which new knowledge is being in a field. There are other possible
measures such as the slope of technical progress curves (Fusfeld, 1970) that
might be more appropriate for applied science and technology. These should
be investigated in greater depth.

To our knowledge, there are no objective measures of subsystem interdependence. Subjective estimates are possible, and in fact are used by every
good project, who should take this measure into account in assigning project
tasks. Harris (1987) has shown that valid estimates can be made and that
project performance has a very strong inverse relationship to subsystem
interdependence. Harris's research reinforces previous research in this field
(Thompson, 1967; Van de Ven et al., 1976) that interdependence and the

289

resulting interface problems seriously affect performance. It also emphasizes the need for solutions to the problem of coordinating work in highly interdependent projects.

In partitioning a project, the project manager should be attempting to minimize the interdependence among subtasks. That is only common sense. Such a partitioning reduces the need for coordination, the responsibility for which falls primarily on the project manager. This is particularly true, when a portion of the work is to be subcontracted (von Hippel, 1988). By partitioning in this way, the project manager reduces the difficulty of his own assignment. There are other parameters to be taken into account in the partitioning process, for example, the availability of personnel with specific talents, experience or knowledge. These cannot be ignored, but subsystem interdependence remains one of the principal criteria for dividing up and assigning tasks. Project managers, themselves, thereby have considerable control over the portion of the organizational structure space committed to project organization.

But this only addresses our understanding of the static model of Figure 12.1. Research is also needed on the dynamics of the process that results from the introduction of information-communication technology. We need to know much more about the magnitude of contributions that information technology can make to both coordination and technical currency. Information technology can potentially provide some help in fulfilling these two key functions of communication in R&D. However, it is not a panacea, and its limits must be explored. At the same time, we must learn far more about the nature of the work itself. This is particularly true for white-collar work (Fleishman & Quaintance, 1984). Context-free typologies of communication-related information technologies should be quite useful for better matching of technologies and white-collar tasks.

Practical Implications

Even though the suggested model has not been tested empirically some of the implications could help practitioners in the choice of organization and communication-related infrastructure. Managers of a variety of functional departments, including marketing, finance, and manufacturing, can use the model not only to determine the preferred organizational form for a given task situation, but also in the choice of information technology to effectively complement and support that choice.

In R&D particularly, the model leads to choices that run completely counter to standard industrial practice. In choosing organizational form, the normal practice is to consider but one of the three parameters of the model. That is the most easily measured one, project duration. In deciding whether to keep engineers in their departments or to form a project team, project duration is often the determining criterion. If the project is a relatively short one, say six months, the decision is usually to leave the engineers in departments. To form a project team for such a short duration project is deemed to be too disruptive. Conversely, if the effort is to be a relatively long one, say six years, then the effort is likely to take on a strong identity of its own and a project team is formed. In following this practice, management not only neglects two of the three parameters but, accordingly to the model, they decide in the wrong direction on the one parameter that is considered!

The model proposed herein has therefore profound implications for management. Certainly it should be investigated empirically and supported or rejected on that basis, but if supported, it should dictate a very different basis for structuring research and development organizations. Still, we have yet to mention information technology in this section. Information technology should be used to augment the organizational structure that is chosen and to offset the losses incurred in the organizational trade-off. The model argues, *ceteribus paribus*, that longer efforts be organized functionally. Information technology will allow the point at which an effort becomes identified as "long term" to be extended. Similarly, the model argues that more complex, interdependent projects be organized in project teams. Information technology will allow the point at which interdependencies force this to occur to be extended. In other words, projects of greater complexity and interdependence can be performed in a matrix of functional departments.

Two of the task variables that determine the effectiveness of organizational choices are internal to the organization and are quite subject to management action. They are subsystem interdependence and task duration. The former can be influenced by decisions related to task modularity. For instance, one of the most common methods to reduce interdependence between subtasks in software development is to create quite independent software modules, which interact in a very specific and predictable way. If the interface between the routines is well designed, the teams designing and programming each of them can work in a totally independent fashion, with minimal coordination. Similar concepts can be applied in nonsoftware tasks (von Hippel, 1988).

Task duration is considerably more to difficult to manipulate. It is dependent upon the magnitude of the goal and the tractability of the problems that will be encountered. However, even given these constraints, a decision can be made after considering the rate of change of the underlying technologies and the interdependencies within the project to modify the goals or to accept interim solutions to some problems in order to shorten the duration of the project effort.

Of the three parameters, dK/dt is the only one not subject to at least some potential management influence. But even in this instance, there can be some of technologies to be employed. These may differ in their rate of change, in which their choice can be, in part, influenced by the two other parameters.

Finally, even at the writing of this article additional advances in information technologies offer new capabilities to organizations and raise new questions. For example, how can information technologies assist in meeting R&D needs for creativity? Can it provide effective alternatives to popular but discredited techniques such as brainstorming? These and other questions await empirical trials and further rigorous investigation.

Notes

1. A recent review of these issues, including the re-interpretation of Allen et al. (1979, 1980), can be found in Hauptman (1988).

2. The type of information that software developers deal with is apparently more amenable to transmission through this medium. Hardware developers often need graphical representations to communicate their problems or ideas. This type of representation, at this writing, remains difficult to transmit through bulletin boards or electronic mail. The queries posted on bulletin boards by software developers, on the other hand, often seek particular programs or specific sets of code, and these can be more easily transmitted (George, 1987).

References

Allen, T. J. (1984). *Managing the flow of technology*. Cambridge: MIT Press.

Allen, T. J., & Cohen, S. (1969). Information flow in R&D laboratories. *Administrative Science Quarterly, 14*, 12-19.

Allen, T. J., Tushman, M. L., & Lee, D.M.S. (1979). Technology transfer as a function of position in the spectrum from research through development to technical services. *Academy of Management Journal, 22*, 694-708.

Allen T. J., Lee, D.M.S., & Tushman, M. L. (1980). R&D performance as a function of internal communication, project management, and the nature of work. *IEEE Transactions on Engineering Management, EM-27*, 2-12.

Cuadra Associates (1984). *Directory of on-line databases*. Santa Monica, CA: Cuadra Associates.

Daft, R. L., & Macintosh, N. B. (1981). A tentative exploration into amount and equivocality of information processing in organizational work units. *Administrative Science Quarterly, 26*, 207-224.

Fleishman, E. A., & Quaintance, M. K. (1984). *Taxonomies of human performance*. New York: Academic Press.

Fusfeld, A. (1970). The technological progress function: A new technique for forecasting. *Technological Forecasting*, *1*, 301-312.

George, F. (1987). *Usage and motivation of a large electronic bulletin board*. Unpublished S. M. thesis, MIT Sloan School of Management, Cambridge.

Hauptman, O. (1986a). Influence of task type on the relation between communication and performance: The case of software development. *R&D Management*, *16*, 127-139.

Hauptman, O. (1986b). *Managing software development: Communication as a success factor*. Cambridge, Massachusetts: Unpublished doctoral dissertation, MIT.

Hauptman, O. (1988). *The different roles of communication in software development and hardware R&D: Phenomenological paradox or atheoretical empiricism?* Boston, MA: Harvard Business School Working Paper 89-028.

Harris, M. S. (1987). *Project performance as a function of subsystem interdependence for multi-site projects*. Cambridge, MA: Unpublished S. M. thesis, MIT.

Hayes, R. H., & Wheelwright, S. C. (1984). *Restoring our competitive edge: Competing through manufacturing*. New York: John Wiley.

Hiltz, S. R., & Turoff, M. (1978). *The network nation*. Reading, MA: Addison-Wesley.

Katz, R., & Allen, T. J. (1982). Investigating the Not Invented Here (NIH) syndrome. *R&D Management*, *12*, 7-19.

Marill, T. (1980). Time to retire the telephone? *Datamation*, (August), 185-186.

McKenney, J. L. (1986). *The influence of computer-communication on organizational information processing*. Boston: Harvard Business School Working Paper 1-786-040 (Rev. 6/1986).

McKenney, J. L., Doherty, V. L., & Sviokla, J. J. (1986). *The impact of electronic networks on management communication—An information processing study*. Boston: Harvard Business School Working Paper 1-786-041.

Pelz, D. C., & Andrews, F. M. (1976). *Scientists in organizations: Productivity climates for R&D* (revised edition). New York: John Wiley.

Perrow, C. (1967). A framework for the comparative analysis of organizations. *American Sociological Review*, *32*, 194-208.

Picot, A., Klingenberg, H., & Kranzle, H. P. (1982). Organizational communication: The relationship between technological development and socio-economic needs. In Bannon, L., Barry, U., & Holst, O. (Eds.) (1982). *Information technology impact on the way of life*, 114-132. Dublin: Tycooly International.

Siegel, J., Dubrovsky, V., Kiesler, S., & McGuire, T. W. (1984). *Group processes in computer-mediated communication*. Pittsburgh, PA: Committee on Social Science Research in Computing Working Paper Series, Carnegie-Mellon University.

Smith, R. B. (1985). *The twenty-first century corporation*. Speech given at the Economics Club, Detroit, Michigan. September 9, 1985.

Sproull, L. S., & Kiesler, S. (1986). Reducing social context cues: Electronic mail in organizational communication. *Management Science, 32,* 1492-1512.

Steinfield, C. W. (1984). *The nature of electronic mail usage in organizations: Purpose and dimensions of use.* Presented at the annual meeting of the *International Communication Association*, San Francisco, California.

Steinfield, C. W. (1985). *Explaining task-related and socio-emotional uses of computer-mediated communication in an organizational setting.* Working Paper, School of Communication, University of Houston.

Stevens, C. H. (1981). *Many to many communication* (Working Paper 72). MIT Sloan School of Management, Center for Information Systems Research, Cambridge.

Thompson, J. D. (1967). *Organizations in action.* New York: McGraw-Hill.

Tushman, M. L., & Nadler, D. (1978). Information processing as an integrative concept in organizational design. *Academy of Management Review* (July), 613-624.

Van de Ven, A. H., & Delbecq, A. L. (1974). A task contingent model of workunit structure. *Administrative Science Quarterly, 19,* 183-197.

Van de Ven, A. H., Delbecq, A. L., & Koenig, K., Jr. (1976). Determinants of coordination modes within organizations. *American Sociological Review, 41,* 322-338.

von Hippel, E. (1988). *Task partitioning: An innovation process variable.* Cambridge, MA: Sloan School of Management, MIT, Working Paper 2030-88 (June).

Whithey, M., Daft, R. L., & Cooper, W. H. (1983). Measures of Perrow's work unit technology: An empirical assessment and a new scale. *Academy of Management Journal, 26,* 45-63.

PETER G. W. KEEN

13. Telecommunications and Organizational Choice

Overview: The Targets for Research and Recommendation

This chapter outlines an agenda for helping managers and their advisers in large organizations use telecommunications to maintain organizational health. It focuses on two targets of opportunity:

1. Creating or restoring organizational simplicity at a time when large companies and public agencies are reaching a limit of complexity but not of growth. Telecommunications offers the chance to deal with a number of common organizational pathologies, including depersonalization of senior management, field/head office tensions, subservience to documents, and fragmented organizational knowledge.

2. Providing the base for evolving the federated organizational structure of the next decade that is the natural outcome of current and emerging business trends, especially among multinational firms. Telecommunications eliminates the dichotomy between centralization and decentralization and allows centralization-with-decentralization. It also provides a base for organizational redesign and reclustering. The federated structure is directly analogous to the United States. It is not a tightly coupled global organization, and there will still be business units maintaining many of their autonomous activities. There will also, though, be the simultaneous or parallel evolution of national, standardized processes.

The selection of these targets reflects a view of what is needed in organizational research on telecommunications and how it should be carried out. The statements below are in effect the axioms for this chapter:

1. Traditional approaches to studying and predicting the impacts of information technologies will not provide much help to firms in making choices about telecommunications strategies. No methodological fine-

tuning will resolve the problem that the impacts, even when important and far-ranging, may not be apparent for well over 20 years.

2. The agenda for research needs to focus on clarifying the areas of organizational effectiveness that open up a strong potential for applying telecommunications as a primary force for improvement. Even when we cannot directly predict impacts and outcomes, we can at least direct the deployment of the telecommunications resource toward important organizational goals.

In many respects the approach outlined here reverses the sequence of much organizational research in this area, which takes a technology or type of application (end-user computing, airline reservations systems, decision support systems, etc.) and asks in what way it affects organizational structure or processes. The analysis may then point toward recommendations for policy, planning, design, implementation, and use.

This chapter suggests an approach that moves backward from desired or needed impact to available and usable technology and applications. The starting point is to identify important and urgent targets of opportunity for using telecommunications to make a major impact on the direction of the organization. This rests on answering three basic questions:

1. What forces and pressures are organizations having to deal with where management choices will significantly influence effectiveness? Here *effectiveness* is defined as a combination of competitive positioning—ensure economic health—and the ability to maintain a "culture", create a "structure", ensure "leadership", and provide "quality of working life"—that is, ensure organizational health.

2. Is telecommunications a major potential means to this end? Can managers be shown a strong causal, correlative link between their decisions concerning telecommunications and the health of their organization over the next ten years?

3. Can the potential be turned into reality through the management process? (If not, there is little reason to raise the issue.)

The goal of this chapter is influence and, hence, prescription. Its aim is to help managers make choices. It views telecommunications as both an important and an urgent item on the management agenda. The two are not always correlated. Many executives see telecommunications as important but not urgent.

296

Is Telecommunications "Different"?

This chapter draws on descriptive research only to a very limited degree, because there are few previous studies that can guide the manager in developing telecommunication strategies. Telecommunications is somehow different from other aspects of information technology in terms of the dynamics of organizational change. In particular, it is clearly different in the context in which choices about it are having to be made.

1. The opportunity to apply the technology on a wide-scale basis, in terms of geography, range of services, and scope of change in work, has come at a time of obvious environmental turbulence: intense cost pressures, internationalization across industry after industry, deregulation or the anticipation of deregulation, and the breaking down of traditional industry boundaries. This means that telecommunications is interlinked with factors of business change that in themselves are new and complex.

2. Telecommunications is largely an enabling technology. It provides an information highway system. Personal computers, office technology applications, electronics customer delivery, videoconferencing, document interchange, and the like are the traffic. It will be hard therefore to measure the impact of telecommunications in, and of, itself.

3. The technology and its economics are evolving so rapidly in some areas that in a very short space new uses, and hence later impacts on organization and work, are emerging in a fairly compressed time period.

All this adds up to an era of discontinuity. It is discontinuity that makes telecommunications "different." We can no longer talk about "managing" change; that is merely reactive when the pace of environmental pressure is continuous and accelerating. The issue is how to get ahead of the change curve. Managing change means reacting to the environmental factors that signal change. Taking charge of change involves looking ahead across the discontinuity and making very basic decisions about business, organization, and technologies without relying on extrapolations from the status quo. The thesis of this article is that telecommunications is a major element in managing discontinuity. It is this that makes it different and that makes prediction so difficult.

long-term implications of telecommunications, firms have
.s now. They cannot easily draw on experience to guide them.
ɔrganizational use of telecommunications as more than just
pa₁. onal overhead is too short. Its more recent use as a force that
can create sustained competitive advantage provides only special examples,
not average ones (see Keen, 1986; Runge, in press).

The very idea of using telecommunications for business innovation means
not automating the status quo but explicitly trying to change entire aspects
of the organization or its interactions with its business environment. Most
businesses recognize they need to have strategies for telecommunications.
They can guess at the organizational outcomes or simply go ahead and later
deal with unanticipated consequences. But they have to make the choices
anyway.

They need research that helps guide those choices. The results of studies
of the organizational impact of information technologies over the past 20
years show how hard it is to assess, let alone anticipate, how technology and
organization interact. We seem to underestimate the pace of technical
change and overestimate the rate of social change.

Of course change occurs and continues. However, despite the obvious
growing appearance of workstations on the office landscape and the importance of computers and communications to basic aspects of operations as well
as innovations in markets, products, and services, organizational structures
and everyday work life do not seem very different today from what they were
20 years ago. Predictions of the cashless society, the office of the future, and,
most recently, the diffusion of artificial intelligence into every aspect of
decision making turn out again and again to overstate both the pace and
degree of the organizational impact of information technology.

The main problem is almost certainly one of time perspective. Leavitt and
Whisler, for example, forecast the coming demise of the middle manager as
early as 1958, due to computers. The forecast looked unconvincing through
the 1970s. Business in the 1960s had emphasized decentralization rather
than centralization and computers had mainly affected clerical operations,
not management functions. But in the mid-1980s most large firms are indeed
explicitly aiming at and getting reductions of 20% in middle-management
staffing.

There are many forecasts being made by researchers concerned with the
impacts of information technology on the nature of future organizations and

the nature of work. They expect major effects. Huber (1984), for instance, asserts that we are entering a "postindustrial" environment marked by increased turbulence, complexity, and knowledge. He sees a need for faster and more frequent decision making and hence for improved participation. He also sees a need for increased control over the way in which complex decisions are made and for formalization of the processing of nonroutine information.

There are many other predictions and assertions that, like Leavitt and Whisler's, need more time to validate than firms have time to wait. The example of Huber's conception of improved decision making and Howard's (1985) warnings of a *Brave New Workplace* and Gregory's (1982) "Race Against Time" point to entirely different managerial options and responsibilities.

The differences are increased rather than reduced if one adds such work as that of Winograd and Flores (1986), which is well-grounded in philosophy and backed by practical experience in providing telecommunications-based tools for improving communication and coordination. Winograd and Flores challenge the rationalistic decision paradigms that underlie much of the analytic management literature. They view the organization in terms of recurrent conversations and organizational performance in terms of the effective management of conversations. They, like Huber, see the importance of telecommunications as the enabling system for improving organizational decision-making processes, but their implicit messages to managers conflict with those of mainstream academic work in this area.

Even the basic conceptions of organizational theory have different implications for understanding how, and if, telecommunications can be expected to change organizational structures and processes. Theorists who view organizations in terms of an information processing paradigm generally assume fairly tight coupling between subunits. Galbraith (1973, 1974) was an early exponent of this view, which is an attractive paradigm for information engineers.

Weick's conception of loosely coupled organizations (1976) and the garbage can model associated with March (Cohen, March, & Olsen, 1972) challenge this entirely. They see much weaker links between information and decision making and their models imply that formal telecommunications systems will have little impact on effectiveness.

Many other examples can be given of both the inconclusive messages from previous studies and predictions of actual impacts of information technology and of the different assumptions and assertions of recent studies of future impacts. The point here, though, is not to either attack or endorse any of them but to highlight the view of research that entirely motivates the rest of this article. The main argument is easily summarized: Telecommunications can be harnessed as a major new force for organizational design and redesign, and all large organizations need to exploit the opportunities it opens up. However, these organizations recognize that there are no easy rules and proven procedures. Telecommunications and business and organizational risk go together.

The Basis for Strategic Choices

Investments in telecommunications by large organizations represent—or should represent—a conscious choice to spend capital to improve some aspect of their activities. Up to now, investment decisions have been forced mainly by competitive pressures; economic, rather than organizational, health has been the motivator. It is impossible to understand the dynamics of competition in the travel, airline, and financial services sectors without recognizing the key role played by telecommunications. In all these industries, risky choices about telecommunications are being forced on firms. Their decisions are largely based on business needs, and organizational issues are secondary.

At some stage, perhaps in the late 1990s, there will be less need for choice and less business risk involved in the investment. In place will be a comprehensive and stable infrastructure and range of services, for which ISDN (Integrated Services Digital Network) is the blueprint. Organizations can then take for granted the availability of a comprehensive and flexible information transportation system just as they now do the car and plane transportation base. They will not have to make many choices about telecommunications, only about its uses. They may well then be more concerned with organizational rather than purely business issues.

Until then, though, telecommunications will pose many problems of business choice, in terms of competitive options and timing (Keen, 1986). Even while business issues drive the investment decision, organizational issues will be on the long-term agenda. Telecommunications inherently involves organizational, as well as technical change.

Although it has been the business issues that have driven the strategic telecommunications choices, there are signs that a new set of issues is becoming recognized.

1. Many organizations have already made the step shift in investment and business commitment to telecommunications. They have the back-

bone network that is a long-term business resource. They made the shift in response to business pressures or opportunities, but they can now focus more on organizational pressures and opportunities. Ownership of a comprehensive telecommunications delivery base thus changes the economics of innovation; it is easier for an airline to add hotel reservations to its reservations system than for a hotel chain to create its own.

2. It is becoming clearer that the firms who are cited as innovators in the use of telecommunications for competitive advantage did not really "innovate." Instead, they applied the technology to the core drivers in their business. For American Airlines, SABRE was the order entry system for handling the basics of its business. American Hospital Supply's system supported its single most important activity, making sales calls. Automated teller machines are a conservative, not radical, force; they protected the banks' most basic transactions and relationship with their customers.

This means that telecommunications already affects the core part of their organization, where the work that constitutes their identity is handled. They have already begun a process of quite radical organizational change. In banking, cash management and fee-based services change the corporate banker's skills and roles. They redefine the selling process and customer relationship. They bring the bank's back office and operations and its marketing units together. They alter the basis for compensation and measure of profitability. This is a simple example of the often hidden organizational changes implicit.

Howard (1985) suggests this change is too often badly conceived and introduced. If that is so, telecommunications may be damaging aspects of organizational health and remedial action is essential. Where it is not so, the opportunity is there to use the installed systems at the core of the business to improve organizational health even more.

Telecommunications and Organizational Simplicity

The rest of this chapter shifts from review to recommendation. It answers the three questions raised in section 1.

This section discusses an area strongly affecting organizational effectiveness, where the answer to each question indicates a major potential role for telecommunications. It concerns the relationship between environmental complexity and organizational complexity and the chance to reduce complexity to simplicity.

The forces that have created or threaten to create discontinuity are pushing large organizations in both industry and government to a point where they are reaching limits of complexity but not of growth. They are still manageable, but too often only through adding resources, procedures, and layers of staff that do not contribute to their mission and sometimes even impede it. They are increasingly cumbersome and viewed by inside and outside observers as failing to meet the demands of a difficult era.

There can be little doubt that the problem of complexity will increase because of continued pressure toward:

1. globalization and extended lines of communication, coordination, and operation across times zones and locations;
2. breadth of activities in terms of markets, services, products, customer demands, and anticipation and response to competitive pressures; and
3. time stresses created through geographic dispersion, shortening of planning, development and delivery cycles, increased environmental volatility, and drastically reduced reaction times.

Some consequences for complexity are shown in Figure 13.1, all of which are targets for exploiting telecommunications. They include:

1. Tensions between the field and head office.
2. Depersonalization of management: Senior executives do not meet their staff; the CEO's business message and company news are sent via memo, not communicated directly.
3. Fragmented understanding: No single individual may have a complete picture of the system, but many may have vested interests and perceptions.
4. Inefficient team and project work: When work is distributed and lines of communications extended, then obviously coordination becomes costly and expensive.
5. Subservience to documents: The virtual ritualization of documents: Claims, travel expense forms, requisitions, and so on can take over from the work process they are intended to support.

These pathologies are well recognized, and many firms have already made progress in attacking them. The tools of integrated information technologies offer powerful support for doing so. Telecommunications and workstations help speed up information access and delivery and bridge geographic locations. Newer applications of videoconferencing, corporate videotext, CD-ROM, and electronic data interchange extend the opportunities to deal with the pathologies listed in Figure 13.1.

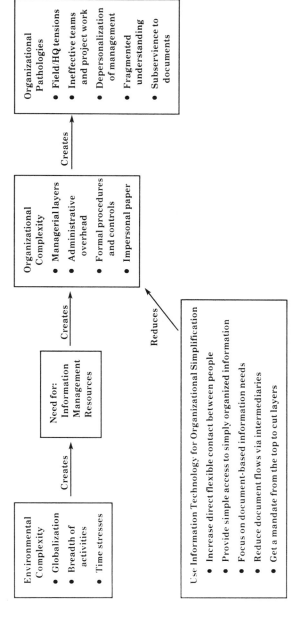

Figure 13.1 Information Technology and Organizational Simplicity

303

Organizations now place the same emphasis on using telecommunications and associated technologies and applications for creating organizational simplicity as they have in the past for using it for competitive advantage. Telecommunications will form the basis for the new enabling systems that help CEOs redesign their organizations through the 1990s. Videoconferencing, for instance, seems likely to be a key tool for repersonalizing management, enhancing team work across locations and even company boundaries, speeding up the distribution and sharing of news in fast-moving business contexts, and for management education and reeducation.

These enabling systems have not been used widely in these new ways. Even though videoconferencing and videotext have been available for years, they have not generally been used to address the problem of complexity. Instead, organizations have historically provided information management resources to meet the demands of complexity through adding layers of management and staff, administrative overhead, formal control and reporting systems, and the substitution of impersonal paper for people in communication.

Two of the main reasons that telecommunications can be deployed over the coming few years to restore simplicity are that video is a natural and direct medium of contact and, equally important, recent technical developments have eliminated several barriers to mass use. Fiber optics reduces the economic barrier and VSAT (very small aperture terminals) open up what may be termed end-user telecommunications. VSAT may well be to telecommunications what the personal computer has been to computing (Goodstein & Sulser, 1987).

An incentive for using telecommunications for organizational simplicity is the elimination of intermediaries, procedure guardians, and administrative overloads that are part of complexity. This is obviously a starting point for overall strategic organizational change and a major source of momentum for rethinking the organizational status quo. Once firms see this as a priority target for improvement, they are in general able to cut headcount among middle level staff by 20%. That figure occurs again and again in reports on office technology, corporate restructuring, and successful productivity and quality drives.

Incentive is also a problem. The impacts of eliminating so many people who have served their firms well must be considered. A major need in research is to address how middle management can be redeployed or reeducated, not just dumped.

Organizational simplification requires more than displacement of people. It has to improve the process that created the need for the people. Just cutting out bodies is not the same as removing excess layers. What seems to have happened since the 1950s, with the speed and permanence of a glacier, is that many middle-level functionaries, whether or not they are called *managers*, have become little more than information coordinators and intermediaries. They become repositories of information and indispensable.

They are indispensable only until communication is made more direct. Hercules corporation is an excellent example of why videoconferencing is now a major force for organizational improvement. Hercules has cut six to seven layers of management through its well-established, organizationwide communications systems. The CEO, Alexander Giacco, directed the deployment of a corporatewide capability that affects every aspect of "meeting", with 25 videoconferencing locations spanning London to California. This was a direct response to Giacco's concern for managing complexity. The firm's scattered locations led to delays, bottlenecks, inconveniences, and essentially flat productivity among its 8,500 white-collar staff.

The Hercules example is striking but not atypical. Layers can be cut while improving overall effectiveness. Several European firms have eliminated at least a level of management in their sales organization by using the simple and—in the United States—neglected technology of videotext.

There is often a mutual cause and effect between delayering and using technology to bridge communications gaps. One helps the other. Wells Fargo reports cutting out two levels in its personnel function because information moves freely up and down without intermediaries. Electronic document interchange, surely a strategic and proven business opportunity for all firms, is also an organizational opportunity. Purchase departments are cut from hundreds of people to dozens.

A Strategy for Organizational Simplification

The second question, in section 1, asks if managers can be shown strong causal links between their own decisions to sanction telecommunications investments and a real chance of improving organizational effectiveness. The strategy suggested below sketches out answers.

The basis of the strategy is to use information technology, to

1. increase direct, flexible contact between people
2. cut down on the need for information intermediaries
3. provide simple access to information, simply organized
4. focus on peoples' needs for document-based information
5. reduce document flows, and barriers to tracking, locating, and controlling document-based work flows
6. get a firm commitment from the top of the organization to cut layers of management; at the same time provide resources to soften the organizational strain and personal damage this brings through phased timing, buy out, education, redeployment, etc. (The *etc.* can be added only through better research in this area.)

The last point is not peripheral. Organizations do not delayer themselves, nor do well-entrenched administrative procedures relax under the logic of simplification. They are too often dominated by social inertia, which dampens out efforts to change them. The firms that have successfully used telecommunications to increase organizational simplicity seem to be able to do so only when the leadership adds its weight to the push. This assertion, based mainly on an informal review of articles and autobiographies needs testing through research on the role of senior managers in setting telecommunications strategies.

When the organizational end is clear, telecommunications provides many means of achieving it. For Hercules, the end was organizational simplicity and the means videoconferencing. For the European firms mentioned earlier, the means was videotext. For Wells Fargo, it was a mixture of fairly standard applications of office technology, end-user computing, and online data base management systems. In every case, the enabling force was the combination of top management fiat plus information technology—neither alone may be enough to challenge inertia on the one hand and avoid simplistic headcount cuts that damage productivity on the other.

Summary and Caveats

All this may sound like the late 1970s paeans to an office of the future that simply never came to pass or a reassertion of the technocrats' belief in organizational engineering via information technology plus tough-minded management. It also reflects the risk involved in making assertive recommendations not backed up by descriptive research. In defining a practical strategy for creating organizational simplicity, it is important to appreciate the linkages between cause and effect implicit in Figure 13.1:

1. Environmental complexity creates a need for additional information management resources; when those resources are based on adding people and procedures, they increase complexity, which creates organizational pathologies.
2. To reduce those pathologies, information resources must be added in a way that explicitly does not generate complexity.

This means that many efforts to apply traditional office technology and end-user computing will compound the problem. Similarly, delayering without cutting out formal procedures, or cutting out formal procedures and paper while maintaining superfluous layers, merely raises unmeetable expectations and discredits the argument that information technology in itself is a force for productivity. It is not.

It seems to be true, though, that targeting a strategy for simplicity directly at the pathologies that result from complexity can be a stimulus for reducing layers of management administrative overhead, and so on. The European firms mentioned earlier, who used videotext to link the field and regional offices, only later realized that as a result they could reduce layers of management and administrative overhead.

It may well be that a combination of top-down, senior management-sanctioned programs plus bottom-up experimentation and local innovation generates the maximum impetus for radical organizational change. The top-down approach can easily lose momentum and may not get middle management's buy-in but at least breaks open the status quo. The bottom-up strategy may similarly be quickly dampened by inertia but generates learning and activism instead of passive reaction to management mandates.

The suggested strategy for creating organizational simplicity does not focus on any specific technologies or tools but it highlights ones, such as videoconferencing, that have not been viewed by most information services (IS) units as in the mainstream of their work.

The suggested strategy also implies a fairly radical shift in IS attention, from managing "data," mainly as numbers and messages, to managing documents. People who know little or nothing about computers view it more naturally in terms of the documents they work with: purchase orders, lists, letters, manuals, forms, and the like. They organize and access their own information resources mainly through a simple hierarchical equivalence of filing cabinet/folder/paper-clipped papers. Traditional applications of information technology have not focussed on the document as the unit of information.

It is partly the role of documents in organizational life that has added to complexity even in an environment of online data and transaction processing. It is this that makes document-based SIS—simple information systems—rather than MIS a target of opportunity, with CD-ROM, videotext, and standards for electronic document interchange becoming powerful new strategic tools.

More detailed examples of companies that have successfully used these tools are the subject of an ongoing study being carried out by the International Center for Information Technologies, together with an analysis of high-payoff emerging opportunities. Several points are already clear:

1. Videoconferencing, properly designed and managed, is a major vehicle to support organizational redesign, especially for helping CEOs get their personality and message across to the field, for ad hoc problem-solving, for team and project work in a distributed environment, for product launches and training, for cost-effective and efficiently distributed education, and for increasing software productivity.

2. The CD-ROM revolution happened but many IS organizations have not exploited it—or even noticed it. The technology is stable and the economics attractive; it offers a major opportunity to make manuals, product information, archives, and so on easy to (a) access, (b) cross-reference and browse through, and (c) simplify in terms of management and use.

3. VSAT (very small aperture terminals) may be to telecommunications what PCs have been to computing, and as with PCs, the opportunity VSAT opens up for organizational and business innovation is easily overlooked by technical staff who extrapolate from the status quo. VSAT offers the relocatable branch office, crisis management communication, corporate news distribution, and full-scale hinterland computing (Goodstein & Sulser, 1987).

4. American firms can learn a great deal from how European organization use corporate videotext. In the United Kingdom, for example, Thomson's Holidays is the European equivalent of American Hospital supply, but via videotext—a simple, low-cost, readily available and easily installed technology.

5. Electronic Document Interchange (EDI) is already commonplace in a range of industries, especially groceries and transportation. The mutual wish of companies to reach agreements means that the pace of EDI

will accelerate and that the X.12 standard will be the universal base for inter- and intraindustry transactions.

Organizational simplification benefits almost everyone—the losers are the 20% of middle management who will be displaced in just about every Fortune 100 firm. The human cost cannot be evaded, but in the longer term, organizational simplicity means reduced costs, higher morale, a more empowered management, more responsiveness and flexibility. The technology is already available, the opportunities both proven and still emerging, and the payoffs clear.

The Federal Organizational Structure

The final main line of argument in this chapter concerns telecommunications and organizational structure. The concept of the federated organization is based on a number of trends in large multinationals that individually do not add up to overt changes in structure but that together seem to indicate a major longer-term change in what we mean by *organization*. Some examples are:

1. The decision by a few firms, such as Unilever, one of the world's largest fast-moving consumer goods firms, to consider getting rid of their head office within the next 5 years and to distribute functions. Telecommunications will be used to provide corporate coordination.
2. The growth of what may be called *faceless markets*, such as NASDAQ, where a complex and large securities trading association operates as effectively and efficiently as any previous floor-based equivalent such as the New York Stock Exchange, without the members ever having to meet each other. Here is "organization" without location.
3. The many instances of firms increasing decentralization and at the very same time increasing central coordination. Toyota of America is typical. The company installed minicomputers in dealers' offices and provided a range of systems to improve the decentralized units' efficiency. The central staff used the telecommunications network to pull to the center daily information that allowed them to reduce "information float"—the time gap between an event occurring and the planners and decision makers knowing about it.
4. The growth of "cooperative processing." This not the same as distributed processing and relates to organizations deciding to locate such functions as finance and engineering in particular locations and using telecommunication to give other units access to facilities.

5. Citibank's international corporate banking organization was, for many years, as lean an organization as any in the world. There were few corporate staff and far less management reporting and reports than in most "well-run" multinationals. Yet communication across the corporation was smooth, fast, and obtrusive. It is no coincidence that at that time, Citibank's international group had the most comprehensive and wide-ranging telecommunications network in international banking.

6. One of the world's top five petrochemical firms is fully commmitted to decentralization of its business operation. At the same time, every single financial transaction over $500 is processed via a central computer on the East Coast of the United States. It is the firm's telecommunications network that allows this central coordination without disruption to local units' autonomy.

The message in the trends listed above is for leading firms to rely on their telecommunications infrastructure to ensure that they can adapt their structure and processes to manage discontinuity. They do not have to make decisions about how to manage corporate functions or coordinate across units and geography in terms of physical location. They have the chance to create a federated organizational structure.

The large firms that can use telecommunications to create the federated structure will not be locked into a fixed organization. They will be able to redesign and reorganize without having to relocate and rebuild. The assertion made here is that the backbone international network will be one of the central determinants of a multinational's organizational flexibility.

Conclusion: The Agenda for Organizational Research

The two themes of organizational simplicity and federated structures point to the truly strategic implications of telecommunications for the future in large organizations. If they are even approximately correct, they require such firms to move fast now to be positioned for the early 1990s. They also imply that in the competition for scarce investment capital, telecommunications holds high priority.

Assertion is obviously not enough to justify action. The role of research needs to be defined to provide reliable guides for action. The three questions that formed the framework for the line of argument in this chapter can be translated to an outline research agenda:

1. WHAT ARE THE FORCES AND PRESSURES ORGANIZATIONS MUST DEAL WITH?

We need research on the causes and consequences of discontinuity and on strategies for taking charge of change where we cannot predict and control environmental stresses. That research will almost certainly be based on studies of lessons from recent shocks. The airline and banking sectors will be the historical data base for understanding what happens when the destabilizing forces of internationalization, deregulation, and time stress interact with telecommunications.

2. WHAT IS THE POTENTIAL CONTRIBUTION OF TELECOMMUNICATIONS?

To answer this we need far more intellectual and empirical research on definitions and measures of organizational effectiveness in an era in which telecommunications is a strategic factor in any aspect of organizational designing. We do not yet know how to measure the business value of the communications infrastructure.

The two themes of organizational simplicity and federated structures can be studied descriptively—through case examples of successful exploitations of the nonmainstream technologies and tools of videoconferencing, corporate videotext, document interchange and the like, plus prescriptive analyses of issues of high payoff opportunity identification, planning, design, implementation and use.

3. CAN POTENTIAL BE TURNED INTO ACTUAL?

No research is needed here. The answer is simply "Of course." One of the reasons that telecommunications will move higher and higher on the organizational priority list is that the technology is moving faster and faster away from being a blockage to action.

Telecommunications will be the basic tool for organizational design and redesign well before the late 1990s. Firms need to look ahead now and prepare to make strategic commitments. Researchers need to study the issues and options for using telecommunications to take charge of change.

References

Cohen, M. D., March, J. G., & Olsen, J. P. (1972). A garbage can model of organizational choice. *Administrative Science Quarterly, 17*, 1-25.

Galbraith, J. (1973). *Designing complex organizations*. Reading, MA: Addison-Wesley.

Galbraith, J. (1974). Organization design: An information processing view. *Interfaces, 4*, 28-36.

Goodstein, P., & Sulser, D. (1987). Business opportunities of vsat. Unpublished manuscript, International Center for Information Technologies, Washington, DC.

Gregory, J. (1982). Race against time. *Office: Technology and people.*

Howard, R. (1985). *Brave new workplace*. New York: Penguin.

Huber, G. P. (1982). Organizational information systems: Determinants of their performance and behavior. *Management Science, 28*, 18-155.

Huber, G. P. (1984). The nature and design of post-industrial organizations. *Management Science, 30*, 928-951.

Huber, G. P., & McDaniel, R. R. (1986). The decision-making paradigm of organizational design. *Management Science, 32*, 572-589.

Keen, P.G.W. (1981). Information systems and organizational change. *Communications of the ACM, 24*, 1.

Keen, P.G.W. (1985). Computers and managerial choice. *Organizational Dynamics*, AMA.

Keen, P.G.W. (1986). *Competing in time: Using telecommunications for competitive advantage*. Cambridge, MA: Ballinger.

Keen, P.G.W., & Scott-Morton, M. S. (1978). *Decision support systems: An organizational perspective*. Reading, MA: Addison-Wesley.

Leavitt, H. J. (1965). Applied organizational change in industry: Structural, technological and humanistic approaches. In J. G. March (Ed.), *Handbook of organization*. Chicago: Rand McNally.

Leavitt, H. J. (1976). Beyond the analytic manager. *California Management Review, 17*(3), 5-12; *17*(4), 11-21.

Runge, D. (1988). *Using telecommunications for competitive advantage*. Washington, DC: International Center for Information Technologies Press.

Weick, K. (1976). Educational organizations as loosely coupled systems. *Administrative Science Quarterly, 21*, 1-19.

Whisler, T. L. (1958). Management in the 1980's. *Harvard Business Review, 36*(6), 41-48.

Winograd, T., & Flores, F. (1986). *Understanding computers and cognition: A new foundation for design*. Norwood, NJ: Ablex.

Author Index

Subject Index

Adoption of interactive media, 211-213; coercion, 212; positive inducements, 212-214; pricing, 211-213

Advanced information technologies; basic characteristics, 240-241; defined, 238; effects on organizational decision making, 260-264; effects on organizational design, 244-260; effects on organizational intelligence, 260-264; properties, 241-243; use of, 243

Bulletin boards, 251, 284-286
Bureaucracy, 33-34, 37-38

CD-ROM, 308
Centralization, effects of advanced information technology on, 250-253, 309

Change, management of, 295-311

Communication media, and: organizational power, 160; organizational task, 159; social network structure, 157-160

Communication networks: as models of social relationships 151-152; Burt's theory of structural action, 147; communication network metrics, 152-153; structuration, 147

Complexity, 302-304, 307
Computer conferencing, 205, 277
Conduit metaphor of communication, 145

Control, 29-44; and information, 43-44; and computers, 29-31; classes of control, 41-43; dimensions of control, 30-31; and organizational structure 35-36; organizations and control, 32-37, 39-44; preprocessing, 38-41; rationalization, 37-39; standardization, 40; technology, 34-35

Coordination, 282, 284-285, 290

Critical mass: collective action, 201-203; communities, 209; described, 196, 213-216; heterogeneity, 206-207; individual costs, 204; for interactive media, 203-208; and universal access, 213-214

Decentralization: effects of advanced information technology on, 250-253, 311

Decision making: effects of advanced information technology on, 260-264; participation in, 245-247; quality of, 262-264; size and heterogeneity of decision units, 247-248

Deskilling, 49
Discretionary database, defined, 221

Discretionary information: as public good, 219-221; asymmetries, 225, 229-230; contribution costs of, 222-224, 228-230; defined, 219; payoffs from, 222-223; subsidies for, 223-224; system size, 224, 230

Document search and retrieval systems, 282-286

Electronic document interchange (EDI), 20, 99-101, 308

Electronic mail, 72, 76-77, 91, 120-123, 129-132, 159-160, 195, 200, 205, 206, 213, 249, 263, 277-278

Emergent communication networks, 162-165

Emergent perspective on organizational actions, 150, 161-162

Environmental scanning, 260-262
Equilibrium, 223-224
Equivocality, 74-75, 77-79
Expert systems, 174-176, 258

Facsimile, 206
Federated organizational structure, 309-310

About the Authors

Thomas J. Allen was a Research Associate with the M.I.T. Sloan School of Management from 1963 to 1966 and is currently a Professor in the Management of Technology Group. He has been involved in a series of studies of the problem solving and communication behavior of research and development engineers and scientists. The first of these studies employed instances of parallel research (two or more groups working independently on the same project) as a mechanism to provide control for the substance of research problem sources, etc., used by the groups. This was followed by studies of laboratory communication networks and the factors which determine their structure and effectiveness. This investigation has led into such diverse areas of concern as the interaction between organizational structure and behavior, the role of the technical gatekeeper in technology transfer, and the influence of architectural layout on human communication behavior. He later applied similar methods to a study of international technology transfer. Professor Allen is currently engaged in an extensive study of matrix organizations and the aging of technical groups. He is the author of the well-known book *Managing the Flow of Technology* (1984) in paperback.

James R. Beniger is Associate Professor of Communications and Sociology in the Annenberg School of Communications and the Department of Sociology, University of Southern California. His current research interests include information technology, communication theory, and societal change—with particular attention to the implications for social control, popular culture, and the arts.

Terry Connolly is Professor of Management and Policy at the University of Arizona, where he also coordinates the Decision Behavior Laboratory. His academic background includes degrees in electrical engineering, sociology, and organizational behavior, and he has held faculty appointments at Georgia Institute of Technology, University of Illinios and University of Chicago. His primary research interests are in decision behavior in organizational settings, and the effects of information processing technologies on them. His publications on these and related topics include two books and more than 60 journal papers and book chapters.

Noshir S. Contractor, Ph.D., Annenberg School of Communications, University of Southern California, is Assistant Professor in the Department of Speech Communication at the University of Illinois, Urbana-Champaign. His research interests include application of systems theory to communication, the role of emergent communication networks in organizations, and information technologies in the workplace.

Richard L. Daft, Ph.D., holds the Ralph Owen Chair in Business Administration at Vanderbilt University, where he specializes in the study of organization theory and management. He is a Fellow of the Academy of Management, and has served for three years as associate editor of *Administrative Science Quarterly, Academy of Management Journal, Academy of Management Review, Strategic Management Journal, Management Science,* and *MIS Quarterly.* Professor Daft is currently pursuing studies of organization design, organizational innovation and change, strategy implementation, and organizational information processing.

Gerardine DeSanctis is Associate Professor of Information Systems at the University of Minnesota. She received her Ph.D. from Texas Tech University in 1982. Her current research interests are computer-supported decision making and systems implementation in organizations. Her articles appear in journals such as *Management Science, Data Base,* the *Academy ofManagement Journal, Information and Management,* and the *Communications of the ACM.* She is currently an Associate Editor for the *MIS Quarterly, Information Systems Research,* and *Management Science.*

Eric M. Eisenberg is Associate Professor of Communication Arts and Sciences at the University of Southern California. He has been published frequently in the areas of language, emergent communication networks, and strategic communication in organizations. His article, "Ambiguity as strategy in organizational communication" won the Speech Communication Association Outstanding Publication Award in Organizational Communication. His most recent research focuses on how individuals achieve transcendence through organizing, in the absence of shared attitudes and beliefs.

Janet Fulk (MBA and Ph.D., Ohio State University) is Associate Professor at the University of Southern California in the Annenberg School of Communications. She serves on the editorial boards of *Communication Monographs* and *Leadership Quarterly* and has published recent articles in *Journal of*

Applied Psychology, Organizational Behavior and Human Performance, Communication Research, and *Communication Yearbook.* Her research interests include the processes and effects of implementing new communication technologies in organizations, superior-subordinate communication, and the management of professional and technical expertise in organizations.

Oscar Hauptman is an Assistant Professor at the Harvard Business School, Production and Operations Management group. He received his B.Eng. and M.Sc. from the Israel Institute of Technology—Technion in Industrial Engineering and Management, and Industrial Management, in 1976 and 1982, respectively. He holds a Ph.D. (1986) from the Sloan School of Management, M.I.T. in Management of Technological Innovation. His research and publications are in the area of technology-based entrepreneurship, communication and R&D management, and information technology and software development. He has published in *R&D Management, Research Policy, Management Science, Journal of Product Innovation Management,* and *Communication Research.* His current research is about the process of technology forecasting by top managers.

George P. Huber is the Fondren Foundation Chaired Professor of Business at the University of Texas at Austin. His research focuses on organizational design, decision making, and information systems, and he has written three books and more than 70 other publications on these topics. In 1983, his pioneering article on the nature and design of post-industrial organizations was awarded First Prize in the International Prize Competition sponsored by the Institute of Management Sciences. For his research contributions in the area of decision making, Dr. Huber has been elected a Fellow of the Decision Sciences Institute. He has served as the editor of *Management Science's* Department of Information Systems and Decision Support Systems, and in policy-level positions for the Institute of Management Sciences, the International Federation for Information Processing, and the Decision Sciences Institute. Dr. Huber is currently the principal investigator of a five-year study of organizational change, design, and performance being conducted by researchers in California, Michigan, Oregon, and Texas.

Peter G. W. Keen is Executive Director of the International Center for Information Technologies, Washington, DC., and Distinguished Visiting Professor at Fordham University. Prior to founding ICIT, he was on the faculties of the Harvard Business School, Stanford University and the Massachusetts

Institute of Technology. He is the author of *Competing in Time: Using Telecommunications for Competitive Advantage* (1988) and coauthor of *Decision Support Systems: An Organizational Perspective* (1978) and *Transforming the IS Organization* (1988). His current research focusses on Business Design through Information Technologies: meshing the competitive, organizational, economic and technical components of the effective use of IT into a new management process. BDIT represents a new profession, management education curriculum, and research agenda. He is an adviser to senior executives and government policy makers to large organizations in North America, Europe, and Latin America. In 1988, Information Week identified him as one of the top ten IT consultants in the United States.

Robert H. Lengel is an Associate Professor of Management at the University of Texas at San Antonio. He received his B.S. in Aero Space Engineering from Penn State in 1968, an M.S. in Engineering Sciences, an MBA from Rensselear Polytechnic Institute in 1978, and a Ph.D. from Texas A&M in 1982. Dr. Lengel has conducted research related to organization design and related communication processes. His work on the concept of information richness has offered new insights into the role the medium of exchange plays in information transfer and the design of Management Information Systems. This research has been published in *Management Science, MIS Quarterly, Communications Research*, and the *Academy of Management Executive*. Dr. Lengel is now exploring the complexities of the human/technology interface and the effects on organizational performance. The ethics of technological control, the dynamics of leadership and the relationship of both to the implementation of strategy and technology transfer are now areas of special interest. In addition to formal research, Dr. Lengel is active in consulting and executive development programs. His professional affiliations include the Academy of Management, the Administrative Management Society, Phi Kappa Phi Honor Society, and Beta Gamma Sigma Business Honor Society.

M. Lynne Markus, B.S. industrial engineering, University of Pittsburgh; Ph.D. organizational behavior, Case Western Reserve University, is Assistant Professor of Information Systems at the John E. Anderson Graduate School of Management, University of California, Los Angeles. Her research interests include the implementation and organizational effects of information systems, office automation, and electronic communication media. Prior to joining the faculty at UCLA, Dr. Markus was a consultant with Arthur D. Little, Inc. and Assistant Professor at the Sloan School of Management, Massachusetts Institute of Technology. She is the author of *Systems in*

Organizations: Bugs and Features and has recently contributed articles to *Management Science, Communications of the ACM, Management Information Systems Quarterly,* and *Interfaces.* She is a member of the editorial boards of *Information Systems Research, Management Information Systems Quarterly,* and *Office: Technology and People.*

Laurie Mason is a fourth-year doctoral candidate in the Institute of Communication Research, Stanford University. Her research has centered on empirical studies of juror attitudes and behavior in libel lawsuits, with particular reference to meaning in messages, especially implied defamation, and evaluation of libel defendants. Recent papers include "Partisan and Non-Partisan Readers' Perceptions of Political Enemies and Newspaper Bias" (*Journalism Quarterly,* in press; with C. Nass), "Testing Some Judicial Assumptions of the Fact/Opinion Distinction in Libel" (*Journalism Quarterly,* Spring 1989; with J. Cohen, D. Mutz, and C. Nass), and "False Impression Libel: Implication or Inference?" (paper presented at the annual meeting of the Law and Society Association, Summer 1989).

Clifford Nass is Assistant Professor of Communication in the Institute for Communication Research, Stanford University. His current research includes information processing systems models of the information economy and organizations, social categorization and social models of computers, and statistical algorithms. Recent publications include "The Lid on the Garbage Can: Institutional Constraints on Decision Making in the Technical Core of College-Text Publishers" (*Administrative Science Quarterly, 34*(2), 190-207; with B. Levitt), "Following the Money Trail: Twenty-Five Years of Research Into the Information Economy" (*Communication Research, 14,* 698-708), and "Work, Information, and Information Work: A Retrospective and Prospective Framework" (*Research in the Sociology of Work: Vol. 4. Hi-Tech Work* (pp. 311-333).

Marshall Scott Poole is Associate Professor of Speech-Communication at the University of Minnesota. He received his Ph.D from the University of Wisconsin-Madison in 1980. His current research interests are computer support for meetings, group decision making, conflict management, organizational communication, and interaction analysis methodology. Recent publications include a volume coedited with Randy Hirokawa, *Communication and Group Decision-Making* and the book *Working Through Conflict,* written with Joseph Folger. His article, "Group Decision-Making as a Structurational Process", coauthored with R.D. McPhee and D.R. Seibold, won the

Golden Anniversary award for outstanding scholarship from the Speech Communication Association. He has served on the editorial boards of *Human Communication Research, Communication Monographs, Communication Research*, and *Academy of Management Review*.

Joseph Schmitz (M.A., Michigan State University), is a doctoral candidate at the Annenberg School of Communications, University of Southern California, and is Visiting Professor at Pepperdine University where he teaches research methodology and organizational communication. His research interests include the effects of social interaction on organizational behavior and the processes and social consequences of adopting new communication technology in the work-place and in the local community.

Charles W. Steinfield (M.A. and Ph.D., Annenberg School of Communications, University of Southern California) is Associate Professor and Ameritech Fellow in the Department of Telecommunication at Michigan State University. He serves on the editorial board of Communication Research, and from 1988 to 1990 he served as the chairperson of the Human Communication Technology Interest Group of the International Communication Association. He has published articles in *Communication Research, Communication Yearbook, Telecommunications Policy*, and the *Annual Review of Information Science and Technology*. His research interests include the implementation, use, and impacts of information technologies in organizations, strategic use of telecommunications, and the management of international telecommunications networks.

Brian K. Thorn is Assistant Professor in the Department of Industrial and Manufacturing Engineering at the Rochester Institute of Technology. His academic background includes undergraduate study of industrial engineering and graduate study of industrial and systems engineering with emphasis on individual and organizational decision behavior and applied statistical methodology. His current research efforts focus on the development of statistically based procedures to improve the decision making ability of individuals and groups within the organizational setting. He has coauthored a number of papers on information acquisition and processing with Terry Connolly.

Linda Klebe Trevino is Assistant Professor of Organizational Behavior in the Department of Management and Organization at Pennsylvania State University. She received her Ph.D. in Management from Texas A&M Universitysity in 1987. Professor Trevino teaches management and organizational behavior to undergraduates, MBAs, and doctoral students. Her current research focuses on two primary areas: ethical decision making and organizational justice (including a justice perspective on discipline); management communication and new information technology (particularly electronic mail). Her research has been published in the *Academy of Management Review*, *Communication Research*, and *MIS Quarterly*. She has presented her research at numerous professional meetings including the Academy of Management, the Organizational Behavior Teaching Conference, and the International Communication Association. Dr. Trevino has served as an expert witness, and has consulted with a number of large organizations. Her professional affiliations include membership in the Academy of Management, the American Psychological Association, and the Society for Business Ethics.

Robert W. Zmud is Professor and Thomas L. Williams, Jr., Eminent Scholar in Management Information Systems in the Information and Management Science Department at the College of Business, Florida State University. His current research interests focus on the impact of information technology in facilitating a variety of organizational behaviors and on organizational efforts involved with planning, managing, and diffusing information technology. In addition to his numerous articles on these topics, he has recently co-authored two research monographs: *Transforming the IS Organization: The Mission, the Framework, the Transiton* and *Information Technology Management: Evolving Managerial Roles*. Dr. Zmud currently is an editor with two journals, *Organization Science* and *Communications of the ACM*, serves on the editorial boards of two journals, *Management Science* and *Decision Sciences*, and previously served on the editorial boards of two others, *MIS Quarterly* and *Systems, Objectives, Solutions*. Both his Ph.D. (University of Arizona) and his S.M. (M.I.T) degrees are in management.